Raising a School

Foundations for School Architecture

Raising a School

Foundations for School Architecture

Rena Upitis

WINTERGREEN STUDIOS PRESS
Township of South Frontenac
Ontario, Canada

Wintergreen Studios Press
P.O. Box 75, Yarker, ON, Canada K0K 3N0

The author and publisher wish to thank the following for permission to reprint previously published material appearing in this book:

Photo of Sinarmas World Academy, courtesy of Fielding Nair International
Photo of Seabird Island School by James Dow, courtesy of Patkau Architects

Every effort has been made to contact the copyright holders, students, and adults who appear in this text for permission for to reprint borrowed material, quote interviews, and use photographs. We regret any oversights that may have occurred and would be happy to rectify them in future printings of this work.

Canadian Cataloguing in Publication Data
Raising a School: Foundations for School Architecture

ISBN 0986547301 EAN-13 9780986547300
Upitis, Rena Brigit, 1958–

I.   Title.

Legal Deposit—Library and Archives Canada 2010

Book design by R. Upitis

to raise: to put or take to a higher position; to increase the amount of value or strength; to construct or build up; to cause to be heard or considered; to set going or bring into being; to rouse from sleep or death; to bring up or educate; to remove a barrier or embargo; to cause to appear; to come in sight of; and, to extract from the earth.

excerpts from the Concise Oxford English Dictionary, 1986

Other books by Rena Upitis

This Too is Music (1990)

Can I Play You My Song?
The Compositions and Invented Notations of Children (1992)

Creative Mathematics: Exploring Children's Understanding (1997)
(with E. Phillips & W. Higginson)

Who Will Teach? A Case Study of Teacher Education Reform (2000)

Listen to their Voices:
Research and Practice in Early Childhood Music (2007)
(with K. Smithrim)

Contents

Preface ix

Architecture as Pedagogy 1
 An Antidote to Crime: Musical Theatre for an Inner-City School 1
 Crime Rates, Prisons, and the Day Job 5
 Architecture and Cultural Values...8
 Montessori, Reggio Emilia, and Steiner Schools 11
 Hard Architecture, Small Acts of Beauty, and Resistance to Reform.........12
 Building Costs and Social Costs: What We Can Learn From School Toilets 17

Conversation..21
 Co-Designing, Dewey's Occupations, and Languages of Learning.............21
 Five Barriers to Conversations Between Architects and Educators 26
 Collaborative Conversations 31
 Flaws in the Consultative Process 32
 Triumphs of Conversation and Design: One Architect, Two Schools.........34
 Concluding Conversation 42

Play...45
 The History of Kindergartens and Other Schools for Young Children.........46
 Education Influences Architecture: Froebel's Gifts and Wright's Designs 50
 Architecture Influences Education: Steiner's Waldorf Curriculum..............51
 Architecture as Teacher: Reggio Emilia Schools 52
 Responding to Natural and Inner Worlds...53
 Beyond Playgrounds: Spaces In-Between...60
 Schools for Play, Learning, and Living 63

Romance 65
 The Romance of Learning 66
 Romanticism, Complexity Science, and Johann Wolfgang von Goethe.............67
 Romanticism and Views of Science and Learning.......................................69
 Waldorf (Steiner) Schools..71
 Complexity Science and Classrooms 74
 Models of Learning: Moving to an Idea-Centered Complexity Perspective............75
 Models of Building: Complexity Science and Architectural Patterns 79
 The Natural World and Complexity: A Myriad of Symbiotic Relationships............84

Body **91**

    Lifelong Learning and School Architecture 91

    Taiko Drumming: An Example of Meaningful Learning...........................93

    Taiko in Schools: Artist Roles and School Architecture............................96

    Embodied Learning in the Absence of Schools 98

    Connecting Mind and Body...101

    Beyond Embodied Knowledge: Ritual and Spirituality 105

Value...**109**

    Standardized Educational Testing and Dual Forms of Accounting.........110

    Towards a Holistic and External Form of Educational Accounting.........112

    Architectural Accounting: Internal and External Approaches 114

    Towards a Long View of Building Costs and Values 118

    The Intersection of Architectural Costs and Educational Values............121

    Environmental Costs of Building Schools 122

    Waterharvesting: Childhood Play and Sustainable Water Technology.....125

    The Ultimate Accounting 127

Nature...**129**

    Place-based Education and School Architecture..131

    Belonging: Social Cohesion, Beauty, Regional Surveys, and Manual Activity 139

    Pedagogy of Place and Ecological Footprints...145

    Ecological Triumphs: Uniting Head, Heart, and Hands 147

    Becoming Both Architect and Gardener 152

Dwellings **155**

    Humble School Buildings: A Feeling of Home..156

    Fostering Social Cohesion Through Architecture 158

    Humane Architecture: Light, Colour, Sound, and Furniture..................159

    Students' Views on Humane Architecture 165

    Dewey's Utopian Schools: Places to Dwell 167

    A Community Sensibility 169

    Creating Dwellings for Living and Learning: From the Inside Out 171

    Dwelling Activities and Dwelling Tools 177

    Raising a School...179

References **181**

Acknowledgments **197**

Index **199**

Preface

I have always had a love-hate relationship with schools. I have crossed the thresholds of hundreds of school buildings over the past half-century—as a student, of course, but also as a parent, as a teacher, as a visiting artist, as a researcher, and as an educator of teachers. I love schools, in part, because there is something oddly comforting and about them. They look the same, they smell the same, and even when I find myself in a school that is completely new to me, there is always something strangely familiar about the students and teachers— I've seen them all before.

But there is something peculiarly disconcerting about schools as well. The very fact that schools are so readily identifiable and familiar is disturbing. Why should a school in urban Montreal look just like a school in northern Alberta? Or southern England, for that matter? The fact that many schools are virtual clones of one another is, I think, a central flaw of school architecture. In this book, I explore an approach to the design of schools that is in marked contrast to what occurs in most Western countries when a school is about to be renovated or raised up from the ground. My plea is a simple one: let's think about how we can build schools in ways that honour both a geographic sense of place and the kinds of learning that human beings find most deeply engaging. This book is not simply about school architecture: it is about meaningful learning, it is about human relationships, and it is about how we live upon the earth.

This book appears at a time when media attention is focused on student performance and high-stakes testing. I make the claim that problems with education are not only about curriculum or teacher competency, but are also about the ways that we build schools. For school buildings, too, serve as teachers. The ways we build and inhabit schools send powerful messages to all who pass through their doors. School architecture profoundly influences the outcomes of education. For a century and a half, we have built schools that lack adequate natural light, comfortable furniture, inviting entryways, and green spaces. There has never been a more important time to break this damaging trend. We will build more new buildings in the first half of the 21st century than have been built in all of recorded human history. For the next several years, construction will begin on two new schools every day in the United States alone, and that doesn't even take into account school renovations. If schools are aesthetically, pedagogically, and environmentally deficient, they will sap the life right out of students and teachers and everyone else who enters them.

In the chapters that follow, I examine a wide range of educational debates and architectural trends spanning centuries of practice. There are stories embedded throughout this narrative—stories from philosophers, artists, scientists, parents, architects, teachers, and students. Some of these thinkers are well known; others are not. But one way or another, their stories are deeply compelling. Many of the accounts come from a wide range of literature that relates to school life. Others come from personal interviews that I was privileged to conduct with parents, students, teachers, and architects associated with school buildings in Canada, Australia, Germany, and the United States. Some of these interviews were casual conversations—such a chance encounter with a stonemason who helped build the Carillon Tower in Canberra, Australia, some thirty-five years prior to our meeting. Others were formal interviews, arranged long in advance, with key stakeholders in the school architecture profession. These various accounts reveal some important foundations for school design—the need to pay attention to natural settings, the need to provide facilities that encourage learning through play, through conversation, and through the body, and the need to involve a broad community in designing and even building the places that become our schools.

The schools that are featured throughout the book—both inspiring examples and unfortunate ones—span several countries and continents in the developed world. But my intention in providing examples is not to suggest a cut-and-dried approach for building an elementary school or for designing a Kindergarten play space. Rather, my intention is to inspire the reader to think about school construction and the profound impact it has on the quality of students' learning and the well being of the larger community. All over the world, we have the opportunity to design schools in fundamentally different ways. This book provides ideas for re-thinking school design and for provoking all of us to take part in that design process.

When I was in the final stages of writing this manuscript, I had the good fortune of encountering an editor who asked just the right sorts of difficult questions, offering a host of suggestions that have improved the manuscript immeasurably for the reader. She urged me, for example, to take on the role of tour guide through this complex topic, making the book both deeply personal and wide-ranging. "And be sure to tell us your qualifications as tour guide," she insisted. So herewith are my qualifications: I am a teacher. I have taught elementary school music, private piano and music theory, and courses in the arts, mathematics, and research methods to university students. I am a carpenter. I am a fledgling designer, having come late to the profession of architecture, and in rather informal ways. I am a parent of school-aged children. A writer. An educational researcher. And I try—to the extent possible—to live an artist's life. Many of my days are spent writing and conducting research and teaching, but for some portion of every day I also attend to the aesthetic, to the natural world, to beauty. And I love to learn. For it is when I am learning something new, embarking on a fresh passion with its attendant challenges, that I feel most fully alive. Isn't this what we wish for students in our schools as well? And so, it is with these sensibilities that I offer myself up as a tour guide to the topic of school architecture. To begin that journey, I open the first chapter with a narrative that illustrates the profound ways that the nature of schools and school grounds affect student learning.

Rena Upitis
January 23, 2010
Paddy's Lake, South Frontanc, Ontario

Architecture as Pedagogy
Crime, Culture, and Compliance

I begin with the contentious suggestion that there is a link between crime and school architecture. Windowless concrete containers surrounded by barbed wire fences, looking more like prisons than schools, can hardly be thought of as inviting environments for students. I give examples of school-like prisons (and prison-like schools), including an American school where I once taught, as well as a 19th century prison built in New South Wales that was converted to a high school and is still in operation today. I explore ways that architecture embeds cultural and educational values, using both prisons and schools to illustrate this notion. Three prominent early childhood education approaches, reflected in Montessori, Reggio Emilia, and Steiner schools, are introduced as examples where both cultural and educational aims are explicitly linked with architecture. I then show how small acts of beauty can change the nature and experience of the built environment. The chapter closes with a discussion of how design decisions, based on attempts to save initial building costs, can have long-term negative effects for students and teachers.

An Antidote to Crime: Musical Theatre for an Inner-City School

Be careful where you park. Those were the first words I heard from the teacher in the classroom next to mine. I had just been hired to teach music at Hennigan School in Boston—my first real job—and I figured parking was the least of my concerns. I was wrong. That warning, spoken in 1985, haunts me still.

I soon learned where to park my car. Some nearby streets were relatively safe, meaning that at the end of the day there was a good chance of finding my car with the windshield intact and the tires undamaged. But the best place to park was just a few yards from the front door of the school, right in the middle of the concrete walkway leading up to the steel front doors. Picture driving over the sidewalk curb onto a broad and crumbling concrete expanse, where, thanks to the cars that parked there daily, not even weeds could grow.

To secure a parking spot on the concrete walkway meant arriving at the school before the other teachers. But that was a small price to pay, because the other safe alternative was to park in the gated lot behind the school. I found it almost unbearable to park there. Every time I heard the gate thud behind me I faced the possibility, however remote, that the bell at the back door of the school might not be working. I imagined being stuck there in limbo, unable to enter the school and unable to leave the locked compound.

On the first day of school—as on every day thereafter—I was greeted by the resident police officer. With profound sadness, I wondered why there was a need for police protection at a school for children who were all under ten years of age. However, during my first walk down the hallway of the primary wing of the school I began to understand.

Outside the Grade 1 classroom, I came across a decorated bulletin board with a banner in place, awaiting the art and stories of the young students. The title on the banner? "Why I Will Not Bring Guns And Knives To School." Two days later, the board was filled with children's work. The drawings—of guns aimed at teachers' heads—were explicit. The two-sentence stories were chilling; stories like: "This boy, he was bad. When the teacher came inside the classroom, he killed the teacher." I was dumbfounded by everything in that display: the content provided by the six-year-olds, the necessity of having a curriculum unit on weapons for children so young, and the detailed depictions of handguns and machine guns, knives, and switchblades. This is not a scene that can be dismissed as something from the past. It is a scene of the present. Similar schools—with similar first-grade topics—still populate school landscapes. Formidable signs on schools throughout America warn "NO GUNS" (Taylor, 1995a, p. 50). Scarcely what one would call welcoming.

And so, on that warm September morning, I was frightened and humbled. I doubted my ability to engage these children on any level, much less teach them something about music. I questioned how my hard-earned diploma in piano performance from Canada's Royal Conservatory had prepared me for this challenge, or how the decade I had spent as a studio piano teacher had any relevance at all. Sure, I could teach young middle-class children how to play the piano and pass piano exams with flying colours. But I had no idea how I was going to teach music to this group of children, many of whom came from unimaginably impoverished environments. To complicate things further, Hennigan was a self-declared "rainbow school" because every skin colour under the sun could be found there. Many of the children were African-American or Hispanic. At the time, I knew next to nothing about the cultural values and experiences of children from backgrounds different to my own. As the kids would say in those days, "Zero. Zip. Zilch. Nada."

Breakdancing was all the rage at the time.[1] I knew next to nothing about breakdancing. Most students of the students could recite reams of rap lyrics as well, with stunning nuances in phrasing and expression. I knew nothing about rap, either. But I learned as much as I could and incorporated breakdancing and rap into the music curriculum.

For a handful of kids, the experiences they had with school music were transcendent: children who might otherwise have ended up in one of the many state prisons instead got bitten by the music bug, and found ways to craft joyful lives with careers in the arts and in other fields—like the student who wrote to me a few years ago telling me about her acting career in New York City. However, far too many of those students did end up in state prisons, scarcely a decade after being in my classroom. I will never forget asking one of my former students, then in his twenties, about the fate of some of his school friends, children I had taught and admired. His answer? "They're doing, dealing, or dead."

Because I now know that some of the happy outcomes of my teaching days at the Hennigan School were so short-lived, the memories of how we spent our days in the classroom have particular poignancy for me. Along with the children, I learned African and Appalachian dances in addition to raps and breakdancing. We created choreographies in response to music of many kinds. The children learned to play instruments and to make instruments with their own hands (Upitis, 1990). They improvised. They composed music, using what was then new technology to hook up synthesizers to computers. Some of them came in early, each morning, to listen to me practice the piano. They heard me play music by Mozart and Chopin, music they not heard before, but decided was "pretty good music." By that time, I had decided their music and dancing were pretty good, too. Very good, in fact.

We started a new tradition at the school the first year I taught there: staging elaborate musicals, in a *real* theatre at the Massachusetts Institute of Technology (MIT) in Cambridge. Cambridge was across the river from where the school was located, and most of the children I taught had never ventured there before, even though MIT was only a few subway stops away. For that matter, most of them had never been in a real theatre anywhere. Everything about the place was new—fold-down fabric-covered seats, fancy lights, and heavy velvet curtains drawn across the stage. Some teachers expressed trepidation about bringing the students across the river. I was duly warned: "The students will trash the place," and, "That will be the end of this experiment."

The students did not trash the place. In fact, they reacted to the architecture with reverence and awe. As we walked through the doors of the theatre, there was hushed silence. A few of the children sat on the plush indigo chairs,

---

[1] Breakdancing, part of the Hip Hop culture developed in the South Bronx in the early 1980s, is a highly acrobatic and creative form of movement. Often performed in public places accompanied by a "boombox," the pioneers of breakdancing were young and male. Most were Black or Hispanic and lived in urban areas—in short, they were the students I taught. Breakdancing is also associated with other elements of Hip Hop, such as Graffiti and Deejaying.
http://www.wikipedia.org/wiki/Break_Dancing (Retrieved September 7, 2005).

carefully pulling down the seats before gingerly taking their places. Others walked up to the stage, brushing their hands across the smooth and glistening wooden surface. Some would lie down on their backs on the stage, staring up at the lights. Still others marveled at the curtains, peering behind them, fold after fold, trying to figure out where the curtains ended. There was no question that this was a *real* theatre. And there was no question that being in a real theatre meant the students were involved in a real musical: a musical of value. And—at least for those few golden days—the work they did was therefore also of value.

I was acutely aware of the magical powers of the theatre. As we prepared for the performance, there was no issue of "controlling" the students. They operated as a self-organizing group of little ants in an anthill. One cluster of children took care of props, another cluster ran impromptu rehearsals of some of the less polished scenes, and another group worked out how to manage the curtains and lights. At one point, a technician from MIT walked in and, looking perplexed, asked, "Is there anyone in *charge* here?" not because of difficulties, but because this group of 150 youngsters seemed to be self-regulating—a topic I will explore at length in a subsequent chapter.

The musical was astonishing. The students performed at a level far beyond what I had taught them. Most important of all, the building inspired them. The building supported their work, and in that way, the building was one of their teachers too. And on the night of the performance, the building welcomed their families.

It was more than the theatre that inspired the students. The MIT grounds, just beyond where the theatre was located, were also important. There were vast playing fields with green grass—and not a smashed bottle in sight. Every afternoon we spent there, over one hundred children ran and played for a solid hour before we began rehearsals. The outdoors spoke to them, too.

It has been well over two decades since the year of that first musical. Much has changed. The state curriculum has been re-vamped at least ten times, teachers and principals have come and gone, and extraordinary technological advances have been made. But one tradition remains. There is still an annual school musical in a real theatre produced by the teachers and students of Hennigan School. The tradition—kept up long after I left the school—owes something to the primacy of the arts and to the dedication of a handful of teachers. But equally important was the availability of a suitable performance venue. Hennigan School, like countless other schools in North America, had a "cafetorium." The cost-saving cafetorium has a cafeteria doubling as an auditorium—though one with terrible acoustics, awful seating, and the lingering smell of greasy fries and bad pizza. Many teachers and students have made do with such facilities with surprisingly good results. But why spend all that energy making do? Despite the availability of their own cafetorium, Hennigan teachers have always chosen to produce the musicals in venues designed specifically for theatre, for beautiful and important performances.

Crime Rates, Prisons, and the Day Job

As I have already noted, not every student at the Hennigan School reaped the benefits of those performances in the long term. Far too many of my former students committed crimes—some petty, some serious. They became data points in the big bank of numbers that comprise crime statistics in America.

There are many ways to talk about crime, and using numbers is certainly one of them. If you lived in the United States in the year 2007, the chance of being murdered was slim. Expressed as a percentage—0.00056%—the number is so small, it's hard to contemplate; it's less than 1 in 10,000. In fact, the overall murder rate in the United States that year was 5.6 people per 100,000 (Disaster Center, n.d.). Expressed another way, though, the statistic seems much more sobering. A rate of 5.6 per 100,000 means that—in one year alone—16,929 people died at the hands of another human being. That number, too, is impossible to contemplate. As are these: in 2007 there were nearly 10 million reported incidents of property damage, over 6 million incidents of theft and larceny, and millions upon millions of assaults and other acts of violence. That's just one year. That's just the United States. That's just the *reported* incidents. Even though crime rates fluctuate dramatically—in 1980, over 23,000 people were murdered in the United States, which has a way of making 16,929 look good in the media reports—we're still talking about a lot of murdered people.

Crime in the United States accounts for more injuries, death, and loss of property than all natural disasters combined. The State of California spends more money on the construction and maintenance of prisons than it does on all institutions of higher education (Bauman, 2000). If prisons teach anything at all, they teach inmates the culture of the penitentiary environment, "and of such environment only... the very opposite of rehabilitation" (Bauman, p. 210). Criminologist Zygmunt Bauman described California's Pelican Bay as a high-tech prison that has been designed as a place where immobilization is brought close to a state of perfection. He wrote, "Pelican Bay is not a school of anything [and] what the inmates *do* inside their solitary cells *does not matter* at all. What *does matter* is that they stay there" (p. 212). In these "schools of crime," a now classic term coined by Donald Clemmer (1940) in the middle of the 20th century, most of the inhabitants are from the least affluent segments of societies, and are imprisoned primarily for minor crimes. Many prison inhabitants are also young.

In Canada, more than 84,000 young people were charged with criminal offences in 2003. And I *do* mean young people: in the report that I am quoting from, Statistics Canada lists the charges for youth between the ages of 12 and 17 (Statistics Canada, n.d.). It is the same in the United States. In Anacostia, one of the more depressed districts of Washington, D.C., fully half of the male residents between the ages of 16 and 35, at any given time, are in prison, or waiting trial, or on probation (Bauman, 2000). In the United States, the total number of people in prison or awaiting sentencing *exceeds* the number of students in all institutes of higher education (Bauman, 2000). Prisons—like schools—are enjoying an unprecedented building boom.

After I left Boston, I returned to Canada to my home in a small village near Kingston, Ontario. I still play the piano. I still teach children and young adults.

But I have shifted the bulk of my teaching from the elementary classroom to teacher education and research. I work at Queen's University, in a building across the road from what was, not long ago, the Prison for Women. From the top floor of our building's library you could see over the tall and forbidding concrete walls right into what was once the prison yard. The former Prison for Women—one of five or six prisons and other "correctional" facilities in the Kingston area—is a grim reminder of society's underbelly. In the spring of 2008, the prison walls started coming down when the building was purchased by Queen's University for an Archives Centre. Watching those walls come down and people's faces light up was an astonishing process. The walls, we discovered, had been not only hiding a lovely limestone building (the best of prison architecture), but also blocking a beautiful view of Lake Ontario. And blocking the southern sun—views and light that no one in the prison or the university had seen for at least a half-century.

Having stared at the concrete walls of the prison across the road for decades, I had become desensitized to the very presence of the walls and the people they enclosed. And I am desensitized to the other prisons in Kingston—a city that has been called, only partly in jest, the prison capital of Canada. At best, the prisons of Kingston remain in the periphery of my vision. Anthropologist Mary Catherine Bateson (1994) says we display a sort of blindness as we focus on our narrow goals and press ahead. We pay attention to only a fraction of what is before us, blocking out our peripheral vision with no sense of a larger picture. Bateson writes about how her father, Gregory Bateson, wondered if this phenomenon was a flaw of human perception or whether it developed because of the mechanistic and reductionist view of the world that permeates the psyche and actions of our communities. I suspect it's the latter, and I am convinced that school architecture contributes to this reductionist view of the world.

British-born anthropologist Gregory Bateson's work on systems theory is also relevant to the notions of learning presented in this book. His remarkable ways of thinking about the many dimensions that affect human behaviour were influenced by his early anthropological studies in New Guinea and Bali in the first half of the 20th century. For the next several decades his work crossed disciplinary boundaries, including those of cybernetics, ethnography, anthropology, environmental studies, psychiatry, animal communication, biological evolution, and systems theory. Relevant to the current discussion are Bateson's observations about play, exploration, and crime—and, as it turns out, architecture and schools.

In *Mind and Nature: A Necessary Unity*, Bateson made a distinction between "crime" and "criminal actions" (Bateson, 1980, p. 138). He said that society acts as if crime could be extinguished simply by punishing criminal actions, although he claims the opposite is the case. The statistics cited earlier support Bateson's view—the more we punish criminal actions, the more the crime rates soar. There is a profound difference between changing the structure of a system and merely messing around with its components. Context is also profound: action takes meaning from context (Bateson, 1980). For instance, jumping over fences could be play—or it could be trespassing. Let me illustrate with an example.

Urban Free Flow is the somewhat subversive pursuit popular with a sector of urban youth. It is an activity that is intimately connected with architecture and cityscapes, and with the physical urge to climb and jump and run so prevalent among young people—especially athletic males in their late teens and early twenties. Criminal actions, like trespassing, are integral to the enterprise. But the youth who take part in Urban Free Flow are not criminals.

I first learned about Urban Free Flow, also known as Parkour, from a musician friend whose 21-year-old son was a Parkour enthusiast in Ottawa, Canada's capital city. The practice involves arbitrarily picking two points on a city map, and then going from Point A to Point B using the most direct route possible. The route, of course, is usually anything but direct, because Parkour is practiced in highly built-up urban environments. Moving from A to B requires climbing, jumping, straddling, running, and pulling up. Climbing over handrails, park benches, walls, fences, roofs, trees, and even houses is part of the game. There is a series of moves associated with Parkour and a specialized set of terms and jargon ("grunt" or "newbie" refers to someone new to Parkour, while "slam" means to fail in the execution of a particular technique).

The practice began in France—*parcours du combatant* has become "Parkour"—and has spread to North America and other countries. Parkour enthusiasts admit the practice is not legal, as trespassing is often involved, but they insist it isn't "officially illegal" either. Thus, Parkour involves two inherent risks: physical injury and conflict with the law. These are precisely the two things that make my friend anxious about her son's involvement in Parkour. But she still applauds the practice. Why?

My friend sees Parkour as a highly physical, intellectually challenging pursuit. She says on the best "runs," her son experiences a sense of oneness—a feeling of "flow" as he moves through the built environments. I suspect that this is the same sense of flow associated with involvement in artistic practices or in spiritual experiences identified by Csikszentmihalyi (1990). My friend also says that Parkour has given her son and his peers new ways of balancing competing desires, of understanding the need for social and legal constraints, of thinking about how urban landscapes are created and connected, and of developing strategies for overcoming physical and psychological obstacles. She says it helps her son negotiate volatile situations, for he must speak convincingly and calmly with security guards and police officers unfamiliar with Parkour.

So if Parkour is not crime, is it play? Or art? And what about graffiti? While I understand that defacing public buildings is not something to be celebrated, some of the great expanses of concrete in large urban centers have certainly been improved by the graffiti they have invited. Indeed, there have been many art exhibitions dedicated to the celebration of graffiti artists and their work. The way we frame activities like Parkour and graffiti, in the sense that the notion of framing is used by Bateson (1972), will "trigger either pictures of self-absorbed, potentially violent, amoral teenagers or inexperienced junior adults experimenting with identity in order to assume their role in the community" (Gilliam & Bates, 2001, p. 3). Interesting choices.

American professor Mary Rose O'Reilley (1993) wrote a book about teaching young adults called *The Peaceable Classroom*. In that book, she returns time and again to wondering whether university English courses can be taught so that people might stop killing one another. This question was first posed to her when she was a graduate student of Professor Ihab Hassan at the University of Wisconsin-Milwaukee. She describes how she and her peers, upon hearing the question, shuffled their feet and wondered if they had heard wrong. But for O'Reilley, the question became an enduring one. Through a complex weave of anecdote and analysis, O'Reilley concludes that if educational experiences are to be relevant and oriented to nonviolence, then they must acknowledge the inner life of students. She distrusts "any pedagogy that does not begin in the personal … and does not conclude in the communal" (O'Reilley, 1993, p. 60–61). O'Reilley's standards for schooling are high. In contrast to most experiences of schooling, experiences she describes as "endless torture by exquisite boredom" (p. 54), O'Reilley says we should expect nothing less of schooling than Augustine's description of his rhetoric class, where students laughed and talked, read books together, disagreed without ill feeling, and otherwise kindled fires to make a community.

O'Reilley argues that most human problems are architectural problems, stating that the cultural agenda of education can be read like a text from the physical arrangements of school classrooms. As she so provocatively writes, "The arrangement of our classrooms should tell us, if we do not consciously know, what horizon we have set for the next generation" (p. 40). O'Reilley also holds the view that curricula can solve the ills of society. I do not share O'Reilley's optimism that school and university curricula can achieve this task. People's characters are shaped by many more factors than the influences of curricula alone. But I do share O'Reilley's view that architecture is a teacher. And this causes me to ask: how much does school architecture contribute to the life outcomes for the students who have spent years attending schools? Better yet, how can school architecture support the healthy development of students?

Architecture and Cultural Values

Cultural values and expectations are reflected in architecture of all kinds, and expectation is a powerful teacher. In the times before the printing press, buildings were a primary medium for communication (Bradley, 1998). The medieval cathedral, architect William Bradley claimed, was a stone and glass testament embracing the teachings of Christian thought. Every aspect of the building conveyed meaning — the forms, the sculptures, the ornamentation and other details were all designed to further the messages of the church and to shape the beliefs of its followers.

Winston Churchill also knew how architecture gave meaning and shape to human activity and social interaction. He is well known for his utterance: "First we shape our buildings, then our buildings shape us." Less well known is the context in which he spoke those words. After the House of Commons was bombed in 1941, there was discussion of how the building would be rebuilt. In a meeting in the House of Lords on October 28, 1943, Churchill argued vehemently for the building to be re-created in its old form. He regarded its horseshoe shape as ideal for debate. He also insisted that it be built, once again, with an insufficient number of seats for its members. Most of the time, the House was empty, but at critical moments it would fill beyond capacity, which, in Churchill's view, created a sense of urgency impossible to achieve in a room that was not bursting at the seams.

Schools shape us, too. The architecture of schools affects the social interactions, physical growth, emotional development, and intellectual attainments of its students. School architecture embodies the values of education and the pedagogical approaches that resonate with such values. Buildings both enable and constrain the learning that will occur within their walls and on the surrounding grounds.

The most prominent ideology of education over the past century, and still present in contemporary schools, is that of socialization. Starkly put, schools have been built for young people to be trained to fulfill the roles society intends of them (Lamm, 1986). In this ideology, education is seen as most effective when it is efficient and organized, preparing young people for the bureaucracy of work. This is sometimes called the factory model of schooling. But schooling of this type equally prepares people for work in armies, hospitals, and—I daresay—universities. Canadian journalist Margaret Wente talks about how large high schools were invented during the industrial age, not so subtly suggesting maybe that's why they look so much like factories. She laments how schools have changed little since the 1950s when everyone seemed to agree bigger was better. She observes that when small rural schools closed, high schools bulked up. Classes grew, and "principals morphed into personnel directors and safety wardens" (Wente, 2004, pp. 142-143).

In factory-like schools, teaching—like the buildings—tends to be boxlike and linear. Transmission teaching dominates: standing at the front of the classroom, the teacher transmits knowledge to the students who are sitting quietly facing the teacher. This kind of teaching works best when the teacher can see everyone at once, and so, classrooms are created as a series of boxes, the most pervasive example being one of double-loaded classrooms down a single long hallway. Professor Kenneth Tanner from the University of Georgia (2000) cites Columbine High School in Littleton, Colorado, as a disturbing example of this type of architecture, a school that had an alarming history of violence as the site of the 1999 massacre of 12 classmates and a teacher by two teen-aged boys. This school model has been criticized not only for the ways in which it limits learning and is architecturally uninspired, but also for the security hazards that come with such large buildings and their labyrinths of hallways (Tanner, 2000). Tanner's suggestion to create easily supervised spaces is in keeping with British architect Mark Dudek's (2000) praise for Frankfurt's Eckenheim day care centre, where an elegant crescent-shape design makes security effortless. I observed the same sort of crescent-shaped construction in the Willunga Steiner School near Adelaide, South Australia, where the two semi-circular Kindergartens give teachers a clear and charming view of the kitchen, play areas, gardens, and toilets.

Tanner (2000) says that smaller schools with ample exits would help meet the growing concern for security in American schools. But smaller schools are in direct conflict with the prevalent ideology of socialization. Large schools exemplify economies of scale, later echoed in the bureaucracies of work for which students are being prepared. And large schools are often multistoried, with the earlier grades on the lower floor. Students rise—physically and symbolically—to the higher grades as they become older, sometimes lording it over those beneath them. In David Orr's (1992) troubling book, *Ecological Literacy*, he suggests such schools are not only about socialization for a bureaucratic existence, but are also about human dominance over the natural world, a topic I will revisit many times in this book.

Acculturation is another prominent ideology of education and architecture (Lamm, 1986). There was a clear message, for instance, in the many schools built throughout the 1930s and 1940s with separate entrances and playgrounds for boys and for girls. This building practice was but one way of telling us all that young male and young female pupils were to be treated differently. Separate staff entrances reinforced yet another type of social hierarchy.

Buildings can also be fashioned to reinforce other values, such as the importance of a classical education. Henry Kendall's book, *Designs for Schools and Schoolhouses,* was first published in Britain in 1847. He urged schools to use a Gothic style, making almost no reference to how the interior spaces of the buildings should function. Kendall's work lives on. Imposing structures, grand staircases, and Greek columns are all designed to let students and their parents know that education is important, particularly if it echoes something of the education of ancient times. In contrast to Kendall's emphasis in England, Dudek (2002) notes that in the United States the concerns were safety related. At the same time that Kendall wrote his seminal work, Henry Barnard, the first United States Commissioner of Education, was concentrating almost exclusively on issues of health and safety.

A broader set of perspectives were taken into account during the same point in school architecture history by the British architect surveyor Edward Robert Robson, who integrated architectural, educational, and safety concerns in his 1874 book *School Architecture: Practical Remarks on the Planning, Designing, Building and Furnishing of School Houses* (as cited in Dudek, 2002). His suggestions about using vernacular building materials and choosing suitable furniture had wide influence in London and other metropolitan boroughs throughout England.

Then there are the not-so-subtle religious messages transmitted by traditional and contemporary schools alike. For example, many of the first one-room, frame schoolhouses in England, Canada, Australia, and the United States looked like churches. These schools had a small peaked tower on the roof that housed the student-summoning bell and left the impression that school was not only for "readin', writin' and 'rithmetic," but for reverence. Reverence for learning, possibly, and reverence for the teacher as well.

Montessori, Reggio Emilia, and Steiner Schools

I find it intriguing to contrast primary and secondary schools that look like factories, Greek temples, or mini-churches with the schools built for the youngest of our school-aged children. Whether the program is a state-funded Kindergarten, a Montessori school, a Reggio Emilia day care, or a Steiner school,[2] the buildings associated with these approaches often stimulate the imaginations of students and teachers alike. Not coincidentally, the approaches of Reggio Emilia, Montessori, and Steiner, while different in a number of respects, share fundamental features and histories (Edwards, 2002). One, the founders of each approach articulated an explicit vision and corresponding curriculum, still followed in contemporary versions of these schools. Two, each approach was developed in Europe in direct response to violence, with the goal of creating citizens motivated by peace and civility. And three, teachers involved with these approaches recognize children as intelligent, creative, and complex beings (Edwards, 2002).

Rudolf Steiner, the enigmatic Austrian-born philosopher, architect, playwright, and scholar, also felt that most of society's problems were rooted in its architecture. Steiner once said that it would be impossible to eliminate crime and wrongdoing without changes in the architecture around us (Raab, 1980). Steiner (c. 1922, translated by B. Bellemore, personal communication, May 16, 2005 and by M. Baxter, personal communication, June 14, 2005) stated:

> However much study may be devoted to the elimination of crime and wrong-doing in the world, true redemption, the turning of evil into good, will in the future depend on whether true art and architecture are able to generate a definite cultural atmosphere that can so fill the hearts and souls of human beings—if they allow this atmosphere to influence them—that liars will cease to lie and disturbers of the peace will cease to disturb the peace of their fellow citizens. Buildings will begin to speak.

Steiner and O'Reilley aren't the only ones who have coupled crime with architecture. One of the guiding questions at a conference held at the Faculty of Architecture of the University of Sydney—a conference with delegates from every continent on the planet—was whether better design of the physical environment could reduce crime (International Symposium of Environment, Behaviour, and Society, 2006).

To this day, throughout Europe, and especially in Germany, Italy and Spain, high priority is placed on pre-school education (Dudek, 2000, 2002, 2007). It is in Europe where the contribution of architecture to education is most likely to be acknowledged by architects, educators, and the general public (Dudek, 2002; I. Williams, personal communication, February 16, 2009). In contrast, reports on school effectiveness in England and the United States rarely mention the quality of the built environment. Correspondingly, there are few architectural casebooks on schools; in the casebooks that do exist, most of the examples come from

---

[2] I use the terms Waldorf school and Steiner school interchangeably in this book; both designations are used throughout the world. Waldorf refers to the location of the first school developed by Rudolf Steiner in 1919 at the Waldorf-Astoria Cigarette Factory in Stuttgart, Germany.

Europe.[3] Those examples are often featured in more than one collection, probably because there are so few innovative examples to describe. Predictably, all of the books on school architecture include a sample or two of Steiner, Montessori, and Reggio Emilia schools.

In all three of these of these approaches, students are seen as being influenced by natural and environmental forces that open pathways for learning. Teachers depend on carefully prepared environments that are aesthetically pleasing and support the students in their growth—and don't look anything like brick boxes. There is much to learn from these movements, and their voices should be heard in contemporary philosophical debates—debates about curriculum, debates about architecture, and debates about learning for a lifetime, not just about learning during the early years. At the heart of many of these debates is the tension between what have been called traditional and progressivist views of education, which find their parallels in the architectural movements of modernism and organic expressionism (Dudek, 2002).

Hard Architecture, Small Acts of Beauty, and Resistance to Reform

I begin this section by examining ways that schools can be unwelcoming, through harsh materials and designs, and lack of maintenance. Next, I consider how even small acts of defiance in beautifying a space can begin to sensitize people to the ways that architecture affects students and teachers. This leads to the final discussion where some of the reasons for resistance to changing the very nature of contemporary school architecture are explored.

Hard Architecture

Thus far, I have spoken about school architecture and educational ideologies. But schools of all types—brick rectilinear boxes, imitation Greek temples, inviting hobbit-like Kindergarten spaces—can either be beautifully maintained and respected or rundown and unsafe. And far too many schools, especially the common brick and concrete boxes, are made worse by poor maintenance. What cultural values and expectations are reflected in school buildings that have been allowed to fall into neglect? Or that look like prisons? Anne Taylor (1995b), Director of the Institute for Environmental Education at the University of New Mexico, pointed out:

---

[3] I refer to two such casebooks throughout this book, both by Mark Dudek. The first of these, published in 2002, is *Architecture of Schools: The New Learning Environments.* Oxford: Architecture Press The second book, published in 2000, is *Kindergarten Architecture: Space for the Imagination* (2nd ed.). Independence, KY: Spon Press. I have chosen to focus on Dudek's work not because his cases are any different or better than in other books, but because his text is more thorough and thoughtful than the text that accompanies most other casebooks. Casebooks that focus more on the buildings than on educational issues include such volumes as *School Builders* by Eleanor Curtis, 2003, published by Wiley-Academy, West Sussex, England. Still another type of casebook, *Inventing Kindergarten* by Norman Brosterman (NY: Harry N. Abrams, Inc. 1996), features one kind of educational philosophy—in this instance, that of Froebel—and while providing a suitable corroborating text, for my purposes, the perspective is not wide-reaching enough for the views that I have taken in this book.

We expect schools to prepare children for living in a democratic society, yet we provide learning environments that resemble police states—hard, overly durable architecture, giant chain-link fences, locked gates, guards, and even guard dogs. Such architecture fails to encourage the sense of ownership, participation, or responsibility required for a democracy. (p. 69)

Taylor and others (e.g., Schnebli, 1998) have written about how architects were commanded to design classrooms without windows in order to save energy and reduce vandalism, as well as to allow students to concentrate without being distracted by views from the outside. In addition to being unpleasant, such architecture also carries an insidious message: overly durable and hard architecture tells children that this is what they have to look forward to—life in cold buildings that will repress their bodies, minds, and spirits. The suggestion again here is that schools prepare people to spend their days in factories, office buildings, university lecture halls, or prisons. Indeed, many criminologists argue that there are far fewer "genuine criminals" in prisons than there are people who have simply become victims of the social production of crime. The cycle of becoming assimilated into prison culture begins early, and becomes a self-perpetuating system (Clemmer, 1940). The first school I taught in was very much like what Taylor describes. I wonder, now, how much the school itself had to do with the social production of crime for the young children I taught.

David Orr, Chair of the Environmental Studies Program at Oberlin College, Ohio, has written about how university campuses directly affect what students learn. In an article titled *Reassembling the Pieces: Architecture as Pedagogy* he describes the typical university building as full of straight lines with nothing to reflect the site on which it is located (Orr, 1999). With only minor modifications, university buildings could easily be converted for use as factories or prisons.

The converse is equally true. After all, Queen's University purchased the former Prison for Women. Then there is the Glen Innes High School in northern New South Wales—opened as a school in 1927, but first erected as a prison in 1884. All of the original buildings—the cellblock, a governor's residence, and a workshop—are still used for teaching or storage spaces. The building never operated as a jail, because in the same year it was built a new rail line opened, making it more convenient to send Glen Innes prisoners to a larger prison 100 kilometers further south. According to a former teacher of English and History at the Glen Innes High School, this is not the only school in New South Wales based on a converted 19th century prison (E. Mayhew, personal communication, April 4, 2005).

Small Acts of Beauty

I have a colleague at The Australian National University in Canberra who is a musician and composer, as well as a professor of musicology. She believes that it is the healing and sublime qualities of music that make working in university music buildings tolerable. We began to converse regularly on the subject of university architecture during the months I spent working on her campus. She had long-held concerns about the state of the lecture theatre and could often be heard bemoaning the inadequacy of the technology or complaining there wasn't even a lectern available.

When I began talking regularly about this book, there was a period during which she became visibly upset about "the sheer ugliness of the place." A few weeks later, she took direct action. Up to that point, she had been writing "endless e-mails," asking for broken furniture to be removed and for a whiteboard to be installed in the seminar room. One afternoon, I rounded a corner and caught sight of her, sleeves rolled up, painting the department's bulletin board. She had secured some paint and an old roller from the university service staff and was busy putting on the first coat of turquoise paint over the dull and ancient tan board. When she came to talk with me after the paint job, she expressed her delight at the number of students who stopped and admired what she was doing, commenting on how nice it was to have a "bit of colour" in the hallway. How stunning that a small change like a painted bulletin board can be received with such pleasure. Microbiologist René Dubos, along with economist Barbara Ward, wrote the pivotal book *Only One Earth* (Ward & Dubos, 1972). Dubos once said, "The worst thing we can do to our children is to convince them that ugliness is normal" (as cited in Orr, 1999, p. 139). It can't be right to convince university students and their professors that ugliness is normal, either. Grey, sterile, and windowless classrooms cannot be the best places for learning, no matter how inspiring the professor nor how gifted the students nor how captivating the curriculum. As Swiss-born essayist Alain de Botton (2006) asked:

> If one room can alter how we feel, if our happiness can hang on the colour of the walls or the shape of a door, what will happen to us in most of the places we are forced to look at and inhabit? What will we experience in a house [or school] with prison-like windows, stained carpet tiles and plastic curtains? (p. 13)

The experience I had with my university bulletin-board-painting colleague reminds me of another tale about incremental changes in school architecture. Paul Barnett is an Australian architect whose business derives about half of its work from school designs and school improvements. I had several opportunities to speak with him over a two-year period. About five years before I interviewed Barnett for the first time, he was occupied with a so-called "minor new works contract" to make repairs to the Wanniassa High School in Canberra. This was a school in dire need of rejuvenation: doors and walls had been kicked in, various areas of the school had been vandalized, and the roof leaked in nineteen places. Some of these leaks had been there since the building was opened. Any repairs had been accomplished quickly and crudely. For example, someone had tacked on some reinforcement mesh to cover some of the gaping holes in the walls. The building was drab and lifeless: dull and stained carpets and peeling paint marked the windowless classrooms and corridors.

Barnett understood that the task at hand was to repair the broken walls and fix the leaking roof, but his goal was to do more: he wanted to introduce elements of beauty. In his words, the building called for "a signature, at least at the entryway to the school." His attention to the entryway was not accidental: in his university days Barnett had studied the architecture of Aboriginal peoples and was drawn to learning more about other traditions as well, such as the Sufi influences on Persian architecture.

In the Sufi tradition, the gateway or entryway has particular significance as a symbolic gesture, evidenced by elegant gateways to buildings and cities (Ardalan & Bakhtiar, 1973). Gateways need not be elegant or elaborate to carry deep meaning. Mary Catherine Bateson (1990) wrote of the ways in which the Bushmen moving through the Kalahari Desert created temporary shelters to guard against the below-freezing night temperatures. The need for shelter was easily met by scooping a shallow dip in the desert sand and lining it with grasses, where, with the addition of body warmth, those who were sheltered there would be safe from the wind and cold. But the shelter was not considered a home—even for a night—without the addition of a hearth and an entryway. A sideways-leaning curved branch, with one end embedded in the sand, was regarded as the necessary minimum to define an entrance.

Whether an elegant gateway or a simple curved branch, the entryway—as Barnett knew—would signal a great deal about the school building he was refurbishing. But he was accustomed to encountering difficulties when trying to convince project managers and members of the education department to install something that they saw as frivolous—like coloured glass, as he hoped to do in this case. And the cost of the glass? Twelve dollars for each of a dozen pieces. Just over a hundred dollars for a project with a budget of over a half-million dollars, where a quarter-million was dedicated to roof repairs alone. But because the project was about fixing things, not about beauty, some of the people associated with the project were adamant that adding coloured glass fell outside the mandate of school repairs. However, Barnett argued long and hard for the glass because one of his explicit aims in the renovation was to attend to beauty.

Eventually, the glass was approved, partly because of Barnett's persistence and partly because the principal of the school cared enough about the school and its occupants to support the gesture. Others were supportive as well, including the project manager. Barnett describes the victory as pivotal. In the ensuing years since the glass was put into place, his group has become known for their aesthetic sensibilities in school refurbishing. School officials who contract Barnett's design group these days *expect* coloured glass, ceramic mosaics, decorative wrought iron, sculptural steel elements, curved walls, and shaped timbers, along with leak-proof roofs and solid doors.

Barnett acknowledges that these incremental accomplishments—teal carpet instead of bland grey, coloured mosaics on an exterior concrete wall—"are not the stuff of award-winning architecture." Gregory Burgess, who *is* an award-winning Australian architect with a glowing international reputation, made precisely the same point upon receiving an honorary doctorate from the University of Melbourne. He said it takes ingenuity and imagination to counteract low budgets and lack of vision. In his view, architecture operates in a world where there is often little care and where most commissions are unglamorous. Burgess (2005) added that these commissions often unfold with difficulty, and architects who take on such work complete it quietly and effectively, remaining "unacknowledged in our celebrity-obsessed society" (p. 3).

So, while Barnett's refurbishing work may not be award-winning, it is the stuff of caring. And it brings a glimmer of beauty to schools. The cost of beauty in projects like these is often not more than a few thousand dollars tacked on top of a half-million dollar contract. This seems a small price to pay. When I visited Wanniassa High School—many years after these renovations were made—I was delighted to see the school was not only well maintained but also fundamentally attractive. The investment in the glass and teal carpet paid off, after all, if it inspired students to care enough about their school not to vandalize it a second time.

Resistance to Architectural Reform

There are also pedagogical reasons for why school design has not fundamentally changed in 150 years. Wente's earlier observations about factory schools are resonant with the speculation by Seymour Papert, computer scientist and educator, in his 1993 book, *The Children's machine: Rethinking School in the Age of the Computer*. Papert mused that a time traveler from the 1890s would find most things incomprehensibly changed if she were to land here now, but would have little difficulty recognizing a classroom or a school. Why have there been so few changes in classroom structures?

A study conducted by members of the Thomas Jefferson Center for Educational Design at the University of Virginia reveals four plausible explanations (as cited in Bradley, 1998). First, most school construction is set in motion to renovate unsafe or overcrowded facilities. The catalyst is not to create a more exciting learning environment, but to fix a roof or get rid of the hideous trailer-like and uncomfortable temporary classrooms often referred to as "portables." Second, school districts producing innovative designs often meet with opposition because of the perception that innovative design is more costly. Third, schools districts see no need to change when test scores are high and parents are satisfied. Finally, Bradley's study suggests that the general public— parents, business people, stonemasons, lawyers, chefs, secretaries, retailers, and even teachers and students— do not think much about how our built and natural environments influence education. It is amazing to me that we don't think more about the construction of schools, given that annual school construction budgets in the United States ring in at over $20 billion and two new schools are completed *every* day (Abramson, 2006; Abramson, 2007). Even in a slow U.S. economy, annual school construction hovers close to $20 billion a year, a far higher amount than was predicted by economist Kermit Baker (1998) not even a decade earlier, when he wrote an article for *AI Architect* predicting that school construction was on a steep upward trend.

Yet time and again, I run into situations that convince me that people pay no attention whatsoever to school architecture. I gave a seminar based on one of chapters of this book while it was still in its embryonic states. Afterwards, one of the senior professors who had attended the session wrote to me, saying, "I, for one, had never thought about the effect of school architecture on my own education, but I'm sure now it was profound. It provokes me to consider the spatial arrangements over which I have some control in my own teaching." My intent is to provoke others to do the same.

Building Costs and Social Costs: What We Can Learn From School Toilets

Here is another seemingly mundane, but highly significant issue. When I was in the middle stages of writing this book and our family was living in Canberra, I spent many hours at the Orana Rudolf Steiner School in Weston Creek talking with members of the school community about their views on school architecture. Not surprisingly, I heard common sentiments, echoed time and again, about particular architectural considerations Steiner thought important: the use of oblique angles and rounded corners so students feel enclosed and safe, the use of certain colours to create feelings of warmth, and the presence of natural objects to develop reverence for living things. But one of the most interesting conversations I had about school buildings was with a primary school teacher who, in response to my question, "Is there anything else you wish I had asked you about?" said she wanted to talk about toilets. By toilets, she was referring to the shared areas—variously known as bathrooms or washrooms or water closets—where there are a number of toilet stalls for students. These are the toilets we see in every school, and in other public places like movie theatres, parks, and shopping malls.

This teacher—who had taught in the elementary grades for over 30 years— said toilets invite threatening and cruel behaviour. Such behaviour begins almost from the very moment children begin to use school toilets. The toilets are prime sites for chasing games, bullying, teasing, and taunting. This is true even in Steiner schools, where there is an overarching emphasis on human rights and civility. Children think they will be safe in the toilets but find they are not— other children climb up and look over the stalls or crawl under them in their all too successful attempts to bully the occupants. Less serious, but off-putting nonetheless, was this teacher's description of the physical difficulties young children can have in simply reaching the toilet in time. Even in schools where the toilets are cleaned regularly, there are occasions when children will say they "can't go in there because it smells." Ruefully she commented, "I can't tell you the number of times I've mopped up the boys' toilet because a little boy didn't get there on time." Toilets can be a long way from classrooms.

I asked about architectural solutions to the proximity issue and toilet teasing. Would classroom toilets alleviate the problems? "Yes," this teacher answered, "they would." She went on to describe a classroom where there was a toilet built in, not for the teacher's use alone, but for the use of the students as well. She claimed there was never a bullying incident when the toilet had a soundproof door and was designed to be comfortable and inviting. Later, I went to see the toilet she had described. The room was painted white, and the floor was covered with terra cotta tiles; there were wooden towel racks and plants on a small shelf above the sink. I found myself thinking such a toilet would be inviting in universities as well—where now, instead of bullying behaviour, what

I encounter in the stalls in every university building I have worked in or visited is a flyer with information on what to do about harassment, abuse, or rape.

After my conversation with the Australian teacher, I regularly asked teachers, architects, and parents about washroom facilities in schools. Some of the comments were good reminders that toilets can also be positive places to congregate—socially engaging sites for students out of the teacher's earshot and vision. But more often, stories emerged about how toilets were trouble. A school administrator at a Steiner school in Vermont ruefully observed, "That's where all the mischief happens." An architect told me his 17-year-old son simply avoided using the high school toilet because of the smell of smoke and the bullying by the smokers. Another parent, who lives in the village of Bega, New South Wales, talked about choosing a high school for her daughter based entirely on the toilet situation. "What's the point," she asked, "of sending your child to school if the toilets are filthy by nine o'clock in the morning and smell of marijuana?"

It is not just students who are unhappy with school toilets. A doctoral student on my research team had an opportunity to interview teachers at a school in southern Manitoba (J. Brook, personal communication, January 15, 2009). As she began the interview, she made it clear that the teachers were free to speak about any topic related to the architecture of their school. One teacher responded, "You mean I can talk about the fact that there is only one staff toilet for 50 teachers?"

So why don't we have more toilets? Or toilets in every classroom? The short answer, of course, is that plumbing is complicated and expensive. And yet, if we were to factor in the costs that are more difficult to quantify—teacher time spent on patrolling and maintaining toilets and the social costs paid by students, perhaps classroom toilets would not be so extravagant after all. It comes down to what we value.

The adults I interviewed are not alone in thinking that issues around toilets are wrapped up with fundamental issues of human existence. Not only do toilets contribute to the social structures that develop in schools, they require enormous resources of power and water to maintain. Nel Noddings, well known in educational circles for her 1992 book, *The Challenge to Care in Schools*, wrote this:

> Sanitation is a topic of central importance today, and focus on it requires information from science, history, sociology, political science, health, aesthetics, and religion. If the topic were taken up in history (and it rarely is), it would be a mere footnote to some chronological account of political struggle. But studied as a major concern for all living beings today, sanitation can be a challenge to both practical and theoretical thought. How does a toilet work? How much water does each flush require? ... Can the gray water from washing machines be used on the garden? (p. 145).

If we admit the pervasive phenomenon of bullying in toilet areas, the inadequacy of toilets in terms of proximity and number, and the enormous draw on natural resources to maintain them, then it seems clear that effort should be devoted to designing affordable and functional classroom toilets.

An ingenious solution to the bullying problem is offered at the Casuarina Steiner School in Coffs Harbour, New South Wales. There, a crescent-shaped half-glazed wall at the back of the classroom separates the classroom space from the toilet stalls and from a storage cupboard as well. This arrangement allows the teacher to be in view of the classroom when she goes to the storage cupboard and also to see the children as they approach and leave the toilets. Because of the natural light flooding the classroom area, this arrangement has the additional advantage of making the toilet and storage areas bright and inviting without using artificial light.

Figure 1. *Half-glazed wall, Casuarina Kindergarten (photo by author)*

In the late 1960s, American psychiatrist Robert Coles (1969) put together a striking collection of students' thoughts on school architecture. An adolescent named Arthur, living in an urban ghetto, fervently believed each classroom should have its own bathroom. He said:

> They should have [a bathroom] for our homeroom, one for each one, and then we wouldn't be walking all over, and it would be ours; and that goes for eating, too. I mean, why couldn't they have a kitchen for us, like at home? My mother said if they can build these fancy apartment buildings so you can each have your refrigerator and your bathroom, they could do it for us in school, and then the whole place would be better, because we'd have a nice room and you wouldn't have to go a mile and then find a big bathroom and you can get lost in it and by the time you get back you've missed everything they've been talking about. (pp. 49–50)

The same student said of his school, "The whole place, it's pretty bad. I'll tell you why, I will. My sister said it was like a jail the other day... I step and fall, because the floors are no good ... and it's like in a war, in a battle (p. 49)." Coles' 1969 findings were echoed by Canadian researcher Neil Gislason (2009) four decades later when a student made this comment about his former high school:

> They got gates and all that stuff, then they got hall monitors doing this—they'll put you in detention like this [snapping his fingers]. ... They have police in there—police sitting by doors, all that ... it was just too crazy for me. ... They had gates [around the courtyard], like 11 feet tall. Can't nobody leave. I was like, man, I feel trapped in here. It just didn't seem like a place I wanted to be. (p. 124)

Doing battle? Not a place I wanted to be? Well, yes. Ugly schools sap the life right out of students and teachers and everyone else who goes there. School buildings tell students and teachers what societies value, what kinds of learning are important, and ultimately, what kinds of human beings we wish our students to become. Right now—no matter how valiant the teachers' efforts—a lot of our school buildings are teaching students some awful lessons: about compliance, about which subjects matter most, about dominance over other people, and about dominance over nature—lessons that American high school teacher Bill Bigelow sums up with the phrase "how my schooling taught me contempt for the earth" (Bigelow, 1996, p. 14).

School architecture needs to be radically re-thought. Such a re-thinking is not just about improving lighting or creating better storage spaces, adding a bit of colour to a university bulletin board, building classroom toilets, or even about creating better school theatres. We need to design buildings and landscapes that resonate with our biological and aesthetic sensibilities, because the ways that students experience schools will forever shape the paths their lives will follow.

Conversation
The Languages of Architecture and Education

This chapter opens with a description of American philosopher John Dewey's views on how people learn through conversation, inquiry, making things, and artistic expression. I invoke the Reggio Emilia notion of the Hundred Languages of Children as an image for the kinds of conversations that are needed for schools to be designed in more participatory and conversational ways. In this chapter, and the three that follow, I focus on how children and adults learn and how their learning interacts with architectural design. Based on the premise that conversation is a powerful way of learning, I make the claim that school design should involve conversations with a diverse group of stakeholders— architects, designers, builders, administrators, teachers, students, and the public. Some of the barriers to these kinds of conversations are explored, and the importance of developing ways of communicating to bridge these disciplines is addressed. The extraordinary work in participatory design that some architects have undertaken, notably the work of Australian architect Gregory Burgess and German architect Peter Hübner, is highlighted.

Co-Designing, Dewey's Occupations, and Languages of Learning

Our family lives in a renovated 19th century limestone schoolhouse. The deep-silled windows facing to the east, west, and south, capture the warmth of the winter sun and guide the cooling summer breezes. In winter we heat primarily with wood, just as was done in the days when the building was a school for the village children. The schoolhouse has a bell tower, the peak of which is the highest point in the village. At the time of purchase, the property had a ball diamond, too, but it has since been replaced with a septic field. And there have been other changes. When our first child was born, it became clear that what had been a fine living space for a childless couple would be less functional for a growing family. We began to plan for an addition to our home.

Planning the addition involved many long and satisfying conversations with Stanley King. Stanley is a Vancouver-based architect, officially retired, but working just as diligently now as he did for many decades before his retirement. Stanley is the founder of the Co-Design Group, a loosely affiliated assemblage of artists and architects from Vancouver and Calgary who have, for four decades, conducted intensive community workshops for the design of public spaces (King, 1989). Their mission is more than architectural: through their work, they strive to increase community vitality and unity. They are known for helping to advance plans mired in controversy and for bringing harmony to communities in conflict. Their work tends to focus on the revitalization of downtown streets, derelict harbours, and neighborhoods.

The Co-design approach also worked for the addition to our home, and I have every reason to expect it would work for school design as well. Talks and drawing sessions with Stanley took place in his Vancouver home, in our home, on long walks through parks, and at cosy restaurants. Over time, we came to know one another well, and Stanley's extraordinary success in advising us regarding the design of our addition was, in large part, based on those special conversations. And those conversations—like most good ones—depended on much more than the words we spoke. For there are hundreds of ways we communicate our most intimate thoughts and profound feelings. A casual nod or a sideways glance can communicate more meaning than the most eloquent speech. When I use the word "conversation" in this chapter, I mean the exchange of spoken words (including those almost imperceptible gestures carrying an abundance of meaning), and also written words and images—sketches, computer drawings, articles, photographs, books, statistics, charts, essays, emails, and office memos.

John Dewey, one of the most quoted American educational philosophers of early 20th century, had much to say about learning and about what he called the occupations of childhood. Conversation was one of them. He identified three other important occupations for children: inquiry, making things, and artistic expression (Dewey, 1900/1956). Dewey described how children learn through play, through movement, and through imaginary worlds. He observed how the instinct for investigation grows out of these early forms of play, claiming that there is "no distinction between experimental science for little children and the work done in the carpenter's shop" (p. 44). He saw children's artistic impulses as yet another expression of their need to communicate. These observations, made over a hundred years ago, are also made every day by parents and teachers the world over. Parents know their children learn through their play, through their constructions, and their investigations. And most children learn to converse—sometimes in several languages—long before they enter school.

This chapter focuses on the first of Dewey's occupations: conversation. We depend on conversation to make meaning throughout life. It is not only Dewey who said so. Russian psychologist Lev Vygotsky (1934/1978) was concurrently saying much the same thing on the other side of the planet. In Vygotsky's view, learning—at all ages—occurs primarily through social interactions. He placed particular importance on the process of scaffolding, claiming that children's social interactions with others, especially the adults in their lives, were at the core of the learning process.[4]

Conversation is most certainly important in the lives of older students as well. A few years ago, I was in Regina, Saskatchewan, collecting data for the fifth year of a study on the effects of an arts education program on teachers and students (Patteson, Upitis, & Smithrim, 2005). Part of the work involved interviewing students. The Grade 8 students I interviewed—teenaged students who were trying hard to look bored and cool at the same time—had been involved with the arts program since they were ten years old.

I began each interview by asking the students to tell me about their out-of-school activities. A few mentioned sports activities; others mentioned part-time jobs. I probed about other activities, such as reading for pleasure. All of the students said they liked to read, describing their reading materials, which ranged from comic books to teen magazines, science fiction to historical novels. Up to this point, the interviews had been low-key and polite, and I was learning nothing new. But when I asked them if they used the computer, and in particular MSN, the room came alive with energy. All of the students started speaking at once in their eagerness to tell me how much they *loved* MSN and about how important it was to talk with their friends. Of all of the things these students did outside of school hours, there was nothing else that held their attention with the same intensity.

When I told this story to a colleague, she asked, "What is MSN, exactly?" Good question. Technically, of course, MSN is simply an abbreviation for Microsoft Network, an Internet service provider. But since it was released in 1995, MSN has been extended to hundreds of other contexts, including MSN Messenger—an instant messaging service where people communicate with one other through their computers in real time. There is more: by the time I interviewed those students in Regina, MSN had become a verb. Just as people say, "I'll go and Xerox that for you" when they're making a photocopy, or "Pass me a Kleenex" when they're looking for a facial tissue, these students would comment, "Make sure you MSN me about that." When I interviewed the Regina students, MSN was driving their social interactions and the social interactions of thousands of other young people just like them. The breadth of MSN is—or rather, was—a brilliant example of how communication evolves with every new technology. For the speed with which MSN has been largely supplanted by Facebook, Internet smart phones, Twitter, and cell phone text messaging is truly astonishing: in a few short years, these new tools have left MSN in their wake.

Other previously unimagined forms of communication are surfacing with the Internet. Wikipedia, most often described as a free encyclopedia that anyone can edit, is a good example of a new form of communication. When I was in the middle of writing this book, Wikipedia was six years old and had over a million

---

[4] While Vygotsky's work was not popular in North America until the 1980s, he was a contemporary of Dewey, and died in 1934.

articles in English and comparable numbers in an dizzying array of forty other languages. A couple of years later, there were over 2 million articles in English. As we approach publication, there are well over 3 million articles in English alone. Wikipedia is a mammoth collaborative work: its readers make thousands of changes every hour, and the history of these changes is archived with every article. What a conversation. What a democratizer: it is not only academics who contribute articles to Wikipedia (thank goodness). And Wikipedia is largely self-policing: nonsense and vandalism are almost immediately removed, and the contributors are banned. It is not a perfect system, of course, and not without its own controversies. But it is a new form of conversation spawned by technology, of that there is no doubt.

In my Regina interviews, after hearing how MSN was central to the students' lives, I moved on to the topic of school. They returned to a subdued discourse. Yes, they liked some subjects better than others. Yes, they wished they had more time to spend in gym and art. Yes, they thought the arts were important. But when asked about the *artists* — the dancers, musicians, actors and artists who had come into their classrooms — once again the room erupted with energy. These students had no trouble calling to mind artists they had only seen a few times, sometimes five years previously. One girl told me her parents framed her Chinese brush painting and hung it in the family room. Another student said his sculpture was displayed on the living room shelf, along with his great-grandmother's silver teapot and other family treasures. The students marveled at the skill of the artists and rejoiced in the unfamiliar ways in which artists spoke, moved, thought, and lived. They wanted more hands-on — and hearts-in — experiences in the arts. Given the importance of the physical, emotional, and social learning associated with authentic experiences in the arts, it seems clear that bringing musicians and dancers and artists into the lives of students is important for learning in the arts, and — more important — for giving students a glimpse of what life as an artist might be like. For the languages of the arts are languages of communication as well. And as Dewey would have it, languages for learning.

The idea that children converse in many languages is artfully captured in the Reggio Emilia exhibit called *The Hundred Languages of Children*, first created by Loris Malaguzzi and his colleagues in the late 1980s (Edwards, Gandini, & Forman, 1993, 1998). The Reggio Emilia approach — which refers both to the pedagogy and the place in Italy where it was first developed — was Malaguzzi's brainchild. After visiting a village near Reggio that had been heavily bombed during World War II, Malaguzzi sought out other educators and parents who were united in their ambition to create schools for a democratic society (New, 2000). They established a number of municipal Reggio Emilia schools even before the passing of a 1968 national law to ensure pre-school education for working families with young children. For the next two decades, Reggio Emilia educators concentrated on two complementary efforts: building more schools and joining regional and national discussions about the aims and methods of education. *The Hundred Languages of Children* exhibit is a result of these several decades of work, where documentation has been painstakingly gathered to promote understanding of children's learning and development. The traveling exhibit features original work by children, photographs of children working in Reggio Emilia environments, transcriptions of children's conversations, and reflections of their teachers. Some of the highlighted features include the very important notion of the role of the environment as teacher, the primacy of the home-school relationship, and children's multiple symbolic languages.

Since it was created in the late 1980s, *The Hundred Languages of Children* has been displayed in close to 50 cities in Canada and the United States alone. The effects of the exhibit have been profound—guidelines published by the National Association for the Education of Young Children are filled with examples from Reggio Emilia classrooms, and scores of American educators have visited Reggio Emilia classrooms in Italy (New, 2000). Australians and New Zealanders have also adopted some of the ideas of Reggio Emilia in their "productive pedagogies" approach.[5] For a school movement scarcely a half-century old, Reggio Emilia approaches have become commonplace throughout many parts of the world. Reggio Emilia educators have been successful in entering the educational debate because they have conversed in the languages of children, teachers, parents, and researchers. Some scholars claim that the greatest legacy of the approach may lie not in the specific educational policies and practices *per se*, but rather, in the ways the movement has caused reflection and debate among educators and the public (New, 2000).[6]

Reggio Emilia schools have been an abiding interest for Howard Gardner, the American psychologist who developed the ever popular notion of multiple intelligences in the early 1980s. Gardner's visits to Reggio Emilia schools span several decades, and he provides a detailed description of the Reggio history and approach in his book, *The Disciplined Mind: What All Students Should Understand* (Gardner, 1999). In that book he highlights the accolades accorded to Reggio preschools in the December 2, 1991 issue of Newsweek Magazine where the Scuola dell'infanzia Diana in Reggio Emilia was hailed as among the best schools in the world.

In contrast to a traveling exhibit, there are instances when the same languages of children have a permanent appearance in schools in the form of artifacts created by students. Not only do these contributions make for a less institutional look, but research also shows that children who are actively involved in shaping and caring for their schools are more likely to enjoy their time there and succeed academically (Hart, 1987; Killeen, Evans, & Danko, 2003; Moore & Lackney, 1993; Noddings, 1992; Olds, 2001; Trancik & Evans, 1995). Permanent student artwork is an extremely effective way for students to cultivate a sense of ownership and pride in their schools (Killeen et al., 2003).

---

[5] Jan Millikan at the University of Melbourne's Department of Early Childhood Studies is well known for her endorsement of Reggio Emilia approaches in the Australian context (G. Daniel, personal communication, March 11, 2005). At the time of writing, Jan Millikan was Pedagogical Director of The Reggio Emilia Australia Information Exchange Inc (REAIE) for Australia and New Zealand (Retrieved July 28, 2005, from http://www.reggio-oz.dd.com.au/introduction.html).

[6] Graham Daniel, a professor from Charles Sturt University made this point forcibly in his keynote address at the Rudolf Steiner Schools Association conference, Orana Steiner School, Canberra, ACT, March 11–13, 2005.

The Mumbulla School for Rudolf Steiner Education in New South Wales provides a charming example of this approach. The Mumbulla School goes from Kindergarten to Grade 6, with just over 120 students in total. Each year the graduating class creates a permanent art addition to their school. These pieces range from stained glass windows to garden furniture to tiled mosaics on the outside walls of the buildings, such as the one pictured below. While these creations are a source of pride for students, they also result in a school alive with the human touch. As I wandered through the grounds of Mumbulla, I felt filled with the life and spirit of the children and teachers who dwell there. I could hear the voices of the students through the artifacts they created.

Five Barriers to Conversations Between Architects and Educators

Specialized Languages of the Disciplines

To be sure, the languages of children—spoken and artistic—are central to this discussion. What of the languages of architects and educators? If we are to seriously consider the ideas presented in this book, we need to attend to the ways in which architects and educators communicate—or more to the point, sometimes fail to communicate. Architects and educators, at some level, speak entirely different languages. As a result, communication is some-times difficult, even when the intention is to converse as fully as possible. Educators may have difficulties describing their notions of teaching and child development; architects may have difficulties describing their visions for buildings yet to be realized. In part, this is

Figure 2. Student art work at Mumbulla School (photo by author)

because there are highly specialized languages associated with each of the two professions, as well as with related professions, such as landscape architecture and psychological testing. Each profession's own jargon and technical terms can make it difficult for someone from outside to understand what is being said.

By way of example, educators often speak of child-centered learning approaches, assessment rubrics, and developmentally appropriate curriculum; while these terms may have some meaning in general discourse, they have *particular* meaning in the education profession. Architects, too, employ terms used in other contexts, such as elements, space, structure, form, and function, but in architecture, these words carry different meanings than in general conversation. To confuse matters more, some words are used in both professions, such as the word "program." By "program," an architect is usually referring to the square footage or dimensions of the proposed building as well as some of the key features regarding anticipated use. For example, an architectural program for a Kindergarten facility might include the total square footage for the facility, the number of students who will attend the Kindergarten, the specification of certain teaching areas (such as wet activity areas), and storage requirements. But by the word "program," an educator is usually referring to the ways to meet a set of curriculum expectations, such as how to approach the teaching of the alphabet or how to help children learn to count objects.

One can easily imagine the confusion that ensues when the word "program" is used in conversations between architects and educators. I was most certainly confused by the term when I first encountered it in an architectural context. Having spent years in the field of education, my sense of "program" was firmly embedded in the educational arena. A few years before I began writing this book, I enrolled as a student in architectural technology at our local college; after decades of constructing cabins and renovating old buildings, I thought it was time to gain some formal drawing skills and to learn more about the language of architecture. In one of my initial courses, the professor used the term "program." It took me a while to realize we had entirely different notions in mind. Since then, I have noticed that architects who are aware of the potential confusion in the use of the word "program" will use the terms "educational program" and "architectural program" to make clear their meaning (Day, 2001).

Images and Words

Architects communicate primarily in images, while educators tend to communicate with words, causing an additional barrier in communication. Architects speak of "reading" a floor plan, which is highly specialized form of image interpretation and not immediately accessible to the layperson. Many people struggle with floor plans—the bird's eye view of the interior of a building, which looks nothing at all like the building once constructed. They also struggle with elevations—the flat two-dimensional side views of buildings—which appear, to some, like the efforts of a child who has yet to master the skill of drawing in perspective. Not everyone struggles, of course; some untrained individuals can read floor plans with seemingly little effort, just as a good chef can taste a recipe while reading the ingredients. A few years ago, when I was working on a floor plan for a proposed Kindergarten, my son, who was five years old at the time, asked me about the flowers on my drawing. I told him the flowers were meant to depict round tables with chairs. Instantly, he understood the orientation and identified the entryway, the storage areas, the toilets, and so on. But this is not a universal experience. I have a colleague who tries valiantly to read floor plans and simply cannot imagine the spaces. He has just as much trouble with elevations: he simply cannot picture how a building would grow from the flat two-dimensional renderings.

Detailing to the Detriment of Craft

The specialized languages of the professions affect communication in yet another way. As the field of architecture has become more specialized, the specifications in the designs and plans have become more involved and complicated. Some architects lament that tradespeople are no longer required to solve problems by invoking the skills of their trades. Rather, they are expected to meekly follow a highly specific and predictable set of plans. This approach lessens both the need and the ability to make decisions, invariably leading to loss of joy in one's work. Sometimes this highly proscriptive approach causes errors that might have been avoided if the tradespeople were more practiced in experiencing judgments about their work.

My friend Kim Turnbull began his life's work as a carpenter. In the past few decades he has developed an abiding love for old windows, and now creates energy-efficient windows to replace historical windows, attempting to maintain the design and function of the original windows while creating a more ecologically friendly replacement. Kim often works with architectural firms hired to oversee a building renovation for its historical aspects. As a result, he constantly shuffles back and forth between the plans of a century ago—which are sometimes not more than rough sketches and elevations—and the highly complicated computer drawings provided by the architects in charge of the building renovation. With unconcealed astonishment, he once told me how the same building depicted with six or seven drawings a century ago is now rendered by over a hundred computer drawings. Those original six or seven drawings were enough for the stonemasons and carpenters of the day who, combining their own knowledge and creativity with conversations with the architect or builder, erected complex buildings. Now, as Kim ruefully noted, the electrician is told where every electrical outlet must go, and the carpenter is told what sizes of fasteners to use for the window installations.

The same escalation on the level of detailing can be observed in other professions. When Baroque composers wrote music for ensemble, one part was written as a figured bass. The figured bass player—often a harpsichordist—was given the basic harmony and was expected to fill in the rest of the notes during the performance. In a similar fashion, when composers in the Classical era wrote concerti, they expected the performers to fill in the cadenzas, encouraging them to showcase both the virtuosity of their instrument and their playing. In newer editions of these works, absolutely everything is specified—notes, durations, dynamics—and very little is left to the discretion and skill of the performer. Consequently, few performers can improvise from a figured bass, and hardly anyone writes—let alone improvises—their own cadenzas. Contrast this to other musical traditions, such as jazz, where improvisation is required and expected.

The phenomenon of increasing the specifications has also occurred in organized sports, such as hockey, where the most skilled players are required to play according to a pre-determined series of moves, thereby curtailing their considerable abilities and skills at improvisation (S. Cherry, personal communication, July 14, 2002). A friend told me that the French Canadian hockey virtuoso Maurice "Rocket" Richard once claimed that he never knew what he was going to do at the blueline. "So how was the defenseman supposed to know?" Richard is said to have asked (L. Scanlan, personal communication, September 6, 2005).

Gender and Communication

The different languages of architecture and education are further complicated by the fact that architecture is predominantly a male profession and teachers are most often women. By most estimates (such as the statistics regularly gathered by UNESCO) over 90% of elementary teachers are women, and at the secondary level, women still make up well over half of the teaching population (United Nations Economic Commission for Europe, 2005). Although men still dominate educational administration, that trend is reversing in a number of countries.

In contrast to the teaching profession, most architects, builders, and tradespeople are men. According to an article in the Wall Street Journal, in 2002, under 20% of the architects licensed by the American Institute of Architects were women, with approximately the same proportion of women as partners or principals in architectural firms (Frangos, 2003). While the number of women enrolled in architectural programs at universities is rising, it is more common for men to join traditional architectural practices after graduation than it is for women. The extent to which architecture remains a male-dominated profession in Australia was made pointedly clear in an editorial in *Architecture Australia* that summarized a century of articles on architectural practices. It ended with the observation that the content of the articles was "always within those boundaries that mark it as a journal of a profession: a *gentlemanly* style of criticism … in the service of those who care for Architecture" (Goad, 2004, italics added).

How is gender an issue? Kathryn Anthony, an architecture professor at the University of Illinois at Urbana-Champaign, says it is helpful for architects to cultivate the ability to listen closely to clients to and then to respond in meaningful and authentic ways. She suggests that women have been particularly successful in listening and responding in such a manner (as cited in Frangos, 2003). This is especially important when one considers the challenges that school architects are now being asked to address—challenges that cannot be adequately addressed without a wide consultative circle. In a later chapter called *Nature*, I discuss a sustainable university building constructed on the campus of Oberlin College, Ohio, under the fierce leadership of environmentalist David Orr. In his description of the evolution of the building, he wrote, "No architect alone, however talented, could design the building that we proposed" (Orr, 1999, p. 143).

Maintaining Rigid Boundaries

One of the factors limiting our conversations about school architecture is the fierce grip members of the different professions attempt to exercise over their professional knowledge and status. I have seen teachers offer disdainful looks to parents who claim to know something about how their child learns. As well, teachers often hold little respect for what university professors tell them about student learning or development. In some ways, this lack of respect is well founded: universities across the Western world are populated with professors of education who have not had contact with school-aged students for decades. Teachers claim these professors are no longer in touch with the "real world," and that their research is not accessible or is of little value to practitioners (Wisniewski, 1998). Fair enough. Nevertheless, parents and professors have something to say about education; they, too, belong in the educational debate.

Indeed, one of the *obligations* of professors is to engage in conversation with accessible language, rather than using words specifically designed to obscure the issues at hand. John Kenneth Galbraith captured this idea remarkably well: "There are a significant number of learned men and women who hold that any successful effort to make ideas lively, intelligible, and interesting is a manifestation of deficient scholarship. This is the fortress behind which the minimally coherent regularly find refuge" (Fulford, 1998). Writing and speaking in plain language is not easy, but it is essential if we are to communicate with people outside our own areas of expertise. Using plain language in no way implies that the ideas are simple-minded. It is a great challenge to present complex ideas without relying on words or scripted exchanges that only a few can understand.

And what of architects? In my experience, the same kinds of scripted vignettes occur between architects as between educators. The first time I attended an architecture conference, I found the experience hauntingly familiar. Except for the differences in topics, I might as well have been at an educational research conference. Some architects presented their work in engaging and accessible ways so that all of us present could understand the points being made; this often meant stepping outside the conventional forms of presentation (floor plans, elevations, and cases). However, others were determined to keep the fence around the profession impermeable, and they even said so.

The ways in which architectural ideas are approached in contemporary schools of architecture have evolved in parallel ways to the discourses of teacher education programs. In both cases, theory is rarely developed in concert with practice. More than one architect has lamented that there was a time, decades ago, when newly minted architects were given real problems to solve and were expected to develop design skills as they took on increasingly complex projects. Some claim that the emphasis is now on architectural analysis and philosophy of design, to the point that some novice architects are paralyzed by too much theoretical knowledge and too little practical experience—just like novice teachers (R. Cheesman, personal communication, May 25, 2005).

Architects who are interested in communicating broadly not only recognize the importance of consultation and public participation, but also recognize one of the problems of communication: designs are not easily understood by the very people they are meant for. By way of illustration, there is something of a bi-modal response among architects regarding the use of the multitude of three-dimensional web-based programs now available at the click of the mouse. I have witnessed architects visibly bristling at the thought of clients using such programs and saying, "Well, if everyone used programs like that, everyone would think they could be an architect. We'd be out of business." Others have the opposite reaction, observing, "I can't believe what this program can do. I just spent $13,000 on a program that can't do that. This would be fantastic for communicating with clients and getting their ideas into the design."

Let me be clear that I do not believe that "anyone can be an architect" any more than I believe that "anyone can be a teacher." Rather, I am suggesting that the professions do themselves a disservice by pulling tight the boundaries around their professional knowledge. After parents or professors discuss their ideas with the teacher, it is still up to the teacher to make those ideas a reality, drawing on all of the professional and personal knowledge she has spent decades acquiring. Likewise, after the school principal presents a set of 3D printouts with ideas for a new school to the architect, it is still up to the architect to give form to those ideas, ensuring the building will be structurally sound and aesthetically appealing.

Collaborative Conversations

In this section I examine ways that the rigid boundaries maintained by the various professions, the specialized languages, and the other barriers to communication can be overcome through collaborative conversations and by taking on multiple roles. I do so through the work of Australian architect Bronwyn Bellemore.

Bronwyn Bellemore designed a series of buildings, over a 15-year period, for the Casuarina School in Coffs Harbour, New South Wales. The School is an inviting one: everyone crosses from the parking area into the school grounds over a small wooden bridge which traverses a small stream. The buildings look as if they have grown out of the grounds where they stand: each one, in a different way, invites entry. When we spoke, I began by asking her how many of the school's buildings she had helped shape, and she answered, "All of them." Paradoxically, she also claimed that she was not responsible for the development of any of them. This was not about humility, although that, perhaps, was part of it. Rather, it was the recognition that individuals do not create building designs alone. For Bellemore, school designs emerge from the teaching of mentors and in discussion with members of the community. They also emerge through engagement with ideas appearing in scholarship and in literature, and through imagined interactions with future generations.

Bellemore spoke eloquently and forcefully about how her mentors shaped her own work. One of those mentors was Peter Kollar, her design professor at the University of New South Wales. After fleeing his native Hungary to escape communist takeover, Kollar arrived in Australia in the early 1950s and became one of the most influential and respected architects of his generation. He taught at the University of New South Wales for over four decades, was a prolific writer, and his works on design theory are still regarded as among the finest of their kind. An idea Kollar often wrote about—and one that deeply impressed Bellemore—was the necessity of attending to the spiritual, mental, and corporeal components of human needs in the context of architecture. For him, if any of these aspects were missing or overshadowed by the other components, the outcome would suffer. As he put it: "Leaving the spiritual, the universal out of the architectural endeavour is like leaving the roof off a building. The rest, no matter how secure, strict, daring or entertaining, will, for sure, be washed away by the rain" (Kollar, 1985, p. 8).

Kollar's work was more than theoretical: he placed fourth in the international competition for the Sydney Opera House, and after the winning architect, Joern Utzon, left the project, it was Kollar who saw it to completion, having been a supporter of Utzon's design from the outset. During our conversation, Bellemore asked, "How can you argue with a building like the Sydney Opera House? A building that succeeds on so many levels, in providing the city with a superb venue for the performing arts and that pierces both the physical and subtle planes?" (B. Bellemore, personal communication, May 15, 2005).

Bellemore's commitment to a broad set of underpinnings for school design goes even further: some years after she became involved as the school's architect, she undertook teacher training, and upon completing her studies, spent three years as a teacher at Casuarina School. In all, the number of roles she has played at the school is dizzying—she was a member of the Board, teacher, architect, parent, and she took on a number of administrative positions as well. While I am by no means suggesting that every school architect needs to become a teacher in order to create successful school designs, it is instructive to observe what kinds of schools are created when a broad spectrum of ideas and disciplines have been embraced.

Flaws in the Consultative Process

Over the past decade, a growing number of architects have turned their attention to involving a number of stakeholders in the design process (Bingler, 1995, 2001; Brubaker, 1998; Carey, 2001; Day, 2001; Hill, 1997; Hyer, 2001; Tanner, 2000; Taylor, 1995a). But this welcome trend towards broad consultation is not enough: the admirable attempt to consult fully will fail to produce schools markedly different from the ones we now know unless the consultation occurs *early* and *often* in the process. Further, effective consultation only occurs when the consultative group can truly affect the decision-making process: consultation in name only can never be effective. As one school leader so aptly put it: "Don't try to fool the public by holding a hearing when decisions are already cast in concrete. I have attended hearings like that, and I don't blame parents for pointing out the truth—that they are invited only for a show of involvement. They know that the more detailed the program laid out at a hearing, the more likely the whole plan is already settled upon" (Carey, 2001). And consultation is not always easy from the architect's perspective, either. Despite his overall view that consultation can be a "positive and binding factor" (Dudek, 2002, p. xv) in the creation of new schools, Dudek nevertheless cautions: "Architectural aspirations can sometimes be blunted by the involvement of community groups who play an increasingly significant role in the designation of new school buildings" (p. xv).

Architectural aspirations can also be blunted when ideas originally derived through a deeply consultative process are later emulated without using the same design sensibilities or processes. There was a historical period, early in the last century, when some architects were seeking more social fulfillment through their work, and John Dewey was able to influence the designs of schools accordingly—including those schools designed by American architect Frank Lloyd Wright. Dudek (2002) writes how Wright's interpretation of Dewey's philosophy represented "a flowering of architecture for schools in its integration of two radical new philosophies, one educational, the other spatial" (p. 20). He observes that the approach was much copied but never with the architectural dexterity of the original.

A case in point is the Crow Island School, constructed from 1939–1940 in Winnetka, Illinois. Unlike many architects of the day, the architects involved in the design of the Crow Island School studied the curriculum deeply and consulted relentlessly before designing classrooms and outdoor play areas, along with offices, library, and an auditorium. The school was designed to support the progressivist philosophy of Dewey. In ways remarkable for the time, furniture was scaled to sizes appropriate for children, door handles were placed at levels children could reach, and windows were placed low enough so children could see the outdoors (Tanner, 2000).

This single suburban school had a long and powerful influence on school design: more than thirty years after its construction, it was recognized as a design of enduring significance (Mock, 1944; Shepherd, 1999). Anne Meek wrote about Crow Island School in the 1990s, observing how the messages of the school continued to "support the work of childhood" over a half-century after its initial construction. In her words, the school says to children that the world around them is "durable and safe; it is the dwelling place of the human family. You are a cherished member of that family; you have a part in it. Your part calls for honest responses, joyful effort, and thoughtful contributions" (Meek, 1995a, p. 58).

It is widely acknowledged that the schools subsequently built on this model were watered-down versions of the original (R. Rudzinski, personal communication, January 16, 2005) and built in places with different geographies and needs. While the basic floor plan was retained, special design features— such as the ceramic sculptures adorning the brick walls of the school, commissioned from Lily Swann Saarinen, the wife of one of the architects—were not. One cannot help but wonder how school designs would have evolved if it was the *process* rather than the buildings that had been copied—a process of thoughtful and mindful conversation among architects and educators with contributions to the design coming from members of the local community.

Central to the consultative process is another, perhaps less obvious issue. Consultation will not be effective until we acknowledge that our views of teaching and learning are incomplete and flawed. In the opening chapter, I described the transmission model of teaching as one where the teacher transmits knowledge to students in a veiled attempt to prepare students for the workplace. Most school buildings support this model of teaching and learning. Schools, then, are as much perpetrators of this system as are governments that test the students who attend those schools. Deeply engaged learning involves dynamic systems that change over time—the kind of learning that happens in our adult lives when no one is watching or testing us, and the kind of learning inherent in Montessori, Reggio Emilia, Waldorf, and Froebel Kindergarten environments.

Triumphs of Conversation and Design: One Architect, Two Schools

One Architect's Story: Gregory Burgess

Perhaps ironically, those professionals who have earned respect and accolades from their colleagues are often the ones who are *most* engaged with the people they serve, both within and outside their professions. Award-winning teachers do not teach in isolation, but work with a broad cast of researchers, parents, and members of the general public in making their work meaningful and rich.[7] Likewise, some of the most highly acknowledged contemporary architects create wide and powerful consultative circles. While the time spent in conversation is intense and sometimes difficult, the rewards can be substantial.

Gregory Burgess is one architect who holds that conversation is indispensable to his work. His practice is based in Melbourne, Australia, and for twenty years, his work has been published internationally and been recognized by more than 40 awards including the 2004 Royal Australian Institute of Architects (RAIA) Gold Medal. Peter Davey, editor of the British journal *The Architectural Review*, names Burgess among a select group of architects worldwide—a group including the likes of Frank Gehry, Norman Foster, and Renzo Piano. According to Davey, these architects are "trying to find ways in which human values can be expressed against the alienating and normative forces of the global economy … tend[ing] the flame of hope and carry[ing] the lamp of truth in a world that seems increasingly to have no values other than profit and the market in its grossest form" (cited in Parken, Jahn, Andresen, Landorf, & Goad, 2004, p. 82). A fellow architect and gold RAIA medalist himself, Peter Corrigan, wrote about how Burgess "has attempted to connect us with the old enduring forces, namely nature (the perplexing Australian version), community, belief, decency, rites, meaning, and rituals" (Corrigan, 2004, p. 84).

Burgess takes on projects of extraordinary range. Some are humble in proportion; a few are so large I have difficulty imagining their scope. He has designed private homes and public housing centres, schools, community centres, ecclesiastical buildings, libraries, and health centres. He has designed

---

[7] The Certificate of Excellence recipients travel to Ottawa to receive their award certificates from the Prime Minister. Then they take part in "best practices" sessions where they get to know their fellow recipients and share their award-winning ideas practices. A description of the awards, recipients, ceremonies, and sessions is available at the Industry Canada Prime Minister's Awards website, retrieved July 28, 2004 http://pma-ppm.ic.gc.ca/pub/index.html?iin.lang=en.

award-winning buildings for Indigenous Australians, including the well-known and oft-praised Uluru-Kata Tjuta National Park Cultural Centre in Australia's Northern Territory. His refurbishment of the Sidney Myer Music Bowl, an enormous outdoor performance venue in the heart of Melbourne, has also received several awards (and, fittingly, it was the venue where he received his own RAIA award). His design for the platypus exhibit at the Healesville Sanctuary was recognized by his peers as a stunning example of the use of timber in architecture. I visited the World of the Platypus not long after I spoke with Burgess, and I was completely charmed by the habitat he developed for those enigmatic creatures. The exhibit is built directly on a creek and looks for all the world as if it grew out of the land in accordance with the wishes of the platypus inhabitants themselves.

Burgess' views on participatory design come from a dizzying mix of life experiences. He grew up in the Melbourne suburb of Box Hill, excelled in university athletics, served as a mentor, teacher, and director of the Sophia Mundi Rudolf Steiner School, and took part in government and community forums on art and design: no doubt these experiences have made him the architect and man he has become. Meeting with Burgess was a pivotal event for me; I felt as if I were in the presence of greatness, in the presence of someone deeply connected to his strengths and to his shadow side, to people, to the material world, and to a world beyond that I do not claim to understand.

By his own admission, Burgess has also been shaped by his studies of other architects and thinkers. In a 1996 paper, Burgess discussed Louis Sullivan, the Boston-born architect who became one of the most influential American architects of the late 19th and early 20th centuries. Sullivan left his mark on the city of Chicago with residences, small commercial buildings, and skyscrapers known not only for their structural ingenuity but also for the distinctive ways in which Sullivan embraced natural forms in his ornamentation. Burgess claimed that Louis Sullivan's thoughts on the "nature of consciousness transcend boundaries of culture and link us at once with the ancient mysteries, and with the physics and biology of a postmodern spirituality" (Burgess, 1996, p. 61). Sullivan believed that the power to create was intimately based on the ability to sympathize, to receive as well as to give, to enter into communion with both living and lifeless things. Sullivan's words have guided Burgess in finding the "inspiration, courage and enthusiasm to work with others in a spirit of collaboration, to be open to the unknown" (p. 61). As Burgess is quick to point out, this is a difficult task in a world marked by a "chronic lack of deeper meaning" (p. 61), where artist and architect have developed highly individualized and often idealized images. For him, "the cult of the egomaniac hero architect died some time ago" (cited in Lane, 2004). Burgess has developed an international reputation as an architect who, by all accounts, approaches design through heartfelt collaboration with the clients he serves. He is a remarkable conversationalist.

When I asked him to tell me more about his views on participatory design, Burgess described his approach as an "invitation to the dance." For him, the design process—the dance—is a moving, improvisational entity, where the architect's task is to be open to working with whatever is offered, in a "light-

footed way" to create the unfolding whole. He spoke of buildings as organisms
with their own heartbeat, centre, and step. Pushed to say more about his role in
the dance, Burgess said he sees the architect as the leader of the dance: at the end
of the process, the architect's hand is visible, but the input of a wide group of
stakeholders involved in the conversations is also evident. Burgess claims that
the result is as much theirs as the architect's. Burgess is not alone in using this
kind of moving, musical metaphor to describe the participatory architectural
process. British architect Peter Blundell-Jones wrote about how some of Lucien
Kroll's designs from the 1960s and 1970s—which also achieved international
recognition—were created through a "complex group process involving clients,
future inhabitants, and architects [with an] outcome [that] was deliberately
made unpredictable, complexity was assured by the nature of the process, and
Kroll played the part of orchestral conductor, marshalling and directing forces,
but without always imposing his own will and choices" (Blundell-Jones, 1986, p.
xi).

Is Burgess unusual? It would seem so. When I asked Burgess if the kinds of
methods he was describing were pervasive in his profession, he answered
regretfully, "Not pervasive at all." He ruefully observed how architecture tends
to be a profession of fashion. Burgess views architecture as a social art, an
environmental art, a healing art, a process quite different from "your own little
ego bashing away at something." Burgess told me that he finds the process of
embarking on each new project as "breathtakingly challenging," describing the
uncomfortable feeling in the pit of his stomach of having to begin again, each
time (G. Burgess, personal communication, March 21, 2005).

One of the school complexes Burgess designed was a cluster of three
Kindergarten classrooms situated near the top of a hill, at the Orana School in
Canberra. I was intrigued by this project on two counts: First, I found it
astounding that an architect of such note would be involved in a project of this
kind (when I asked him how he came to be involved, he quite simply answered,
"Because they invited me"). Second, because I will never see the building—the
Kindergarten was destroyed by a firestorm that swept through the school in
January 2003. Only the ghost of the building remains. But what a powerful and
present ghost. When I arrived in Canberra two years after the firestorm,
teachers, parents, and even some of the children still talked about the
Kindergarten, still grieved its loss. By 2005, a new Kindergarten was being built
in a completely different location, and a biodynamic garden was being planted
at the old Kindergarten site. As one teacher put it, "The stories of the children
will live in the garden. Something of the spirit and soul of the building will
remain there, too." This teacher also spoke of how the Kindergarten was "one
with the forest": it was not possible to rebuild the Kindergarten on a site now
stripped of the towering pines that once grew there. For her, the loss of the trees
was even greater than the loss of the Kindergarten building. In describing the
Kindergarten, another teacher told me, "We felt stronger and more alive the
moment we walked through the classroom door." This brings to mind a
wonderful observation by essayist Alain de Botton (2006) when he mused,
"Belief in the significance of architecture is premised on the notion that we are,
for better or for worse, different people in different places—and on the

conviction that it is architecture's task to render vivid to us who we might ideally be" (p. 13). My sense is that the Orana Kindergarten rendered vivid personages in both child and adult.

I asked Burgess why the school community would still mourn the loss of the Kindergarten and why—even though there were ample funds from the insurance claim to re-build—the school administrators and teachers had not chosen to erect the same building once again, albeit on a different site. He seemed surprised that the building had affected the community so deeply and wondered if it was because the community had been so invested in the process, a process which was, at times, drawn out and intense, and involved a great deal of debate and shifting ground until the building "finally found its form." Maybe the struggle of creation also elicited some of the enduring love for the place—like giving birth, where the struggle makes the prize all the more precious. As I was leaving his office, Burgess showed me a model of the Kindergarten rooms. In that model, beautifully fashioned from unbleached pasteboard and other natural materials, I could feel something akin to magic drawing me inside. There are many who describe the work of Burgess as representative of organic architecture: Conrad Hamann (2004), professor of architectural history at Monash University, has written how Burgess "has joined the world's leading responsive architects" (p. 90). His responsiveness to people and land, the past, the present, and the future, has, in turn, created the kinds of responses I had to the Kindergarten model and others had to the Kindergarten itself.

Hübner's Cologne and Gelsenkirchen Schools

I now present two examples of school design by public participation, both led by German architect Peter Hübner. Like Burgess, Hübner is well known for his participatory approach. Equally, Hübner is praised for his ingenious use of recycled materials, demonstrated as early as the 1980s with the design of the Morgenstern School (Blundell-Jones, 2004). In previous buildings, Hübner had used grass roofs, untreated timber, and passive solar heating, in addition to employing recycled materials and incorporating coloured glass and mosaics. The Cologne Waldorf School was to be no exception.

When Hübner was hired to design the Cologne Waldorf School, he began by interviewing Grade 6 and 7 students to determine what, in their view, would constitute the ideal classroom. This interviewing process involved making clay models of the classrooms, the furniture, and the people who would live and learn in the classrooms. The students' contributions to the design were significant. For example, after Hübner described some of the challenges and advantages of using untreated timber for part of the school's structure, the students came up with the idea of using internal columns, and these columns made their way into the final design (Blundell-Jones, 2004). When I visited the school in February of 2009, I was immediately impressed by these internal columns, not only by the elegance and beauty of the structure itself, but by the ways in which the columns defined a central gathering place for the students. In my conversations with the students, they expressed how much they loved the columns, the open space, the views from the various floors, and the connection that they felt with others in their school community as a result of this architectural feature.

Students, teachers, and parents were involved in the finishing work, including floor mosaics, sculptural tiling, and colour washes for the interior walls. I found these elements present in every part of the school: in classrooms, laboratories, hallways, toilets, woodworking areas, and art rooms. In this way,

there are permanent reminders of how participation began with the ideas of the students and extended to the physical engagement of the whole school community. The students engaged in all of Dewey's occupations in designing and building their school: inquiry, making things, conversation, and artistic expression. Conversations, of course, were threaded throughout the process, which took nearly four

Figure 3. Internal columns of the Cologne Waldorf School (photo by author)

years from the conception of the design to the opening of the building, with Hübner spending two days a month in Cologne over the life of the development (Blundell-Jones, 1999; Blundell-Jones, Petrescu, & Till, 2005). Such an approach does not accord well with most school building schedules, but I would suggest that true participatory design takes much more time than conventional approaches to school design and construction.

The participatory approach to design was extended further by Hübner in a subsequent project. In 1993, an international competition for a new school in Gelsenkirchen-Bismarck was held. Gelsenkirchen is a city in the old industrial heartland of Germany, the Ruhr, in North-Rhine Westfalia, where about a third of the population consists of Turkish Muslims. After the decline of the coal industry, Gelsenkirchen fell into decline; unemployment levels hovered around 30%, and the area—especially Bismarck—was marked by considerable poverty. At the time that I visited the school in 2009, the unemployment levels were still by far the highest in Western Germany (around 20%) with much of the unemployment residing in Bismarck's Turkish Muslim population. Indeed, Bismarck has been historically regarded as a "synonym for social deprivation" (H. Lehmann, personal communication, February 21, 2009).

Hübner took an extraordinary risk in his submission. Rather than submitting the traditional site plans, floor plans, elevations, and three-dimensional perspectives, Hübner chose to tell a story about an imagined graduate of the new school, some twenty years into the future, accompanied by some conceptual sketches about what the school might look like rather than submitting the more conventional finished designs. The narrative he spun took the form of a hypothetical speech given by former student Kemal Ozcul upon receiving the European Environmental Prize in 2034. In this hypothetical tale, Ozcul, the son of poor Turkish immigrants, lived in Gelsenkirchen-Bismarck when the new school was built. In accepting the award, Ozcul spoke of how his life had been transformed by Evangelische Gesamtschule Gelsenkirchen-Bismarck (Evangelical Community School of Gelsenkirchen-Bismarck),[8] which he began to attend as an 11-year-old, and where a teacher's work to save the damaged planet had inspired him (Hübner, 2005). Along with other students, teachers, parents, professionals, and members of the local community, Ozcul took part in the building of the new classrooms, communal facilities, and a garden. Upon leaving the school, Ozcul studied ecology at university and returned to the school as a teacher. Some years later, he undertook a forest project in Ankara, for which he was (hypothetically) receiving the award.

In addition to Ozcul's hypothetical speech and the conceptual sketches, Hübner provided details of how he expected teachers, students, and a host of architects to be involved in the design and realization of the school. Hübner's office won the IBA Emscher Park competition for the new school design based on this conversational and participatory approach.

The resultant school is like a village, with a cluster of buildings around a central covered street with a public square at the entrance. Lit from above, the school is bright and inviting. But what I was most impressed by when I first entered the front of the school was the sound of running water—connections to the natural world abound inside the school and out.

As promised by Hübner, students were involved in planning the school from the very beginning. Architects' proposals were based on the students' ideas, and after discussion and adjustments, the students built models based on the architects' drawings. Once the architects took the designs through the approval process and contractors erected the basic structures, the finishing was accomplished through the labours of teachers, students, and parents. Work on the landscape followed a similar process. Landscape architects designed an approximate layout and much of the hard landscape, but beyond that, the rest of the design has continued to evolve as a dynamic and interactive process involving the students and their teachers, and the responses of the landscape itself. After a four-year planning process, the school opened in 1998 with just under 150 students. Each year, a group of a similar size has been added; at the time of writing, there were over 1100 students in the school from Grades 6

---

[8] In Germany, most publicly funded state schools are affiliated either with the Protestant Church (which is called Evangelisch, or Evangelical) or the Catholic Church. The school prides itself on diversity; 30% of its students are Turkish, Turkish is one of the 'recognized' school languages, and Islam is taught as well as Christianity. All students take part in the multi-denominational chapel services.

through 13 (H. Lehmann, personal communication, February 21, 2009), with the
first class involved in the design and building of the school graduating in 2007.[9]

Early support for this extraordinarily full and public participatory process
came from then director of the school, Rainer Winkel, who had taken a leave
from his position as professor at the Universität der Künste in Berlin to serve as
the school's first director. Winkel's own educational philosophy was rooted in
the ideas of John Dewey and Maria Montessori, and he was convinced of the
importance of learning through practical projects involving one's own hands.
The Gelsenkirchen-Bismarck project had political support as well. When Karl
Ganser, then Minister for Development in the North-Rhine Westfalia regional
government, heard of the plan, he helped convince Minister-President Johannes
Rau of the worthiness of the project. Local church administrators also supported
the unfolding of the project with Hübner at the helm.

At the time of writing, the school had been thriving under the directorship
of Harald Lehmann for some years. It was during my walking tour with Herr
Lehmann through the school and its grounds that I began to catch a glimmering
sense of the magnitude of the educational accomplishments of the school—
accomplishments that Lehmann was convinced would not have been possible
without the architecture. He commented on the expression that architecture can
serve as the "third educator"—an expression with its roots in Reggio Emilia
schooling. But, he noted, in most "ordinary" schools the architecture is simply
not that important; "It might be the ninth or tenth teacher." In this school,
however, the architecture provides students with "a place, a home. And that
makes it easier for the teacher. What we have done here would not have
happened without the architecture."

Elements that contribute to a sense of place or a feeling of home abound.
There are comfortable places to congregate: in the library overlooking a pond
teaming with fish, turtles, and ducks; in the open atrium, café-like in feel,
bounded by a wall of plants with olive trees reaching the skylights far above;
and in the classrooms themselves where sofas and cushions are found in many
of the loft-galleries of each of the two-storey classrooms. There is also an
intergenerational presence, as people from the community walk past the various
school buildings on the extensive networks of sidewalks and pathways
(teaching schedules have been adjusted to allow students enough time to
meander from one space to another between classes). And there is running
water, still water, plant, reptile, fish, and animal life—both indoors and out.

---

[9] Background information on the Evangelische Gesamtschule Gelsenkirchen (Evangelical
Community School of Gelsenkirchen) was culled and translated by David Murphy Haglund from
several sources, including the school's website (http://www.e-g-g.de), Peter Hübner's architectural
firm's website (http://www.plus-bauplanung.de/dna/), and Rainer Winkel's website
(http://www.prof-rainer-winkel.de/index.htm). I also learned about Evangelische Gesamtschule
Gelsenkirchen-Bismarck from articles by Peter Blundell-Jones before visiting the school in
February, 2009 and speaking with the school's headmaster, Harald Lehmann. The school is
featured in the collection by Eleanor Curtis (2003) titled School buildings, and by Mark Dudek
(2002) in Architecture of schools.

The school has purposely retained its diverse student population and the population is one that continues to challenge the staff of close to 90 teachers. Each year, 150 new students are admitted; in the most recent intake, there were 370 applications for these coveted spaces. Priority is given to neighborhood children, and the ethnic and cultural make-up of each new class mirrors that of the neighborhood. The current Grade 5 class of 150 had 58 students of "migration background" with most of those students being of Turkish Muslim heritage (H. Lehmann, personal communication, February 21, 2009).

When I asked about the typical graduation rates for some of the least advantaged students living in the region, Lehmann ruefully noted that it was typical for 30% of the Turkish Muslim students to leave school without the minimal formal qualifications that are granted after successfully completing Grade 10. When asked about the graduation rates at his school, Lehmann's humble response was, "We try not to have any student leave without qualification." Put another way, as compared to other schools in the community with 30% failure rates, Evangelische Gesamtschule Gelsenkirchen-Bismarck has graduation rates as close to 100% as one can imagine. Small surprise that standardized test scores have been steadily increasing as well.

During my visit to the Evangelische Gesamtschule Gelsenkirchen-Bismarck I could not help but notice the condition of the furniture throughout the school; 12 years after opening, there was not a mark on the lovely wooden tables in the dining area, and the tile work in the toilets, the furniture in the classrooms and common areas looked like new. I was also taken with a beautiful piece of graffiti artwork that had found a permanent place in the central atrium. I learned of the story behind that piece of artwork from Herr Lehmann. The student who had created the work wanted to have his own art displayed, after seeing some of the more con- ventional work finding a permanent place of the newly restored high school. Lehmann gave him the opportunity to design and paint a piece in keeping with the colours and style of the rest of the atrium. This the student did. And while the student was not entirely transformed by the event, he remained in school despite the odds against him. When asked

Figure 4. Two-storey classrooms of the Evangelical Community School of Gelsenkirchen-Bismarck (photo by author)

why there was no vandalism in the school, Lehmann responded that it was because they students have come to treat the school as they would their home. He told another story to illustrate his point. When there was graffiti sprayed on the inside door of one of the girls' bathrooms, his response was to cover the graffiti with a big piece of white paper, with a message to the effect, "Do you really want our school to look like this? Like other schools with graffiti?" Some of the students responded on the white paper (in Turkish, as was the original message). During the next school holiday, he had the door re-painted. A year and a half later, there was no new graffiti on the door.

That the school has a home and village-like feel is further embodied by the separate spaces for woodworking, pottery, home economics, art, and theatre. There is a bicycle repair shop where Grade 8 and 9 students fix bicycles brought in by students and other community members. The theatre, with its apricot coloured walls and comfortable seating, is sometimes rented by the mayor of the city for municipal events, providing yet another link between school and community. This connected series of buildings simply does not feel like a school. Indeed, in a book describing the participatory process of building the school (Hübner, 2005), Hübner asserted that some visitors to the school, after being toured through the various spaces, ask "where the school is after they have already walked through it" (p. 8). I thought this report a little far-fetched until I returned home and was assembling a slide show of the school with the help of my then eight-year-old daughter. When we finished our work, she said, "It's very beautiful, isn't it? But where is the school?" Case in point.

Concluding Conversation

I have waxed eloquent about Evangelische Gesamtschule Gelsenkirchen-Bismarck. Of the hundreds of schools that I have had the privilege of visiting, it is perhaps the one that has impressed me most. But it is much more than the architecture that is impressive. It is the weaving of architecture and teaching by teachers and administrators committed to education that makes it an exemplary place. And this exemplary project and others are possible only because of wide-ranging conversations and an equally broad base of support. It is because architects like Hübner and Burgess recognize this necessity that such projects even see the light of day.

But architects like Hübner and Burgess are the exception. This exceptional orientation must become more prevalent if the nature of schools and schooling is ever going to change. Incumbent upon all of the stakeholders is to make the effort to learn a little of one another's languages so the most deeply held beliefs and values about learning and living can be communicated and realized in design. Expertise is not lost in this kind of approach: the opposite is the case, as architects, gardeners, teachers, parents, and students learn about other points of view and disciplines.

Even though I have suggested that there are ways to make educational and architectural language more accessible, I am not suggesting that a common language, alone, would alleviate the problem of communication in the design process. We need a common language *and* we need to retain the subtleties of the specialized languages of the professions, the embodied knowledge of the tradespeople, and the many languages of children. The task, then, is to build bridges between languages—what poet Don McKay (2001) has called "acts of translation" (p. 62)—so a multiplicity of expressions can communicate the ideas we cherish most deeply. McKay says we need to think of language as "apparatus, to use and inhabit with an awareness of residual wilderness" (p. 62). For him, good acts of translation do not "supersede the original… nor forget its existence" (p. 62). Or as Shirley Thomson (1999), then Executive Director of the Canada Council for the Arts, so fervently argued at a Canadian National Symposium on Arts Education, we must speak many languages, marshalling our arguments in whatever way makes sense to our audiences.

And we must listen, too. For it is only in the interchange of ideas—through a dynamic system involving people with differing perspectives, beliefs, and skills—that the most provocative and successful ideas will be brought to fruition in school design.

Play

Kindergartens, Playgrounds, and the Spaces In-Between

In this chapter, I explore Dewey's views on the importance of play. After an examination of the historical roots of early childhood education and Kindergartens, I discuss the ways that Friedrich Froebel's Kindergarten materials influenced the work of architect Frank Lloyd Wright. Next, I outline how architecture has influenced early childhood education, using Steiner and Reggio Emilia schools as examples. Children's objects of play and their playgrounds are then examined. The importance of what the outdoor environment has to teach—an issue that gains momentum as the book unfolds—also forms a focus for this chapter. The chapter closes with a discussion of the spaces that lie between buildings, and how they can be developed as places for play, learning, and living.

Let your dreams bind your work to your play.[10]

Play is an undertaking I immediately associate with the days of early childhood. Like others, I have often marveled at how much children learn about the physical world and about interacting with one another through their play. But play is also relevant to learning throughout schooling and beyond. And play is resonant with the pursuits of architecture. I have heard it said that being an architect means being able to spend time in ways reminiscent of childhood play—imagining and sketching, manipulating shapes, and playing with objects. British scholar Mark Dudek (2000) observes how

---

[10] From a song titled *Thanksgiving Eve*, by singer songwriter Bob Franke, © 1982, Telephone Pole Music Publishing Co. (BMI). Stan Rogers, a Canadian singer-songwriter who died in a plane crash in 1983, popularized this song.

childlike pursuits and perceptions fascinated artists and architects throughout the 20th century. He points to a fundamental link between the childhood play experiences for artist Paul Klee and architect Frank Lloyd Wright, and the kinds of creative work they produced as adults. English architectural historian John Summerson has identified a form of play common to children across cultures: children the world over create shelters in their play, using furniture and blankets, or fallen branches from the garden. Summerson says adults do not outgrow the need for this symbolic game, a game likened to the aesthetics of architecture (as cited in Dudek, 2002). Psychologists, too, have suggested that childhood games continue to be carried out through the primary years and even into the beginning years of adolescence and that these games continue to be a source of learning (Hart, 1993).

Architects and educators have observed that the most effective Kindergartens have abundant sensual variety, with "texture, sound, light and colour which challenge and inspire children, rich enough to provide cosy quiet spaces for withdrawal and security, as well as more open communal and social places for group activities [and] an exciting outdoor space, for freedom of movement and physical daring" (Dudek, 2000, p. 7; Tarr, 2001). Dudek's description begs the question: Why do we tend to limit these environments to young children and their teachers? Sadly, the obvious answer is that once children begin grade school, so-called serious schooling begins—schooling with little time or place for play. I am saddened when I hear stories of students in upper grades who, upon pulling out coloured pencils or crayons to decorate or illustrate their work in science or math, are told by their teachers to put the pencils away, with the admonition, "You're not in Kindergarten anymore." But scientist David Hawkins (1965) says the best learning happens in Kindergarten and in graduate school. Perhaps some of the best learning happens in Kindergartens because of the physical environments (I'm not so sure about the physical environments of graduate schools). Dudek (2000) likewise observes that the freedom granted to the youngest children in our schooling systems does not exist anywhere else in the education system. And in a world ever more obsessed with student achievement and standardized testing, these freedoms that are, too, fast disappearing.

The History of Kindergartens and Other Schools for Young Children

Nearly every contemporary Kindergarten and early childhood approach can be traced back to 19[th,] and early 20th century forms of education, where the natural world, artistic expression, inquiry, and the manipulation of physical objects were thought to engender intellectual and moral sensibilities for the growing child. Kindergartens—by which I also mean pre-schools, early learning centres, infant schools, and nursery schools—cater to children as young as three and as old as six, depending on the country and on the broader educational context. The German word "Kindergarten" means a children's garden, and the term works on both literal and metaphoric levels. Dudek claimed the term "originally derived from the notion of the school as a metaphorical garden, [alluding] to the idea of children as unfolding plants" (2000, p. 1). He further suggested that the term points to the affinity young children possess for natural phenomena. While the origin of the term "Kindergarten" is generally attributed to Friedrich Froebel (Dudek, 2000; Herrington, 2001), others, such as Margaret McMillan, one of the most vigorous British proponents of early childhood education in the early part of the 20th century, also described the ideal nursery school as a garden city for children (Dudek, 2000).

The idea of children benefiting from exposure to the outdoors pre-dates even the earliest formal Kindergartens. In the 17th and 18th centuries, church officials, scholars, and lawyers recognized the importance of education for the very young, to cultivate links between children and the natural world and for the development of moral values. Jean-Jacques Rousseau's 18th century humanist views on education—education he thought should take place in a garden because it offered the opportunity to experience, through the body and the senses, the "moral dance between nature and property" (Herrington, 2001, p. 30)—were taken up in another form by the Swiss educator Johann Heinrich Pestalozzi, in the late 18th and early 19th centuries (Dudek, 2000; Herrington, 2001; Wilson, 1969).

Present day Kindergartens are supported by public funding, religious trusts, and private sources. They are often housed in stand-alone buildings with gardens and outdoor play areas accessible to the children and their teachers (Dudek, 2000). In some jurisdictions, specially designed Kindergarten programs have been created to support children from families with lower incomes and to help these children acquire some of the cognitive skills essential to their later schooling. Perhaps the best known of such programs is the Head Start pre-school program in the United States, where billions of dollars of funding have been dedicated to associated programs and facilities (Stormshak, Kaminski, & Goodman, 2002). The reason for this? Evidence suggests that if children lose ground in the first six years, they will never make it up.

The importance of early educational interventions for children from impoverished environments is also an idea with its roots in centuries past. In many cases, the first pioneers for early childhood programs created settings for the children most in need of such experiences. In 1816, Robert Owen set up a nursery school in New Lanark, Scotland, so that children of factory workers would be able to "fill the air with perpetual questionings... [and so they might] not be stinted, rebuked, dispirited ... [but allowed to develop] a continuous elastic spirit, ever enquiring, and ever extending to others the fullness of its own aspirations" (Taylor, as cited in Dudek, 2000, p. 6). A century later, British educator Margaret McMillan argued that children living in impoverished conditions in London needed outside space and physical games to liberate them from their cramped environments. And so, she too developed a form of nursery school education focusing on the outdoors. Some of the earliest nursery buildings, such as London's Deptford Nursery School, established in 1913 for so-called poor and undernourished children by Margaret McMillan and her sister Rachel, were created as centres for social and medical care; the educational goals followed (Dudek, 2000). The architecture for these first centres was anything but inviting—makeshift sheds and shelters were the norm. The importance Rudolf

Steiner (1861–1925) later placed on the Kindergarten years—and in particular on the aesthetic and imaginative aspects of early childhood—has been attributed to a visit he made to the Deptford Nursery School in 1923. Largely as a result of his visit to London, the first Waldorf School in England was opened in 1925 in south London. When it moved to Forest Row in Sussex, it became known as the Michael Hall School, a thriving school that continues to provide leadership to other Waldorf communities to this day.

Johann Pestalozzi (1746–1827) created a school at a farm at Neuhof, Germany, in the late 18th century. There children from poor families could learn the practical skills of agriculture—a considerably less romantic but equally compelling role for the outdoor gardens and landscapes than the one later claimed by Froebel. One of Pestalozzi's striking contributions was the development of a teaching style that engaged children through the arts—song and dance in particular—and in addition to agricultural activities, emphasized learning with objects and through manual activities (Herrington, 2001). He claimed that students would be better equipped to learn throughout their lives if, as young children, they were able to express themselves artistically and were provided with real objects for carrying out operations such as those of arithmetic (Wilson, 1969).

Friedrich Froebel (1782–1852) remains the best-known figure in the development of early childhood education. Part of the reason for his continuing esteem is the extraordinarily rapid and continued growth of Froebel's Kindergartens. Less than a decade after Froebel's first school was opened in 1839 in the Thuringian forest of Germany, 61 Kindergartens had been established in Germany. Many of these were established under the guidance of women of considerable social and economic standing who were able to further spread Froebel's notions in countries throughout the world (Herrington, 2001). Froebel produced a weekly journal, published a songbook, and codified more than 20 of his so-called 'Gifts,' a series of objects for children to manipulate to enable them to learn about geometry, design, and form. But Froebel's methods were not universally accepted. Because his spiritual views "conflated nature with God," the church objected to his teachings, and the use of women as teachers was considered threatening to the family structure (Herrington, 2001, p. 43).

Froebel's Kindergartens emphasized both interior and exterior learning spaces, based on his belief that children learn through physical activity and play (Reitzes, 1998). Froebel himself grew up in a rural environment, and in addition to his studies in architecture, he studied biology, mathematics, and forestry. Although he abandoned architecture as his chosen profession and turned to education, the influences of his architectural studies remained. Froebel was also influenced by the educational principles of Johann Pestalozzi (Wilson, 1969), having visited the Pestalozzi school at Yverdon, Switzerland, where he encountered Pestalozzi's humanist legacy. One of Froebel's practices came from Pestalozzi's method of teaching geography, which was based on Rousseau's "survey method." Simply put, Froebel took his students on a weekly walk through the town and countryside in which they lived, which formed the starting point for later explorations in the classroom. On these walks, children would gather flowers and other artifacts from the natural world, create gardens, and present their findings and Gifts to their parents and teachers. Out of these weekly excursions Froebel developed his teaching approach and materials, including the specially designed Gifts to be used by children.

The influence of Froebel and Pestalozzi reached across the ocean to the United States as well. The first Kindergartens in the United States were based on Froebel's notions: Margarethe Schurz (1833–1876), a former student of Froebel's, opened the first German-speaking Kindergarten in Watertown, Wisconsin, in 1855 (Herrington, 2001). Soon thereafter, Elizabeth Peabody (1804–1894) established the first American English-speaking Kindergarten in Boston, with a program featuring singing, games, and the tending of individual garden plots (Herrington, 2001). Fifteen years later, there were over a hundred Kindergartens in the United States.

John Dewey became interested in Froebel's gardens as early as 1879. When he established the Chicago Laboratory School in 1896 (Herrington, 2001; Mazzone, 1995), Dewey made gardening a special activity as much in accord with Pestalozzi's orientation as Froebel's. Although Dewey appeared to appreciate Froebel's romantic notions of the garden as well as Pestalozzi's practical orientation, Froebel's version came under sharp criticism by American critic William Heard Kilpatrick (1916) who "scoffed at Froebel's symbolic use of the garden" (Herrington, 2001, p. 43). Kilpatrick considered Froebel's view of the spiritual nature of plants as "pure mysticism" (p. 43), suggesting that it would be better to concentrate on the "cultivation of gardens for the sake of produce" (p. 44). Kilpatrick's scorching criticism may explain why the garden and excursion components were eliminated from most American Kindergartens, while schools in England, Germany, the Netherlands, and Japan retained both the gardening and nature study aspects of Froebel's Kindergartens. The situation in the United States has been further exacerbated by the long-standing view held by many teachers, administrators, and parents that pursuits like gardening take too much time away from what are increasingly narrow curricular demands (Herrington, 2001).

In 1876, Kindergartens were featured at the Philadelphia Centennial Exhibition, where Hannah Wright, mother of Frank Lloyd Wright (1867–1959), first encountered the ideas of Froebel. Frank Lloyd Wright (1943) wrote:

> My mother had seen the 'Gifts' in the Exposition Building. The strips of colored paper, glazed and matt, remarkably soft brilliant colors. Now came the geometric by-play of those calming checkered color combinations! The structural figures to be made with peas and small sticks: slender constructions, the joinings accented by the little green-pea globes. The smooth shapely maple blocks with which to build, the sense of which never afterward leaves the fingers: form becoming feeling. … And the exciting cardboard shapes with pure scarlet face—such scarlet! Smooth triangular shapes, white-back and edges, cut into rhomboids with which to make designs on the flat tabletop. What shapes they made naturally if only one would let them! … These 'Gifts' came into the gray house in drab old Weymouth and made something live there that had never lived there before. (cited in Dudek, 2000, p. 60)

Throughout the 20th century, Kindergartens and other related approaches with roots stretching back to the humanist and Romantic movements took hold in mainstream education throughout North America. Meanwhile, Rudolf Steiner

(1861–1925) was developing educational methods in Germany that combined his architectural sensibilities with his observations of children, and applied them through to the end of high school. Maria Montessori (1870–1952) was honing educational methods for young children in Italy that also involved the manipulation of physical objects, with the aim of schooling children to become civil and peaceful beings.

In the next section of the chapter, I describe how education has affected architecture, showing how Frank Lloyd Wright was influenced by Froebel's Gifts. Then, I examine how architecture has affected education, using Rudolf Steiner's work as an example. Following this, the Reggio Emilia approach is considered, where architecture itself is viewed as a teacher.

Education Influences Architecture: Froebel's Gifts and Wright's Designs

Among Froebel's Gifts—described above in the words of Frank Lloyd Wright—were wooden forms for three-dimensional design work, clay modeling materials, and paper for folding. This series of Gifts, presented to children in increasing complexity, were intended to encourage students to develop an ever more elaborate understanding of form, pattern, and symbolism. Beginning in 1835, Froebel spent fifteen years developing the Gifts, based on observations of natural phenomena and the verbal and kinesthetic responses of children to the Gifts as they were being developed. The first two Gifts, the sphere and the cube, were meant to emphasize "action, surface, unity and form" (Wilson, 1967, p. 238). Opposite or contrasting qualities, for example, unity-diversity, movement-repose, space-objects, and whole-part, were set off against one another through the Gifts. The Gifts grew quickly in complexity. The fifth Gift was a three-inch wooden cube divided in each direction by two cuts; each edge was also trisected so each face had nine equal parts, and the entire cube was made up of twenty-seven one-inch cubes. Six of the cubes were further divided: a diagonal cut divided three, and three others were divided into four by two diagonal cuts. Thus, the fifth Gift contained 39 pieces of cubes and sub-cubes, allowing for a large range of explorations by the child (Wilson, 1967).

As we have seen, Froebel's Gifts would become foundational influences for Frank Lloyd Wright. Of all of the topics linking education with architecture, there is more writing on the connection between Froebel and Wright than on any other topic (e.g., Economou, 1999; Herrington, 2001; Kaufmann, 1981; MacCormac, 1974; Rubin, 1989; Sloan, 2002; Wilson, 1967). Dudek (2000, 2007) argued that 20th century views of modern architecture stemmed directly from the many hours Wright spent manipulating Froebel's Gifts. Wright himself acknowledged this debt in his 1943 autobiography, where he said the feeling of the maple blocks remained in his fingers throughout his life.

In his autobiography, Wright described his mother's frequent sojourns to Boston, where she studied with a teacher of the Froebel method. Wright described how, once the housework was done, his mother would sit with her children "at a low mahogany table with a polished top, working with these Gifts" (Wright, 1943, p. 60). Because Wright manipulated Froebel's forms throughout his childhood—long past the Kindergarten years—these explorations were particularly formative (Hitchcock, as cited in Wilson, 1967). Wright was reacquainted with the Gifts again in his adult years when he and his first wife, Catherine, began educating their own children through Froebel's techniques (Sloan, 2002). This was also the time when Wright's former employer, Chicago-based architect Louis Sullivan, was experimenting with free-form organic creations of his own. Scholar Julie Sloan demonstrates how the ninth Gift, a series of steel arcs and rings used to create circular designs, was intimately connected to the pre-Prairie period windows Wright created during this period. She suggests that Wright's interest in the circle might have "been kindled by a combination of childhood memories of the Ninth Froebel Gift and exposure to Sullivan's rich organic ornament" (Sloan, 2002, p. 69). Sloan's work shows how three other Gifts—the eighth (sticks for sticklaying), the fourteenth (weaving papers), and the seventh (quadrangular and triangular tablets), are in harmony with Wright's fabulous leaded glass window designs.

Architecture Influences Education: Steiner's Waldorf Curriculum

For architect and philosopher Rudolf Steiner, architectural principles shaped the development of his Waldorf schools as much as pedagogical ones. Steiner was known for a form of architecture referred to as organic expressionism, where buildings were "liberated from the constraints of the right angle" (Dudek, 2000, p. 62). Steiner education has become one of the fastest growing school movements in the world (Oberman, 1997; Steiner Farm School, 1979). There are now over 1000 Steiner schools worldwide (D. Gerwin, personal communication, January 19, 2009).

In Steiner's view, every aspect of the school—the wooden furniture, pastel colors, natural lighting, and the presence of natural objects in the classrooms, as well as the outdoor spaces—had architectural and pedagogical significance. Waldorf curricula have been described as arts-based: not only is there an emphasis on learning in the arts themselves (e.g., water color painting, beeswax modeling, playing musical instruments, singing), but other subjects, such as language and mathematics, are also approached through the arts. Drawing, stories, chanting, and a choreographed series of body movements known as "eurhythmy" are prominent in Waldorf schools. Waldorf schools also operate without the familiar administrative structure of most schools—there are, for example, no school principals. Teachers make decisions by consensus.

In *Kindergarten Architecture*, Dudek (2000) speaks at length about Steiner's philosophy because he holds the view that Steiner, more than Montessori or Froebel, believed that educational aims could only be achieved through particular architectural forms and environments. In Steiner's case, these educational aims go well beyond the Kindergarten years, for Steiner schools encompass the full primary and secondary years of schooling. Dudek's criteria for evaluating contemporary Kindergarten architecture, which he applies to the 22 cases in his book, are developed from Steiner's notions (Reitzes, 1998). The casebook on school architecture by Eleanor Curtis (1993) also contains several examples of Steiner schools—a disproportionately high number when one considers the relatively small number of existing Steiner schools, many of which were not purpose-built. Dudek has lamented how "the highly metaphysical nature of the Steiner philosophy ... worked against its being adopted by [the] mainstream, [and while] Steiner's basic philosophy was always a little too esoteric for his enlightened methods to be widely adopted ... architects find many aspects of his architectural reasoning capable of producing particularly appropriate architecture for children" (Dudek, 2000, p. 33–35). I agree.

Architecture as Teacher: Reggio Emilia Schools

And what of the Reggio Emilia approach? Teachers in the pre-primary schools of Reggio Emilia focus explicitly on what school environments teach children. In most such schools, there are two teachers, and it is common for educators to use the term "third educator" or "third teacher" to describe how the school building functions as a teacher (Gandini, 1998; Tarr, 2001). Reggio Emilia environments are based, in part, on John Dewey's educational philosophy. Teachers believe that the best environments for children are rich and complex, support relationships between people and ideas, and have a strong aesthetic appeal (Borgia, 1991). As a result, Reggio schools bring elements of the home into the school, elements that scholar Patricia Tarr calls "beautiful objects in their own right" (Tarr, 2001, ¶ 4). Tarr describes how Reggio educators carefully consider the physical environment in light of its educational potential, both in terms of the objects in the environment and in terms of the kinds of spaces for inquiry, such as the atelier (art studio). She comments on how she was struck by the "beautiful wooden table with a large bowl of flowers and wooden sideboard in one of the rooms in La Villetta School" (Tarr, 2001, ¶ 5) and, further, how the role of the arts was clearly evidenced by the atelier and the atelierista (artist-teacher). She contrasted this to North American classrooms where children are prepared for the future world of work with "simplified visual forms" reflecting mass marketing and "craft-store culture" Tarr, 2001, ¶ 6). In Tarr's view, North American schools do not challenge children to respond deeply to the natural world, to their cultural heritage—and most certainly not to their inner worlds.

Speaking about Reggio Emilia schools, American educator Howard Gardner (1999) offered a markedly similar description:

> If you walk into one of the preschools on a given morning, you will first be struck by the beauty and spaciousness of the building. Reggio buildings are ample, open, streaming with light; potted plants and inviting chairs and couches are strategically placed, adding color and comfort to the surroundings. There are secluded alcoves to which youngsters can retreat, interior gardens and common space where the teachers can meet. Most of the classrooms flow easily into one another and spill out into a large central piazza. Passage to the play areas outside the school is also convenient, and in good weather, one will see groups of children playing together on the grounds. On neat shelves are stored literally hundreds of materials—from colored geometric forms to grains of cereal to seashells to recyclable wooden sticks— with which the youngsters may become engaged at some point (or repeatedly)

during the year. Everything seems in place; there is no clutter or mess; and yet, the spaces feel inviting and flexible. (p. 87)

Gardner emphasized that these schools "stand out by virtue of the type and quality of the activities that the children carry out on a regular basis; the deeply caring and respectful ways in which teachers interact with the youngsters and with one another; [and] the availability of the education free of charge throughout the municipality" (p. 87).

Responding to Natural and Inner Worlds

The recurring theme of responding to the natural and inner worlds through play, through inquiry, through the manipulation of objects, and through artistic expression forms the crux of the next section of the chapter. Earlier I referred to the description by David Hawkins of the richness of learning in Kindergartens and in graduate school, which suggests to me that we ought to contemplate how school architecture might contribute to rich learning in the years between these two extremes.

Hawkins is remembered for his classic essay, *Messing About in Science*, first published in 1965. In it, he argued that much more time ought to be devoted to "free and unguided exploratory work (call it play if you wish; I call it work)" (p. 7). He suggested—in a Dewey-like manner—that children should be given materials, objects, and equipment and then be permitted to "construct, test, probe, and experiment without superimposed questions or instructions" (p. 8). Hawkins did not suggest that science learning would end with this kind of unguided exploratory work; rather, he argued that this kind of play would later lead to deeper understanding and more engagement in the learning itself. The late Canadian author Carol Shields also observed how this kind of unstructured time contributes to the creative process. In her poetic and compelling prose, Shields (2001) wrote:

> In a long and healthy life, which is what most of us have, there is plenty of time. There is time to sit on a houseboat for a month reading novels. There is time to learn another language. There is travel time and there is stay-at-home time. Shallow time and fallow time. There is time in which we are politically involved and other times when we are willfully unengaged. We will have good years and bad years, and there will be time for both. Every moment will not be filled with accomplishment; we would explode if we tied ourselves to such a regimen. Time [is] not our enemy if we [keep] it on a loose string, allowing for rest, emptiness, reassessment, art and love. (p. 344–345)[11]

---

[11] The quote, as it appears in this book, came from an earlier version of these thoughts that Shields presented as an invited address upon receiving an honorary doctorate from my home institution, Queen's University. At the time, I was serving a term as Dean of Education, and so, I had the honor of escorting Carol Shields during the convocation ceremony. In the signed copy of the address that she sent to me a few weeks later, she thanked me for being a gentle shepherdess. While I doubt that her generous words describe me accurately, I can't help but note that the images of shepherding are also familiar and welcome in the Kindergarten.

If Hawkins and Shields are correct in their views of how unstructured time bears fruit in both science and art, then physical environments to support messing about and fallow time should also be considered. There are two aspects of the physical environment that support play (or work) of the highest order: (a) objects selected for play, and (b) outdoor playground and learning environments.

Objects of Play

The notion of play invariably invokes an association with the *objects* of play. American philosopher and mathematics educator Nel Noddings (1992) wrote about the importance of objects as a cornerstone of Maria Montessori's educational method; Montessori insisted that children should be free to use objects that were carefully selected, so long as they were used for their intended purposes. Montessori's focus on the objects, over the outdoor world that so captured Froebel, no doubt owes its genesis to the different circumstances in which each of these educators developed their methods. Montessori died a full century after Froebel, and during the intervening years, considerable changes occurred in the circumstances surrounding early childhood education. Froebel located his first Kindergarten in a charming wooded valley; Montessori's first school was "in the most squalid district of urban Rome" (Dudek, 2000, p. 58). Understandably, she cultivated a particular emphasis on the pragmatics of the indoor environments. Such pragmatics included attention to ordinary tasks of daily care, such as personal cleanliness, and a series of gymnastic exercises to help develop coordination. Montessori also felt there should be a proper place— one readily accessible to the children—for storing objects (Dudek, 2000). American educator Nel Noddings describes how Montessori believed a love of order would derive from this kind of caring relationship with objects, and that such physical order would ultimately "induce serenity of the soul, or what Montessori called grace" (Noddings, 1992, p. 141).

While Noddings (1992) makes clear how caring for human-made objects and instruments is not the same as caring for animate beings, in that there is no immediately obvious moral impact in the caring of objects, she nevertheless argues that the treatment of objects has a profound impact on both human and nonhuman life. "When we are careless with things or become obsessed with gross acquisition, we use far more than our share of the world's resources, so our behavior with objects has moral implications" (p. 139). For these reasons and others, Noddings says students must learn how objects work. She suggests that as students begin to examine and use objects in a mindful manner, they invariably begin to examine their own lifestyles. But such examination can only happen if students have a certain level of literacy about objects. In her view, for example, students should know what a fine chisel can do and what happens if a chisel is used to scrape off old paint or to pry open paint tin lids. That is, the study of objects should be related "to how we ought to live, to the obligations we feel as moral people, to our sense of beauty, to our desire to preserve the natural world" (p. 142).

Montessori's notion of ordering objects of play, or facilitative order in Noddings' terms, is a kind of ordering that is given scant attention in most contemporary schools. The implications of this lack of attention to this type of order are moral, utilitarian, and aesthetic. This is not to say, as Noddings has been quick to point out, that schools lack order; in fact, Noddings claims that schools are often all *too* ordered. But the orders are arbitrary rather than facilitative—crayons are stored in neat little baskets far away from the paper because the paper happens not to fit on the shelf where the crayons are kept. The ways objects, buildings, and other human artifacts are arranged is part of the utility and overall effect of the objects themselves.

Noddings describes how the Japanese are known for their "meticulous arrangement of wood, rocks, plants, and water to produce effects of peace and serenity" (Noddings, 1992, p. 139). Arranging living environments in pleasing and efficient ways should begin in the preschool years. Noddings highlights a common scene in a Montessori school where children set a table for a tea party; the children will pick a flower or two to grace the table and use real milk or juice when the time comes to pour tea. This kind of scene is typical of Reggio Emilia and Waldorf schools as well, where respect for both objects and their attendant rituals is cultivated.

Noddings writes about how the physical arrangement of objects is used to connect social and spiritual domains. She describes how goblets, candles, medallions, embroidered cloth, robes, scrolls, torches, stained glass and other objects have been used in ceremonial rites across cultures and time. Bioevolutionary scholar Ellen Dissanayake (1988, 1998) made similar observations in demonstrating how objects and art-making are used to make sense of our physical, social, and spiritual worlds. Noddings (1992) writes, "we do not want our children to spend their days polishing and protecting their possessions, and we certainly want them to use their possessions freely (as Montessori said, freely and properly), [but] we want them to see that future pleasure or use depends on care" (p. 145).

What of the places in which objects are to be stored and housed? Architects Anne Taylor and George Vlastos have spent over 30 years discussing school design with students, educators, parents, and other designers. As a result of those conversations, Taylor and her colleagues have developed a series of zones or spaces they view as essential components for contemporary school design, some of which relate directly to objects central to schooling (Taylor, 1995b). While Taylor and Vlastos focus first on the entryways to the building and to individual classrooms and work areas, they also concentrate on work "zones"— surfaces for writing and drawing, areas for reading and talking, centers for cooking or wood-working. These are precisely the kinds of activities Dewey would claim are essential to the education of students and involve the use of objects in the ways that Montessori and Noddings have so carefully described. Taylor underlines the importance of designing storage systems—with facilitative ordering, one would hope—along with the need for display areas, lounging areas, research areas, and so on.

Outdoor Playgrounds

And what of the outdoor spaces and playgrounds surrounding schools? By the very name "playground," it is clear that play is expected to take place on the grounds. I find the range of school playgrounds extraordinary. Some schools have no playground to speak of, unless the barren asphalt or concrete surrounding the building can be considered a playground. Others have minimal outdoor resources for play—perhaps a gravel lot, or grass field, or a basketball hoop barely dangling from the back wall of the school. But other playgrounds and outdoor classrooms are extraordinarily rich and diverse. A casebook on Kindergarten architecture edited by Aurora Cuito (2001) devotes an entire section to the playground. The book describes both the traditional sorts of playground equipment one might expect to find for children in the early grades, such as swings, slides, teeter-totters, and sandboxes, as well more imaginative play structures—bridges and footpaths, climbing apparatuses leading to playhouses and towers, and play spaces populated with stone and wooden sculptures and plants of various kinds.

Australian educator Annie Ball was trained as an architect, and somewhere along the way she became enchanted with the voyage through childhood. She now works as a landscape designer and lives on the southern coast of Tasmania. In recent years she has concentrated much of her energy on designing play areas for children. We had an extended conversation walking along a beach in Tasmania, a conversation that focused almost entirely on playgrounds for children.

When I asked her about the features she thought were most important for children's playgrounds, her first response was that "playgrounds ought to be a bit dangerous." In almost the same breath, she ruefully observed how the occupational health and safety standards make it difficult to design playgrounds to serve the needs of children in this way. American psychoanalyst Bruno Bettelheim would agree. Some readers may recall that Bettelheim's work caused a stir in educational circles several decades back when, in the context of an ultra politically-correct environment where fairy tales were censored for young ears, he argued for the importance of the genre in developing children's sense of morality and self (Bettelheim, 1976). His views on the physical environment would likely cause a similar stir with those who are overly taken with children's health and safety concerns. Bettelheim described how children's environments need to be safe *and* provide context for adventure, giving the "assurance of being secure there and now, but also ... transmit[ing] to him [*sic*] the sensation that venturing into the outside world does not constitute a risk, whilst the future, though difficult, holds success in store" (Bettelheim, as cited in Dudek, 2000, p. 6). Dudek also laments how a pragmatic ethos has directed the policies of education, an ethos that "focuses upon health and safety legislation at the expense of imagination and experimentation" (Dudek, 2000, p. xvi).

In our conversation, Annie Ball made it clear that the job of the playground, gardens, and other outdoor spaces is to create a mini-world for children where they can explore the diversity of the natural world, using all of their senses and intellectual capabilities. She feels that gardens should reflect seasonal changes, should be abundant enough for children to be able to pick things, and should be filled with a cornucopia of textures and colours, with plants that are both inedible and edible. The presence of edible plants, giving children opportunities to grow their own food and to engage in meaningful, purposeful work, is of central importance to her notions of a good school garden, as it was for Pestalozzi centuries earlier. She also talked about the rich variety of aromas gardens ought to contain—to cultivate in a child the necessary wonder and awe and sense of care for the natural world. She uses native plantings whenever possible, and she plants liberally. She spoke of a school where there was so much deliberation about what might or might not grow that there was a delay of several years before the plantings took place. "If you plant fifty trees, and in twenty years time, you only have one left," says Ball, "then you will have still created a sense of place with that one tree. So why not start planting?" (A. Ball, personal communication, April 20, 2005).

Every aspect of a garden has potential for rich learning, although the nature of learning will vary as students make their way through school. In the earliest years, perhaps the most important learning is reverence for nature; in later years, the topics of science and agriculture, botany and mathematics are naturally sited in school gardens. In Annie Ball's view, the garden ought to become a place of artistic expression for whatever epoch the students might be studying. She spoke about how gardens can help teach about relationships— relationships between people, relationships between people and other living things, and relationships between people and the earth—a nested set of relationships.

I was not surprised by Annie's insistence that outdoor environments must be physically challenging; she does not shirk away from environments where there is a danger of falling. When I later visited one of the Kindergarten playgrounds she helped design, I was acutely aware of the heights children might scale as they made their way through the logs and trees in the garden, and at the same time, I was thinking what a glorious gift it was to those children to be encouraged to climb. As we were speaking about dangerous playgrounds, with a sweep of her hand, Annie waved across the sandy beach where we were sitting and asked what better playground could exist than this one. Just then, a mother walked by with her two children. As they passed us, the toddler caught his finger in the hinge of a plastic truck he was carrying and burst into racking sobs. While we were watching this scene unfold, Annie commented that there was danger on the beach, of course, but so too was there danger in playing with plastic toys that had passed every required safety measure before appearing on department store shelves. We both agreed that children who are encouraged to explore their physical limits often become monitors of their own physical safety. I remember watching my children, as toddlers, choosing to sit down to descend steep slopes without being prompted to do so—a prime example of self-monitoring.

Annie Ball's playgrounds—like the playgrounds of Margaret McMillan's day—include places with low enclosures, cave-like spaces where children can have a "safe running away place." She is fond of tunnels and mazes, but once again, regretfully noted that such enclosures were difficult to create in order to "satisfy the supervision requirements of the health and safety people." Open spaces are important too, spaces where an entirely different form of learning and experience can take place than in the gardens and tunnels and caves.

Annie pointed to the importance of pathways in connecting the various parts of the playground. I have encountered teachers who also recognize the importance of pathways between classrooms and buildings, or more to the point, pathways between activities. As one Australian teacher commented, "The way children move is so important—the journey should be marked in some way by an inviting pathway, by landmarks on the way."

In playgrounds, students can learn to love all kinds of weather—a love for the changing temperatures and climatic conditions of one's home region, a love that should be cultivated from the earliest years. Annie spoke fondly of a Kindergarten teacher who used to wander around a somewhat unruly garden, in the cool days of autumn, gathering bits of broken twigs and dry leaves to feed the small fires she would start later in the morning—fires the children could poke their own sticks into as they watched the flames dance, fires the children could gather around for a bit of warmth. Hearing about these Kindergarten fires reminded me of the fires my younger brother and I used to start when we were children. We were allowed to light fires in the back corner of our semi-rural lot in the full view of our mother, who could see us through the kitchen window as she carried on with the work of the home. I continue the tradition. These days, our own young children play with fire, having been instructed on how to ignite fires safely, and under the careful—though not necessarily obvious—supervision of one of their parents. Sometimes as I watch them poking at the burning sticks, I imagine that it must have been a bit frightening for my mother to let us start those fires, and I am grateful that she understood the importance of such play to our overall development.

Just as Annie Ball understands the value of gardens and play areas well beyond the Kindergarten years, so too do Helen Tyas Tunggal and John Webber understand how the spaces outside buildings and classrooms have the potential for play and learning from the early years through to the end of high school. The two of them run an independent consulting service in Australia for playground design. Their designs for school grounds have won several awards, and after seeing some of those designs, I can understand why. Helen spent 25 years as an educator, including five years as a curriculum consultant and ten years as a teaching principal. At the time of her retirement, she was the school principal of Harwood Island Primary School on the Clarence River in New South Wales, Australia. Before John Webber and Helen began their enterprise in the mid-1990s, he specialized in projects involving environmental rehabilitation where public consultation was a central feature of the work. John contributed to environmental restoration projects and management plans for more than 50 nature reserves throughout New South Wales and served as a landscape architect for the State's Department of Lands. Helen and John share the belief that listening and conversing are central to the design process, and they have demonstrated how virtually every space between buildings has the potential to be used in an ecologically wise and pedagogically fulfilling fashion.

John Webber and Helen Tyas Tunggal have developed a particular process for playground design. They begin work with their clients by offering a full-day workshop to raise awareness about the potential for the school site along with the most prevalent environmental issues. Some months later, they assess the physical features of the site, gathering maps and descriptions of the topography, hydrology, flora and fauna, species diversity, degradation, erosion, and a list of feelings and emotions that students, teachers, and others associate with the site. The process continues with more workshops, where groups of stakeholders identify activities for the site and begin to conceptualize the order by which the design features of the playground should evolve. These features are varied and go well beyond pathways, play spaces, and gardens (H. Tyas Tunggal, personal communication, June 13, 2005). Undertaking this process is a lengthy one: it can take up to two years to come up with the final design, and then several more years to implement it. But as Helen pointed out, "It's not worth jumping the process." She cited several examples where an individual teacher or parent sought to accelerate the development and design process, only to discover that they needed to backtrack in order to come up with a design that would support the curricular emphases of the school and that could be implemented with the available human and fiscal resources.[12]

I examined the "Learnscape" design that John and Helen created for the state-funded Berwick Primary School, located in the southern metropolitan region of the city of Melbourne, Australia's second largest city with a population of over 3 million people. This suburban school, set on a typical school plot, houses approximately 900 students from pre-school through to Grade 6. In consultation with teachers, parents, and students, John and Helen developed a host of learning spaces for the school's students and teachers. As one might expect, they developed play areas for the infants and junior-aged students, an after-care playground, basketball courts, a bike storage area, and a recycling depot. But in addition to these areas, the design included a story-telling place, wetlands, a sculpture park, a rare nature area, a ball wall, a gazebo, areas to display student art, a Koori cultural learning area where students learn about indigenous food, fibre, and medicine plants, a rainforest and bush food forest, and a challenge trail (reminiscent of the notion expressed by Annie Ball that playgrounds should be a bit dangerous). In other school designs in urban, suburban, and semi-rural settings, John and Helen have found ways to include olive groves, worm farms, sensory mazes, butterfly gardens, weather stations, poetry corners, fitness trails, rice paddies, and places for livestock. These Learnscapes mirror both the practical orientation of Pestalozzi and the romanticism of Froebel, a demonstration of how the practical and romantic can co-exist. These are not your ordinary school playgrounds.

The results are not ordinary either. Helen Tyas Tunggal and John Webber's first significant school-based Learnscape, undertaken when Helen was still the

---

[12] In addition to the design of the Learnscapes, a curriculum resource kit has also been developed that focuses on environmental diversity, interactions, change, quality, design, and care and repair, using the Learnscapes as sites to support the classroom learning.

Principal at the Harwood Island Primary School, involved a wetlands restoration project of considerable magnitude. A weed-infested paddock, where Helen recalled that, "even the cows couldn't get enough to eat," was transformed into a wetland that is now home to fifteen different species of native frogs and countless other creatures. The restoration project was recognized with a Rivercare 2000 Gold Award. Helen's contributions to curriculum development in environmental education have been honoured as well: in 1999 she was the recipient of the Gold Banksia Environmental Award for her work in empowering future generations to become competent and involved caretakers of the planet. These are but two of close to a dozen national and international awards given to Helen and John in recognition of their achievements.

Beyond Playgrounds: Spaces In-Between

The notion of valuing spaces around and between buildings is not new, but it has never been a prevalent one. The modern movement in architecture placed an overriding emphasis on the buildings themselves, and it is the tension between the modern and the organic, the back-to-basics curriculum and progressivist educational ideals that has marked the major architectural and educational debates, respectively, for more than a century.

There are exceptions, of course, to this overriding attention to the buildings, such as in the work of 20th century Dutch architects Aldo van Eyck and Herman Hertzberger. Aldo van Eyck developed the idea of the "spaces in-between" as important in school architecture (Dudek, 2002, p. 32). Herman Hertzberger, working first in Amsterdam and later elsewhere in the Netherlands, continued to influence school architecture when he created built environments to "enhance the social relationships between the users, through the organization and detail suggested by the built form" (Dudek, 2002, p. 32). In an article written in 1969, Hertzberger argued that each classroom should be considered as:

> a complete unit, a house in itself. The houses open onto a central space, "the street"; here all activities take place between students of many ages, interrupting the unity of the classroom-groups. ...The most active and complex point of the building is where the classrooms and hall open onto each other. These are the points where the children will work in the hall as though outside in front of the house on one's own ground—outside the security of one's classroom, yet not shut out, still under the eye of the teacher—still belonging. (p. 60–61)

I am not familiar with contemporary examples of richly developed in-between spaces in school design, other than the kinds of playgrounds developed by Webber and Tyas Tunggal and the spaces between the buildings at Evangelische Gesamtschule Gelsenkirchen-Bismarck in Germany. But currently there are architects and city planners involved in residential and commercial architecture who see the spaces between rooms and buildings as the key to comfortable working and sustainable living. These spaces can contribute significantly to the ecological strength of the entire site, to say nothing of the attractiveness of the design. We can learn much from these examples when considering school design.

One fine example is the work of the urban ecologist Paul Downton. Paul lives and works in Adelaide, the largest city in South Australia. Like many other cities—but even more so in Australia where the distances are vast—Adelaide is characterized by suburban sprawl with "inefficient, gas-guzzling, water-profligate housing spread thinly over huge areas with little opportunity for the development of community" (Downton, 2005, p. 26). Paul's answer to this suburban phenomenon is the community-titled development called Christie Walk, located on the site of a former bottle-recycling depot.

Christie Walk comprises 27 dwellings, including townhouses, free-standing homes, and apartments, offering the benefits of both urban and village life. The development features the use of non-toxic and locally available construction materials, plus passive solar and climate-responsive buildings. More unusual is the capture and use of storm water for irrigation, on-site sewage treatment, and the use of photovoltaics that produce enough electricity for the residents, plus a surplus to sell back to the grid. The development also provides more housing and community space on a smaller footprint than the usual urban conventions, with far less overall burden on the environment. Researchers at the University of Adelaide have demonstrated that even those residents with habits that are not environmentally respectful still use far less energy than the norm (Daniell et al., n.d.; Perez & Batten, 2006).

There is no question that the success of Christie Walk can be calculated in terms of overall energy use and sustainability, but at the heart of its success are the spaces *in between* the buildings. Community living and pro-social interactions have been fostered throughout the complex as a result of these spaces. The in-between spaces create the possibilities for "the public and community realm, and determine whether a town or city can come alive and be something other than a mere assemblage of objects" (Downton, 2005, p. 28). When we entered Christie Walk, through an arched gateway with unrestricted access to pedestrians regardless of whether they live in the complex or not, I immediately felt a hushed sense of peace. In contrast to the unending drone of cars on the encircling city streets, the complex is quiet and inviting and has the feeling of a magical village—an oasis in the incessant bustle of city life. As we walked through the community, we met up with one of the residents, and this casual encounter seemed typical and almost to be expected. Indeed, as Paul was designing Christie Walk, he envisioned the complex as being part pedestrian street and part walled garden. And so it is.

The resident we met talked about the ways water is harvested and used, and about the shared gardens, which serve multiple functions. They provide, of course, an aesthetic contribution to the overall feeling of the complex. Because of the emphasis on indigenous and native plantings, they also serve as a city habitat for birds and insects and contribute to the overall regulation of the micro-climate in and around Christie Walk. They also produce abundant vegetables for the residents of the community. The roof garden, with its view of the ocean on one side and the central business district of Adelaide on the other, creates yet another space for calm reflection and informal encounters in the

centre of urban life. As we stood there, Paul observed that this was the first roof
garden of its kind in Adelaide. With a deep soil base, the garden captures water
and solar energy, and like the other gardens of Christie Walk, helps modify the
overall microclimate. Paul alleged that roof gardens are one of the keys to urban
sustainability, reminding me that in some municipalities in England and
Germany, roof gardens are now mandatory for urban construction.

The planned life for the Christie Walk buildings is 100 years, in stark
contrast to North American urban residences and schools often designed for half
that lifespan. Another stark contrast to most developments—especially urban
ones—is that Christie Walk holds *human* activity as paramount. As Paul
observed, here the humans are given the best outdoor spaces. While some cars
are "permitted" to park (there are only 11 spaces for the 27 homes), these
parking spots are hidden away amongst the shrubbery and walls, nothing like
the shrines we typically build for automobiles in urban and suburban settings.
What would a school, designed like Christie Walk, look like in terms of parking?
And the spaces in-between?

Perhaps it would look like one of the schools—or campuses, more to the
point—designed by Fielding Nair International.[13] I'm thinking in particular of a
school in Tangerang, Indonesia, the Sinarmas World Academy (SWA). Members

*Figure 5. Koi Pond at entrance of Sinarmas World Academy, Tangerang, Indonesia (photo courtesy
of Fielding Nair International)*

[13] To see other schools designed by Fielding Nair International, see http://www.fieldingnair.com.

of the SWA community worked closely with educational architects and planners of Fielding Nair International to design a school that would serve as a learning community for the Kindergarten through Grade 12 students and teachers, as well as for members of the larger community. The spacious 5.8 hectare campus is set amongst spectacularly landscaped gardens. Each building—akin to each building at Christie Walk—was conceived as its own learning community, specifically designed to meet the developmental needs of each age group. Pathways between the buildings are as important as the buildings themselves. Each floor contains learning studios of various sizes, arranged around a multi-purpose learning commons. Here, then, is a school with spaces in-between—for living, for learning, for play.

Schools for Play, Learning, and Living

The impact of the work of people like Paul Downton, Helen Tyas Tunggal, John Webber, and Annie Ball stems not only from a conviction about the importance of the built and natural environments for human enterprises, but also from a deep understanding of the nature of the interactions that will occur in the spaces they create. Paul Downton is an urban dweller; Helen Tyas Tunggal is an educator; John Webber is an expert in the growth and decline of ecosystems; Annie Ball is an astute observer of children and their development. Their projects have been extremely successful. They stand in contrast to a story told by Mark Dudek (2002), where a well-intentioned architect—who had scant, if any, background in child development—designed a series of washing-up sinks. The sinks were placed at three different heights, with the intention that the youngest children in the school would use the lowest sinks and the adults would use the highest. From the very outset, even the smallest children refused to use the lowest sinks, reaching instead, to use the sinks created for the older children and adults. This would not be a surprising outcome to anyone who knows something of young children's proclivity to partake in adult tasks. Dudek tells this anecdote, not, as he says, to dissuade architects from attempting to use novel approaches in designing children's environments, but rather to stress that "easy sentiment should be avoided. Overly [sentimental] ideas may merely patronize the natural aspirations of children to behave in a grown-up way within the school setting" (Dudek, 2002, p. xv). For it is through the careful observation of the work and play of children—of the sort undertaken by Froebel and Dewey, Montessori and Malaguzzi, Gardner and Bettelheim, Ball and Webber, Steiner and Pestalozzi—that we can ascertain what kinds of curricula are best suited for students. Only then can we determine what kinds of physical spaces are most likely to support their intellectual, emotional, social, and spiritual growth.

Romance

The German Romanticists and Complexity Science

In this chapter I use the work of the German Romanticist, Johann Wolfgang von Goethe, as a way of contextualizing the educational philosophy of Rudolf Steiner, founder of Waldorf schools. I use Goethe's sensibilities to introduce complexity science as it applies to learning. The notion of "delicate empiricism" used by Goethe and by more contemporary scientists like Barbara McClintock also figures in this chapter. Features of complex systems are discussed in terms of learning and school architecture. For example, the idea that complex systems require both redundancy and diversity is explored in terms of architectural patterns that allow these characteristics to emerge in schools.

> *Mit frischen Blick bemerke freudig.*
> *Und Wandle, sicher wie geschmeidig.*
> *Durch Auen reichbegabter Welt.*
> *~ Goethe*

> Joyfully perceive with a fresh eye,
> and wander, confident and graceful,
> the rich meadows of our world. [14]

---

[14] The translation of Goethe's poem at the opening of the chapter is an unpublished translation by David Murphy Haglund, and reflects some of the central messages of this chapter. Translating Goethe's poetry is a daunting task: there are many translations. The stanza I have selected comes from the poem *Vermächtnis*. A standard translation, by David Luke (1964), reads as follows:

Keep your eyes fresh and open and joyful,
and move with sure steps, yet flexibly,
through the fields of a world so richly endowed.

The Romance of Learning

The word *romance* opens up a cornucopia of meanings. In the context of human dwelling places, romance brings images of gardens and courtyards, alluring pathways, hidden alcoves, tantalizing scents, nooks for quiet conversations, and an overall feeling of invitation, warmth, and beauty. When I think of the romance of childhood, an image of unfettered time coupled with curiosity and opportunities to explore and play is evoked.

What of romance and learning? I once characterized romantic learning as what we do at no one's bidding but our own: it is the learning we do when no one is watching. The call to take part in such learning can be strong and incessant. If we are lucky, romantic learning—an all-consuming undertaking characterized by fear, ambiguity, excitement, flexibility, uncertainty, sensuality, struggle, exploration and surprise—occurs throughout our lives (Upitis, 2003).

The links between romance and learning have been invoked for a very long time. At the beginning of the 20th century, philosopher Alfred North Whitehead wrote a classic work called *The Aims of Education* (1929). In it, Whitehead claimed that learning begins with romanticism. For Whitehead, the "natural cravings of the human intelligence" (p. 50) were expressed in a rhythmic fashion. In the time of romanticism—a stage he observed in children between the ages of eight and thirteen years—students are dominated by a sense of wonder and are absorbed with forming questions and seeking answers and with devising new experiences "amid a welter of ideas" (Whitehead, 1929, p. 50). Whitehead was quick to point out that this stage of development, while characterized by freedom, nevertheless requires guidance and discipline. But he admonished those who would destroy wonder, for in his view, without "the adventure of romance, at the best you get inert knowledge without initiative, and at the worst you get contempt of ideas" (p. 52). According to Whitehead, after the "stage of romance has been properly guided, another craving grows" (p. 52). Because the student has acquired general knowledge from "plenty of independent browsing amid first-hand experiences, involving adventures of thought and action" (p. 52), the student's next need is to examine, more deeply, the subject at hand. Whitehead calls this the stage of precision, a stage readily identified with traditional education at all levels. For Whitehead, romance remains in the background even during the stage of precision: "the organism will not absorb the fruits of the task unless its powers of apprehension are kept fresh by romance" (p. 54). Romance is present also in Whitehead's final stage of generalisation, although there it plays a different role as the learner seeks to apply knowledge in a form of active wisdom.

While Whitehead attached approximate ages to each of these three periods, he noted a large variation within and between individuals for different areas of inquiry. He suggested that this threefold cycle begins afresh with each new endeavour, and thus, throughout one's life, these stages of learning—romance, precision, and generalisation—are present. Whitehead identified a pattern within a pattern as well: "there are minor eddies, each in itself a threefold cycle, running its course in each day, in each week, in each term" (p. 60). Whitehead said this rhythmic pattern was essential to sustaining interest, to developing techniques and skills, and to realizing the fruits of the knowledge gained.

Romanticism, Complexity Science, and Johann Wolfgang von Goethe

The general notion of romance and learning that I have just described is related to the Romantic period of art and music—the time of Liszt and Brahms and Chopin, of Goethe and Blake. In my many years of teaching music history, I have learned a good deal about the connection between the Romantic composers and Romantic poets, about how the words of Goethe inspired the music of Schubert. But it was only in recent years that I learned about the connection between the German Romantic poets and the contemporary field of inquiry known as complexity science, a branch of science I explore throughout this chapter. Complexity science—which focuses on patterns within patterns and systems within systems—provides a relevant and intriguing framework for thinking about learning and about how we build our schools.

Fritjof Capra, physicist, environmentalist, and internationally acclaimed author of such books as *The Turning Point* (1984) writes extensively about ecosystems, which demonstrate all of the organizing principles of complexity science. Capra speaks of the patterns existing at the heart of healthy ecosystems. These patterns are about relationships among species, the phenomenon of self-organization, and the need for flexibility and diversity in order for ecosystems to survive. In other words, healthy ecosystems are complex systems. Capra also writes about our collective global challenge to create sustainable communities, in which social and cultural needs can be satisfied without reducing the chances for life in future generations.

Throughout the history of science, the study of these types of complex systems has always been present, though rarely in the mainstream. Capra claims that whenever the study of pattern is at the forefront, artists have contributed significantly to the advancement of science. He also suggests that the study of pattern comes naturally to children and yet, in traditional schooling, the study of natural patterns has not been encouraged. In his words, "Art has been sort of on the side. We can make this a central feature of ecoliteracy: the visualization and study of pattern through the arts" (Capra, 1998, p. 37).

Capra (1996) connects ecosystems and complexity science with the German and English Romanticists, arguing that the Romantic poets and philosophers returned to Aristotelian traditions (in contrast to Platonic ones) by concentrating on the nature of organic forms. With this background in mind, I now turn to a central figure of the German Romantic era—Johann Wolfgang von Goethe.

Goethe lived in Germany from 1749 until his death in 1832. He himself acknowledged that he was best known as a playwright and poet: "For more than half a century, I have been known as a poet, in my own country and undoubtedly also abroad" (as cited in Mueller, 1952, p. 164). He continued: "The fact that I have busily and quietly occupied myself with Nature in all her general and organic phenomena... is not so generally known, still less has it been accorded any attention" (p. 164). But his 19th century views of science resonate with the theory of complexity science where patterns and relationships are paramount. Goethe recognized that "each creature is but a patterned gradation of one great harmonious whole" (as cited in Capra, 1996, p. 21).

Natural phenomena—of all kinds—interested Goethe. He pursued mineralogy and geology when his official duties for the Duke of Weimar involved overseeing the local mines. He later became interested in botany and in the knowledge of the herbalists he met in the Thuringian forests, where Froebel soon thereafter established the first Kindergarten. The areas of zoology, meteorology, and anatomy did not escape his interest, either; Goethe is credited for discovering the intermaxillary bone in the human jaw (Mueller, 1952).

In 1791, at the age of 42, Goethe published his first essay on optics. The issue of how we perceive colour was one that would interest him until the end of his days. Despite his wide interests and writings in other areas, it was his work on colour that "[gave] him a ... somewhat ambivalent place ... in the history of science, and remains the subject of heated controversy" (Naydler, 1996, p. 18).[15] In contrast to Newton, who sought to explain colour in terms of the measurable angles of refrangibility, Goethe wished to understand colour as it arose in experiences with nature, as experienced by artists.

Goethe's views on colour, light, and shadow are familiar to Melbourne architect Gregory Burgess. Burgess contends that for Goethe, colour represented both the "deeds and suffering of light." Burgess wrote about how shadow and light interplay, describing how, at dusk, all becomes shadow as "it drains light, forms, and colour of their separateness" (Burgess, 2004, p. 98). Burgess also relates light and shadow to culture. During a conversation I had with him in his Melbourne office, he observed how Australia's history has tended to deny the suffering and mourning of its Aboriginal peoples. He said quietly, "We have the mistaken tendency to stand in light with no shadow" (G. Burgess, personal communication, March 17, 2005).

This kind of attention to light and shadow, both literal and metaphorical, accords with Goethe's scientific approach, which has been called "delicate empiricism" (Borcroft, as cited in Naydler, 1996, p. 12; Seamon & Zajonc, 1998). In this approach, the object and observer are not separated, but rather, the observer is engaged in a participatory relationship with nature as he or she interacts with the observed phenomenon. In the latter part of the 20th century, the manner in which Goethe had conducted his studies drew a measure of respect from scientists interested in the quality of human experiences. As British philosopher Jeremy Naydler (1996) wrote: "It is precisely over [Goethe's] methodology that scientists either feel compelled to dismiss him as a poet who made a fool of himself dabbling in matters beyond his competence, or find

---

[15] It is widely agreed that Goethe has been considered in terms of extremes. Jane Brown (2000), from The University of Washington, wrote in an unpublished essay: "Opposing readings of Goethe have developed... as the embodiment of nineteenth-century culture or as utterly out of touch with the world around him... there has been a long tradition of ambivalence toward him."

themselves irresistibly attracted to him as a pioneer of a holistic and qualitative science of nature" (p. 21).

Presumably anthropologist Mary Catherine Bateson (1994) is one who would not dismiss Goethe's approach. She posits that there is something of a spiritual component when one pays close attention, "a humility in waiting upon the emergence of pattern from experience" (p. 10). American writer Annie Dillard (1974), too, wrote captivating descriptions of how she discovered such patterns, notably in her classic work *Pilgrim at Tinker Creek*. She wrote:

> Living this way by the creek, where the light appears and vanishes on the water, where muskrats surface and dive, and redwings scatter, I have come to know a special side of nature. ... When I leave the house the sparrows flee and hush; on the banks of the creek jays scream in alarm, squirrels race for cover, ... snakes freeze, warblers vanish. ... Many of us are still living in the universe of Newtonian physics, [but] I find in quantum mechanics a world symbolically similar to my world at the creek. (p. 95)

Dillard applauds the work of physicist Werner Heisenberg, who proposed the controversial Principle of Indeterminacy in 1927. Heisenberg argued that method and object could not be separated—a notion resonant with Goethe's approach. Goethe did not separate the phenomenon from the observer; he viewed the phenomenon itself as being "caught up and entangled in the individuality [of the observer]" (Naydler, 1996, p. 72).

Romanticism and Views of Science and Learning

Many of us have learned to distrust our immediate experiences of nature, for we have been taught to believe that the world is quite different from how we perceive it. We do not trust our instincts because we have been sold a bill of goods convincing us that the true nature of the world is accessible only to specialists with elaborate equipment. In some mysterious and indirect way, these specialists can access *real* nature—the protons, neutrons, electrons, quarks, leptons, muons, taus, and neutrinos invisible to the human eye. Capra (1996) has argued that the consequences of this deference are colossal. Because we have relinquished our intimate ways of perceiving nature, we have lost an acute awareness of the natural world, and this loss contributes to the continued degradation of the planet. Although the prevalent view of Goethe has been of "a muddle-headed dilettante who made a fool of himself by opposing Newton" (Naydler, 1996, p. 9), some scientists are beginning to see that Goethe was actually a careful observer of natural phenomena (Bortoft, 1996; Miller, 1995). Surely this kind of observation has a place in schools, even while the approaches of Galileo, Descartes and Newton still reign in contemporary scientific education.

For while these approaches still reign, they no longer conquer. Other scientists have honoured the naturalist methods of observation and engagement Goethe saw as fundamental to his scientific work. Barbara McClintock was one such scientist. In the book *A Feeling for the Organism*, biologist Evelyn Fox Keller (1983) wrote about how McClintock spent day upon day making observations while sitting in the middle of a cornfield in her attempts to understand fully the complexities of the genetic structures of corn. McClintock made her ideas about genetics public in the early 1950s, concluding that the controlling genetic elements for corn reproduction actually *moved* from cell to cell as the corn kernel developed, a process she called transposition. At the time, both she and her ideas were described as "obscure, even mad...in spite of the fact that she had long since established her reputation as an impeccable investigator, few listened, and fewer understood" (Fox Keller, 1983, p. 10). McClintock's conclusions were even more suspect because her contemporaries were using tools of biochemistry to explain molecular mechanisms, while she sought a broader conceptual structure using "the techniques more familiar to the naturalist... [observing] the markings and patterns of colorations on the leaves and kernels of the corn plants" (Fox Keller, p. 8). However, scarcely a decade later, a "number of dramatic and unanticipated observations began to appear. Among these was the startling discovery of elements of the bacterial genome which appeared to 'jump around' [with] regulatory properties paralleling those observed earlier by McClintock" (Fox Keller, p. 10). So it turned out that McClintock was right after all. In the late 1970s and early 1980s, McClintock was showered with honorary degrees and awards, and in 1983 she received a Nobel Prize in Genetics.

American historian and critic Lewis Mumford's views of science also seem to be in synchrony with those of Goethe and McClintock. Mumford (1946) claimed there was a need to move away from a "belief in a science of dead things, analyzed, isolated, dissected ... to a belief in a science of living things [where] a qualitative understanding of pattern, form, configuration, history, is as important as statistical analysis" (p. 147). Mumford further claimed that no problem was fully explored until it was understood in relation to its *social* relationship to human purposes.

Chemist James Lovelock and microbiologist Lynn Margulis also possess this patterned and complex view of science. In 1969, British-born James Lovelock first proposed the Gaia hypothesis, which holds that the earth is a single, integrated, living organism: that the earth, in other words, is alive. Novelist William Golding suggested the name 'Gaia hypothesis' after the Greek goddess of the Earth, because he recognized in Lovelock's idea the renaissance of a powerful ancient myth (Capra, 1996). In the introduction to *Slanted Truths: Essays on Gaia, Symbiosis, and Evolution*, written and edited by Lynn Margulis and her son, philosopher and artist Dorian Sagan, mother and son wrote: "No scientist should be deceived by a pretense of objectivity, and no information can be garnered on delicate issues by single researchers acting alone. All science is a highly social, self-correcting, interactive enterprise" (Margulis & Sagan, 1997, p. xxi).

If this view of science has merit—and it has—what are the implications for school architecture? One might well re-write the quotation above, substituting "architect" or "educator" for "scientist," and conclude that education and architecture are also subjective in nature and that suitable solutions on delicate issues cannot be proposed by single architects or educators alone. Education— and the buildings in which education takes place—is Gaia-like: a highly social, self-correcting, interactive, living enterprise. In other words, education can be thought of as a complex living system.

Waldorf (Steiner) Schools

A handful of educators have been aware of Goethe's views and have applied them to schooling. At the turn of the 20ᵗʰ century, Rudolf Steiner, the philosopher, architect, scientist, and teacher who founded the first Steiner school, wholeheartedly embraced Goethe's ideas. In 1884, the young Steiner attended a symposium on Goethe's scientific works and for many years thereafter he was involved in editing Goethe's scientific papers on the natural sciences and colour theory (Steiner, 1921). By 1910, Steiner had arrived at his basic philosophy which has become known as anthroposophy, the study of "the wisdom of man [*sic*] combined with his spiritual being" (Sharp, as cited by Dudek, 2000, p. 63). The first Anthroposophical Society was founded in 1912. A year later, Steiner, along with a cadre of like-minded artists, architects, actors, and musicians, set out to establish a centre for this society at Dornach, near Basel, Switzerland. The centre was called the Goetheanum, reflecting Steiner's admiration of Goethe's thinking. This first Goetheanum attracted artists and architects from several European nations, and provided a space where "artists and craftsmen worked together … entering into the experience of a harmonious building process which defined the essential nature of [Steiner's] philosophy" (Dudek, 2000, p. 63).

In 1919, with the devastation of World War I still at the forefront of people's consciousness, factory owner Emil Mott invited Steiner to create a school for the children of the employees of the Waldorf-Astoria cigarette factory, located in Stuttgart, Germany.[16] Mott's idea was for a new kind of schooling to educate children so they would later create a just and peaceful society. Steiner, too, felt there was a need for "a new social order, a new sense of ethics, and a less damaging way of resolving conflict" (Oppenheimer, 1999a, p. 73). At the time, the school was revolutionary—it was coeducational, it was open to children from any background and ability level, it spanned the range from preschool to high school, and it was independent of external control (Edwards, 2002). Waldorf schools continue to be administratively independent: many of the world's 1000 or so Waldorf schools are loosely affiliated, but operate independently (Barnes, 1991; Oppenheimer, 1999a). As in the first Steiner schools, students at present day Steiner schools are still taught to observe nature and much attention is given to pattern, to rhythm, and to colour.

---

[16] The genesis of the first Steiner school is well known and often described. For a comprehensive view of Steiner schools written by someone who was new to Steiner education, I suggest reading Todd Oppenheimer's article, Schooling the Imagination, which appeared in *Atlantic Monthly* in 1999 and is widely available in print and on the Internet.

After the first Goetheanum was destroyed by arsonists on New Year's Eve night in 1922–1923, a second building was created (Plummer, 2003). Its structure is a twisted three-dimensional surface of poured concrete that registers shifts in sunlight and weather. In this way, the contrast between shadow and light is incorporated in the architecture itself — a tribute to Goethe's notions.

Figure 6. Curved concrete of the Goetheanum (goetheanum.org)

Notions of ephemerality, of light and shadow, are a long way from the current ethos of public schooling with its emphasis on standardized test-ing. Not surprisingly, the ideas of Rudolf Steiner have been met with the same ambivalence as those of Goethe. And in some cases, Steiner's ideas have been met with more than mere ambivalence. A parent in California launched a lawsuit after the Waldorf philosophy was introduced into two local public schools, maintaining that there was an unwritten agenda to indoctrinate children into anthroposophy, which, in his view, was a brand of spirituality with no place in public education (Oppenheimer, 1999a). Other parents have resisted what they view as quasi-religious teachings of anthroposophy. The response of Waldorf teachers has been to say that they do not teach anthroposophy, but rather, that their own study of anthroposophy enlivens their sensibilities and deepens their understanding, which in turn helps them "inspire students with the wonder and curiosity that make for profound learning" (Oppenheimer, 1999a, p. 82).

Sometimes Steiner schools are criticized, even by Steiner teachers themselves, for being excessively dogmatic in their adherence to Steiner's purported views on curriculum and architecture. Although I encountered this kind of dogmatism during my visits to Steiner schools, more often than not I encountered openness on the part of teachers to consider what Steiner's views would have been in the 21st century. Sometimes I met with true bewilderment as teachers struggled with how to proceed so as to keep faith with Steiner in the absence of clear direction. For example, confusion often arises when teachers and architects attempt to interpret Steiner's views on colour. Steiner thought colour in the classroom was significant, and while the first Steiner school in Stuttgart was "not architecturally organic or distinctive, evidence suggests this first building adopted Goethe's colour theories and a number of Steiner-esque details" (Dudek, 2000, p. 64). Many Steiner schools have adopted the pattern of painting the classrooms in the colours of the spectrum, beginning with red in Grade 1, moving to orange in Grade 2, and so on. The ways in which this practice manifests itself are highly varied. One Steiner teacher laconically asked, "Well, we know we're supposed to use the rainbow through the grades, but does it stretch to Grade 8? Or all the way to Grade 12, with various shades of blue and green in between?" Another teacher commented that, for a number of years, a blue classroom was used for Grade 3 students, because it was the best available space and because the school could not afford to "constantly re-paint the walls." She also playfully noted that being in the blue classroom "didn't seem to do the students any harm."

While some of Steiner's views—on reincarnation, for example—can be unsettling to say the least, his contributions nevertheless have a place in the grand educational and architectural debates. Pointing to Steiner's understanding of how complementary colours interact, for example, Dudek concludes: "The struggle to understand colour in psychological and physical terms is ongoing and serious" (Dudek, 2000, p. 120). There are other reasons to consider Steiner's views seriously, not the least of which are the outcomes associated with Waldorf education. As American journalist Todd Oppenheimer (1999a) says, "In the end the measure of a school lies in the graduates it produces" (p. 83). He claims that Waldorf graduates stack up well against their peers in terms of standardized measures and outdo their peers in terms of the quiet confidence and self-awareness they exude in daily living.

Oppenheimer's observations accord with those of Australian architect Rob Cheesman, who told me that upon his first visit to the Willunga Steiner School just outside of Adelaide, he was "taken by the peacefulness of the school." He described how he "could see the children had been building things, that there was order and structure in the place, and that it was peopled with very intelligent teachers. Somehow, the kids in this school seemed to have developed a social glue—a sense of responsibility and morality." He referred to the importance of stimulating the creative intellect within everyday school activities and commended the Waldorf system in this regard.

Paul Stapleton is responsible for the maintenance of the Willunga Waldorf School and at the time that we spoke, his three children attended the school (P. Stapleton, personal communication, May 26, 2005). He said that while some of "Steiner's anthroposophical business baffles [him]," he has no doubt that the curriculum had a profoundly positive impact on the students. He spoke enthusiastically about how his children took part in activities he would never have dreamed of doing in school, describing woodworking projects, knitting and weaving, and archery competitions. He spoke about a week-long trip his 12-year-old son had taken to a nearby national park, along with the rest of his Grade 6 class and their teacher. Stapleton also talked about how pupils respected the grounds. Willunga is not a school troubled by graffiti or vandalism: not only do students take pride in their school, they are involved in maintaining the grounds and buildings. Stapleton described how students help with the cleaning and cooking in the early grades, how they garden throughout their school years, and also, how they create sculptures and other artifacts for the grounds. I took note of a small pond and garden, surrounded by a dragon shaped from straw bale and mud bricks, with benches curling around the interior of the dragon wall. A Grade 12 student from the neighbouring Mt.

Barker Waldorf School created the piece. Small wonder these students do not destroy what they create.

The ideas about learning held by Goethe and others like him resonate in powerful ways with complex systems. With romance, close observation, and quiet reverence as the backdrop, I now expand the discussion of ecosystems, patterns, and complexity science as it relates specifically to architecture.

Complexity Science and Classrooms

Even though Goethe and others had attended to patterns and ecosystems nearly a century earlier, complexity science first arose as an acknowledged field of study in the latter half of the 20th century (Capra, 1996; Maturana & Varela, 1987). It has since been applied to various phenomena in the social sciences (Davis, 2004; Davis, Sumara, & Luce-Kapler, 2007; Johnson, 2001; Mitchell, 2009). Simply put, complexity science involves the study of adaptive and self-organizing systems (Davis, 2004). Complexity science seeks to understand collectives — such as ecosystems — but also ant colonies, pigeon flocks, and trends in the stock market. All of these collectives have organized structures in the midst of flux and disorder, structures that arise with no single member in control of the system (Johnson, 2001). Complexity theory explains how such dynamic systems function when there are many agents or members interacting in both predictable and random ways. These systems are capable of giving rise to new levels of order — of evolving. As Brent Davis, former Canada Research Chair in Mathematics and Ecology at the University of Alberta put it, "self-organized, self-maintaining forms can arise and evolve without goals, plans, or leaders" (Davis, 2004, p. 151).

Because complexity theory seeks to explain how a system functions when there are multiple members involved in some form of self-organization, scholars have applied this orientation to describe learning settings, including social cliques, the classroom collective, and other clusters that form in the school community (Davis, 2004). I can think of numerous examples of teachers speaking about their classes in just such a manner: "Last year I had a class of artists," or "That was the funniest group I ever taught." These teachers were not describing individual students *per se*, but how the class as a whole moved in one direction. In terms of complexity theory, it is a group of artistic students that brings the rest of the students along with them, forming a dynamic and evolving system of artists. The ways a class can take on a personality of its own are explored time and again by Vivian Paley in her descriptions of Kindergarten classes at the University of Chicago Laboratory School, established by John Dewey. In one of her books, *The Girl with the Brown Crayon*, Paley (1997) describes how one child's interest in a character in a children's book became a focal point for class explorations for the entire school year. This characteristic of self-organization, I now realize, was markedly present in the group of students I brought to the MIT theatre many years ago and described in the opening vignette of this book.

Models of Learning: Moving to an Idea-Centered Complexity Perspective

For nearly two centuries, the majority of public schools in North America have been built to reflect a transmission model for learning: put a homogeneous group of children in a confined space (a classroom), process them for a year (fill them with knowledge), make sure they have learned the set and predictable curriculum (test them according to established standards), move them to the next processing container (another classroom), and continue the cycle until they have reached the age at which they are deemed ready to leave school and enter the workplace. Despite the many new theories of learning spawned over the past century — including Dewey's progressivist notions, complexity theory, and the refreshing perspectives of Alfred North Whitehead and Lev Vygotsky, among others — transmission teaching remain. However, a vast number of people — educators *and* architects — have called this model into question (Boss, 2001; Bullock & Foster-Harrison, 1997; Davis, 2004; Day 2000, 2001; Fiske, 1995; Gardner, 1999; Lamm, 1986; Nair, Fielding, & Lackney, 2010; Papert, 1993).

I become ever more convinced that the buildings in which we house students and teachers play a role in perpetuating the transmission model of teaching. School buildings also favour the teaching of what are commonly referred to as the "core" subjects — subjects like mathematics and language — over subjects like music, art, dance, sport, and gardening — some of the very topics that seem to hold such universal appeal over our lifetimes. As a retired Australian teacher sadly observed, "There are no showers in primary schools. Clearly, we do not expect children to sweat or to take part in any kind of serious strenuous physical activity while they are at school" (T. Walker, personal communication, April 19, 2005).

Teachers often *want* to do more with the arts and the natural world, but the buildings and grounds limit them. In my research on teachers' views and practices in arts education, I was taken aback by how frequently teachers said they were unable to do more in the arts because it was difficult to find time to use the gym, or because studio or performance spaces were not available (Upitis, 2001; Patteson, Smithrim, & Upitis, 2002). Perhaps not coincidentally, learning about the natural world and learning in and through the arts are not as amenable to being testing by standardized, paper-and-pencil methods, either.

What are some of the other ways of conceiving of learning that go beyond the teacher-centered transmission model? Many approaches to learning and teaching discussed by philosophers, psychologists, and educators during the latter half of the 20th century moved towards more learner-centered ways of knowing. One such approach is constructivist learning, in which children, given appropriate materials, structures, and guidance from the teacher, are expected to construct knowledge (Driver, Asoko, Leach, Mortimer & Scott, 1994; Driver & Bell, 1986; Duit, 1993; Fensham, Gunstone, & White, 1994). But a complexity science characterization of learning is neither teacher-centered nor learner-centered: more accurately, it is both. Using complexity theory to describe learning means going beyond this dichotomy to *idea-centered* ways of thinking about learning and living. With this orientation in mind, I can make sense of what I have always viewed as perplexing inconsistencies in the Steiner pedagogy. For example, while Steiner teachers make the study of the arts part of the core curriculum, the approach is overwhelmingly teacher-centered, which seems contradictory to a curriculum with a heavy arts emphasis. But when one thinks of the curriculum as idea-centered rather than teacher- or learner-oriented, then the inconsistencies fall away. One can learn about the same ideas from the strictest of teachers or from the most romantic of explorations.

Educators use complexity theory to show how the relationships among individuals, collectives, ideas, and curriculum can be thought of as nested learning communities (Davis, 2004; Fleener, 2002). In terms of the classroom context, the individual learns, but so too does the class as a whole learn—it learns about particular forms of knowledge and interaction, and as noted previously, it takes on a personality of its own. Then there is learning in a broader context still, where, due to the knowledge generated by individuals and collectives, disciplinary knowledge itself grows.

By extending the notion of learner into these nested contexts, by implication, biological and cultural systems shape and are shaped by learners (Davis, 2004; Lakoff & Johnson, 1999; Tomasello, 2000). For millennia, biological bases of knowing have been either ignored or suppressed within most Western discussions of knowledge and teaching. The strong reactions to Goethe's approach are a symptom of this suppression. Complexity science offers a way of bringing those influences back into the discourses of teaching and learning (Davis, 2004). Such a theoretical framework can bring our understanding of learning closer to those romantic ways of knowing we engage in of our own free will, and, in turn, back to a place where the natural world is important in educational settings.

Which features of complex systems enable this kind of dynamic growth and learning to occur? There is wide agreement about key principles accounting for complexity, which include decentralized control, redundancy among the members of the collective, diversity or novelty in the system, neighbour interactions, enabling constraints, pattern recognition, and feedback (Davis, 2004). I now describe these principles, beginning with decentralized control.

Decentralized Control

How is a complex collective controlled in a decentralized way? Here's an example: when someone dives into the ocean into the middle of a school of fish, the fish move away from the diver in a coordinated way, without a single "queen fish" communicating to the group that it is time to move. Rather, the collective moves as an entity. The same situation can arise in a classroom. As some teachers admit, while they certainly *influence* the outcomes in the classroom, they do not *control* the classroom: classroom collectives can be said to respond with a will of their own. Taking a complexity perspective means that teaching is unpredictable: it "cannot be managed into existence" (Davis, 2004, p. 170).

But adopting a complexity perspective on learning does not mean that the teacher abdicates responsibility for influencing the collective. Instead, teachers must "establish a balance between sufficient organization to orient learners' actions and sufficient openness to allow for the varieties of experience, ability and interest represented in any classroom" (Davis, 2004, p. 182). In this way, any teaching approach can support a complex classroom collective, although some approaches are more conducive than others in that they allow the teacher to respond attentively to students, ideas and interests generated in the classroom context. One of the conclusions reached at the 2004 Complexity Science and Educational Research Conference was that teaching and learning should be about expanding the space of the possible, about creating conditions for things to emerge that are not yet imagined. Complexity predicts there will be surprises, an evolution through the known to the unknown (Davis & Sumara, 2006).

Redundancy

For complexity to emerge, there must also be redundancy in the system. Now, the idea of introducing redundancy — given the common meaning of the word — might seem counterintuitive. But it is the redundant — or commonly held ideas and abilities of the members — that make it possible for the system to learn. Here is an example of how redundancy is important. Ants all share common or redundant biological features that make it possible for them to live together in a colony. Similarly, redundancy is present in most classrooms simply because most children are of a similar age: they are at roughly the same stage of physical development, and their knowledge of symbols systems (such as those associated with reading text) is approximately the same. Redundancy in the collective makes the system robust.

Diversity

But redundancy also requires diversity to enable a system to respond in flexible ways to new situations. In the example of the ant colony, while every ant looks rather like the others in terms of its ant-like structure, even the naked eye can observe that some ants are smaller than others and some move more quickly than others. These elements of diversity are necessary features for the collective to respond to new circumstances posed by the environment. Diversity in the classroom can be more difficult to engender, when students share similar cultural experiences and values and are all of a similar age. But when diversity is present — as it was in terms of the cultural backgrounds of the students I taught at the Hennigan School — the stage is set for a complex system to thrive.

Neighbour Interactions

Redundancy and diversity work closely together through neighbour interactions where the members or agents in the complex collective come into contact with one another. In an ant colony, this can mean literally bumping up against one another. In terms of a learning collective, neighbour interactions exist when diverse ideas come into contact — and contradict, harmonize, or amplify one another: "History is rife with examples of ideas bumping against one another to give rise to new, more powerful interpretive possibilities ... this sort of dynamic is present in every significant advance in human knowing" (Davis & Upitis, 2004, p. 126).

Historian and humorist Stephen Leacock (1922/1961) knew about ideas bumping up against each other as well. After extolling the virtues of the student life at Oxford, he concluded that the most important factor for learning was "continued and intimate contact" with fellow students. He wrote:

> Students must live together and eat together, talk and smoke together. Experience shows that that is how their minds really grow. And they must live together in a rational and comfortable way. They must eat in a big dining room or hall, with oak beams across the ceiling, and the stained glass in the windows. … If I were founding a university—and I say it with all the seriousness of which I am capable—I would found first a smoking room; then when I had a little more money in hand, I would found a dormitory; then after that, or more probably with it, a decent reading room and a library. After that, if I still had money over that I couldn't use, I would hire a professor and get some textbooks. (p. 95)

One can imagine, with the right mix of students, that a great deal of learning would happen in Leacock's professor-less university—much like participants learn during conference coffee breaks when no formal papers are scheduled, or how children learn during their recess activities and encounters.

Another way I like to think about the concepts of redundancy, diversity, and neighbour interactions is through the phenomenon of music improvisation. When musicians form a blues ensemble, there must be shared or redundant knowledge about harmonic and melodic structures and a sufficient skill level to play the various instruments. There must also be a level of diversity in the ensemble. This diversity comes from the instruments themselves, of course, but more importantly, from the different solutions each member of the ensemble might bring in creating a coherent piece.

Enabling Constraints, Pattern Recognition, and Feedback

In order for emergence to occur, the collective also requires some enabling constraints, a shared structure. Shared structures for classroom work are often set in place by teachers who are skilled at creating conditions for learning in groups. An example of a musical structure that a high school music teacher might use is that of the 12-bar blues. This enabling constraint is the harmonic sequence of chords that enables musicians to compose a seemingly limitless number of blues tunes. Because of their specialized knowledge, the musicians recognize further patterns associated with meter and harmony. Also, if a particular note or sequence doesn't work, other members of the ensemble will compensate so the whole remains coherent. The notion of members of the group compensating for one another based on the feedback they give and receive brings us back to one of the central notions around complex emergence: the idea of indirect or decentralized control. No single person controls a small music ensemble like this one—just as no single person controls a string quartet, even though the first violinist has particular responsibilities (like a classroom teacher) for influencing the collective.

In the next section, I discuss how complexity relates to school architecture, beginning with a general discussion of how the enabling constraints of architecture can affect the experiences and outcomes of schooling.

Models of Building: Complexity Science and Architectural Patterns

If complexity theory can be used to characterize the emergent and romantic nature of teaching and learning, then the next issue to consider is the kinds of architectural patterns that would allow for complexity to emerge. My use of the term architectural patterns pays homage to the book, *A Pattern Language*, first published in the late 1970s by Berkeley architect Christopher Alexander and his colleagues (Alexander, Ishikawa, & Silverstein, 1977). This book has become a classic text on design. Christopher Alexander's aim was to provide a sourcebook of patterns for the built environment by taking into account the ways in which people move through and live in their environments.[17] By "pattern," Alexander referred to a recurring problem in our environment for which he offered a core solution and related it to other patterns in the environment. Thus, one of the key premises of the approach is that patterns are not isolated entities, but each pattern relates to other patterns. The book offers an architectural language capable of describing complex systems, in the same way that Whitehead's previously described analysis of the rhythm of learning involves an endless variation of threefold patterns at both micro and macro levels.

Here is how the pattern language operates in architectural design. The pattern called *small parking lots*—one of hundreds of so-called patterns in Alexander's book—addresses the problem created by large parking lots. Large parking lots cover the landscape and are generally unpleasant places that "wreck the land for people" (Alexander, Ishikawa, & Silverstein, 1977, p. 504). This *small parking lots* pattern is related to several larger patterns, including *work community*, *green streets*, *main gateways*, and *house clusters*, and to smaller patterns, such as *tree places, positive outdoor space*, and *garden walls*. Indeed, some of the patterns described in the book deal explicitly with design on a macro-level, such as *cities* and *agricultural valleys*, whereas other patterns are at a micro-level in scope, such as the *street windows, alcoves, half walls,* and *fruit trees* of an individual building. In each case, Alexander and his colleagues identified problematic features of the built environment and then described a range of physical and social needs to consider in solving the problem in a humane and pleasing way.

Some architects suggest that Alexander's approach is formulaic and simplistic (and thereby fundamentally flawed). Others say it is simply good design (and therefore not worth special consideration). But I have encountered architects who welcome their clients' use of the approach because it works on both macro and micro levels, because it helps them understand the kinds of behaviours and movement patterns their clients are likely to engage in, and because it gives a sense of the building elements their clients might find

---

[17] At well over a thousand pages, *A Pattern Language* is a comprehensive work, to say the least. Alexander intended for it to be accompanied by another volume called *The Timeless Way of Building*, which provides the theory underpinning the practical outcomes contained in *A Pattern Language*.

appealing.[18] I am convinced that the approach has endured for decades both because of its intuitive appeal to lay people and, equally, because it fits well with a complexity approach to buildings and spaces between buildings.

American researcher Kenneth Tanner has taken a number of Alexander's patterns and sought to find examples of those patterns in school design, seeking to link the architectural patterns with student achievement (Tanner, 2000; Tanner & Anderson, 2002). There is, of course, supreme irony in using achievement measures as a way of assessing the value of architectural patterns for schooling, given the intimate relationship between standardized testing and the transmission model of schooling, which, on the whole, limits rather than enhances complex interactions. Nevertheless, Tanner's research shows how elements of school architecture affect students' experiences of schooling in profound ways. He has applied his theoretical work to develop a compendium for planning educational facilities (Tanner & Lackney, 2006).

Tanner's (2000) initial work involved an empirical study of 44 elementary schools with close to 23,000 students in the state of Georgia. He developed a scale to assess school design based on Alexander's patterns, including *green areas, quiet areas, promenades, play areas, flex zones, small group areas, large group areas, outdoor rooms, acoustics, windows, pathways, living views,* and *natural light,* among others. After taking into account various socio-economic variables, Tanner concluded that some of the best predictors of achievement in language and mathematics were *pathways* (schools that had clearly defined areas for freedom of movement, both indoors and outdoors), *positive outdoor spaces,* and *overall impression.* A year later, Kathleen Yarbrough (2001), one of Tanner's doctoral students, applied a modified version of Tanner's design scale and assessed the importance of the various patterns on students' academic performance in Grades 3 and 5. In Grade 3, the most important patterns predicting academic behaviour were *circulation* and *outdoor learning environments.* In Grade 5, Yarbrough found the presence of *large group meeting areas* to be the most important—meeting areas making it possible for neighbour interactions, a complexity science feature, to readily occur. Another doctoral student, Scott Andersen (1999), applied a version of Tanner's scale to the study of 50 middle schools (Grades 6 through 8). In this research, Andersen found that some of the strongest predictors for academic achievement included *multifunctional areas, play areas, activity pockets, green areas, exit doors to the outdoors,* and *overall impression.* Once again, architectural patterns supporting the emergence of complexity were identified as most significant.

In the sections that follow, I continue to explore the implications for complexity science and school architecture, focusing on some of the key features of complexity. I begin with the one that I view as most important: neighbour interactions. Then I examine redundancy, diversity, and decentralized control in both in terms of architectural features and curriculum.

---

[18] Two of the Australian architects I interviewed who made specific reference to *A Pattern Language,* and encouraged their clients to refer to it, were Paul Barnett in Canberra and Rob Cheesman in Adelaide.

Neighbour Interactions

Freedom of movement facilitates neighbour interactions, so it should come as no surprise to find a relationship between movement and academic achievement, as demonstrated by Tanner (2000). Sara Snyder Crumpacker, an American organizational consultant, states: "Schools should be planned so that users 'bump into' different choices on a daily basis" (Crumpacker, 1995, p. 35). She suggests that buildings should include informal areas to congregate that are "as comfortable as our own family rooms" (p. 40). In order to facilitate the bumping up of ideas—the informal learning that happens as a result of unplanned interactions—architectural spaces like nooks, wings, or alcoves, commonly found in Reggio Emilia and Steiner schools, are needed.

Ironically, the intent of the now largely passé 1970s open concept or open plan classrooms, where classrooms were not walled, was to encourage this kind of informal interaction (Bradley, 2005; Carlton, 1987; Gislason, 2009). During the 1960s and 1970s open concept plans were a prevalent elementary and secondary school architectural form; between 1967 and 1969, fully half of the new schools built in the United States were open concept, and by 1975, in Canada and Britain, roughly 10% of all of the schools were open concept (Gislason, 2009). In these schools, students in one class, while listening to their language lesson, might also experience something of the art lesson happening in the next class area. As many readers will recall, in most cases this kind of architecture did not lead to informal and rich possibilities for learning, but to noise and chaos. Students found it difficult to decipher the many messages they were receiving: there were times when the voice of the teacher from the adjacent area was louder than the voice of the teacher in the immediate space, resulting in what one researcher called a disturbing cacophony of sound (Bradley, n.d.). An Ontario teacher, who had worked in an open concept school for 27 years, wryly told me, "Open concept is great when the students aren't there. And it's OK when you're young and have lots of energy. But it wears you out over the years" (R. Palombri, personal communication, April 6, 2006). Small wonder that most teachers working in open concept settings are quick to put up partitions and bookcases to create contained spaces for their students. Indeed, in many open concept schools built in the 1970s, more permanent walls have now been erected to make the instructional areas more intimate, and the concept was quickly abandoned; by the 1980s very few open concept schools were being constructed (Rothenberg, 1989). Canadian researcher Neil Gislason (2009) argues that part of the failure of open schools is that the pedagogy did not match the architecture: traditional styles of teaching are poorly suited for these kinds of schools. However, even in case studies of project-based Dewey like environments, Gislason found that teacher advisors viewed "noise and traffic as persistent environmental distractions" (p. 130). I would suggest that there is a further problem with the open concept, and that is that open schools do not encourage complex emergence. For it is not the grand caverns that encourage informal learning; it is the romantic nooks and alcoves we most need for the informal conversations that promote engagement.

The bumping up of ideas is also fostered through access to technology embedded throughout a school building. This notion is advocated by Prakash Nair, an American-based school planning consultant and architect who works internationally with his colleague Randall Fielding on school designs. He suggests that deep engagement in learning is supported by the presence of presentation spaces, getaway spaces and niches, and easy access to technology. With ubiquitous access to wireless laptops, students come into contact not only with those people who share the same learning space, but also, with other "classmates" who share similar interests in other parts of the world (Nair, 2002; Nair & Fielding, 2005; Nair, Fielding, & Lackney, 2010). This notion of easy access to technology has been lauded by educators as well (Bullock & Foster-Harrison, 1997), and I view it as a contemporary version of one of the features of Dewey's Utopian book-filled schools (Dewey, 1933/1989). Teacher workrooms for research, collaborative work, and meetings with students also facilitate neighbour interactions and the bumping up of ideas (Bullock & Foster-Harrison, 1997; Nair, 2002).

Redundancy

How might architectural design encourage redundancy, another key feature of complex systems? Crumpacker (1995) refers to redundancy in her suggestions regarding navigation. She claims that lighting effects, visual perspectives, and focal points should draw people into and through a building with ease. Redundancy is also a central feature of Steiner schooling in the form of the ritualized practices and occasions that are reinforced by the architecture. Many of these ritualized occasions are built around seasonal festivals. Teachers at the Steiner schools I visited remarked on how their classrooms and communal spaces had been designed to accommodate the festivals. For example, the two-classroom Kindergarten at the Casuarina School in New South Wales is separated by a series of wooden panels, which are folded back to accommodate the mid-winter festival.

Other forms of redundancy in Steiner Schools are directly embedded in the teaching objects and materials. The youngest children in Steiner schools paint with watercolours in a particular way, using single primary colours in their early explorations, moving later to two colours, and later still, to a full palette of possibilities. As well, redundancy in Steiner schools is found in the architecture, where there is a preference to build at angles greater than 90 degrees, and ceilings are often moulded or curved rather than flat. Steiner schools are not shaped with cubes and boxes, but are built using more organic forms, such as those found in the Goetheanum. Dudek describes Steiner's interiors as "liberated from the constraints of the right angle" (Dudek, 2000, p. 62). Common (or redundant) classroom objects include wooden materials, furniture, and toys, crayons made of beeswax, soft fabrics, and figures made of wool felt—and a palpable absence of plastic objects and synthetic materials. Many classrooms have their own outdoor spaces, gardens with fruit trees, and, where the climate permits, goats and chickens in the yard.

There is something universal (that is, redundant) about Steiner schools the world over, even though Steiner schools are often built and designed with local building materials, and curriculum is altered to suit regional contexts. Ethnographer Mary Henry (1993) observed this phenomenon as she described her visits to two Waldorf schools, three years and two continents apart. On her first visit to a Waldorf school in New South Wales, Australia, Henry wrote about the children's watercolour paintings, the soft fabrics, and the wooden furniture—the same objects and artifacts she found, three years later, in a Waldorf school in Southville, Virginia. Henry says, "Children would not paint blue moons on a yellow background, the whole class, in watercolor, in both the school in Australia and the one in Southville without some guidance" (p. 3). But what is the nature of such guidance? In writing about the institutional memory of Waldorf schools, both Mary Henry and researcher Ida Oberman noted that there are no directing mechanisms in Steiner schools obvious to the eye. Oberman (1997) suggests that Waldorf institutions function more like clans than corporations, for the system as a whole remembers and adapts without by-laws or other bureaucratic measures, with each school attempting to find the best structures and relationships to fit its own circumstances. Oberman also identifies forms of redundancy contributing to the robustness of the system—such as the seasonal festivals, curricular practices, and architectural features I have already mentioned. This is the language of complexity.

Diversity

School architecture can also encourage diversity. One example is the growing trend for schools to serve more than just school-aged students, including the design of spaces to accommodate community members who might be present during school or after school hours. These members include parents, seniors, and special interest groups, bringing diversity to the school through a wide group of interests and needs (Bogle & Diamond, 2004).

Another feature of built environments that encourages diversity is the availability of spaces that support different kinds of learning, as envisaged by Dewey who called for a variety of equipment, workshops, and laboratories (Dewey, 1933/1989). The project rooms, kivas, and atriums described by Prakash Nair (2002) also contribute to curricular diversity. There is a similarity here to some of the early childhood structures too, such as the atelier of the Reggio Emilia schools (Tarr, 2001).

Lucien Kroll spoke of diversity in his book titled *An Architecture of Complexity*. He claimed that architecture is often too homogeneous, pointing to dull, unsurprising, and lifeless housing developments as prime examples. He might have been writing about schools as well when he argued that "diversity encourages creativity, while repetition anaesthetises it" (Kroll, 1986, p. 29). Kroll also suggested: "If inhabitants were to organise their own buildings, they would by their own efforts generate both the diversity and the close relation to the fabric which is lacking" (p. 29).

Patricia Tarr's (2001) description of how children in Reggio Emilia schools are expected to respond aesthetically to the natural world, to their cultural heritage, and to their inner worlds, contains elements of another feature of complex systems, pattern recognition. On this topic, thoughtful school architects have suggested that school design should incorporate rich patterns throughout the school. For example, William Bradley, an architect by training who became an educational programmer for an architectural firm in Virginia, claims that balance, order, symmetry, rhythm, form, space, volume, and scale are the diverse architectural elements for creating pattern. One example he gives is the central corridor in the Hope Elementary School in Hope, Indiana, where a series of arches "articulate the spine, creating a syncopated rhythm that draws the occupant from one end of the building to the other" (Bradley, 1998). Others have also noted the importance of balance and pattern including Christian Rittelmeyer (1992), who surveyed hundreds of German students about their views on school buildings and concluded that schools with a feeling of balance, warmth, and pattern were regarded as attractive and inviting.

Decentralized Control

Several decades ago, architects in Scandinavia pointed to the need to change school design in two fundamental ways: to decentralize administration and teaching, and to create physical environments that would allow for teamwork and greater flexibility in learning and teaching interactions. The importance of opening the school to the larger community was also emphasized (Cold, 1986). In terms of complexity theory, the latter of these directives can be seen as including the community as one of the nested collectives involved in the generation of knowledge. Other architects practicing non-traditional school design also strive for decentralized administrative services (Day, 2000). As we have seen, decentralized administrative control is a feature of Steiner schools too.

The Natural World and Complexity: A Myriad of Symbiotic Relationships

One of the predictors of school achievement, as measured by Kenneth Tanner (2000), was the prevalence of so-called "positive" outdoor spaces, such as green areas in contrast to asphalt parking lots and concrete playgrounds. Others have paid particular attention to the outdoor classrooms created by the spaces between buildings (Bingler, 1995, 1998), as epitomized by the Learnscape designs of Helen Tyas Tunggal and John Webber described in the previous chapter. Still other architects have emphasized courtyards (Muir, 2001). Some have simply suggested that what matters is a variety of outdoor spaces rather than distinct outdoor activity settings (Crumpacker, 1995). And to pay attention to the natural world also implies paying attention to a larger aesthetic. As Dewey (1933/1989) said, attending to the aesthetic elements enhances learning and brings balance and order to daily life.

When I ask teachers at Steiner schools to identify the physical aspects of their schools they like most, they often identify the Kindergartens. They tell me that the Kindergartens are embryonic to the whole feeling and direction of the school. A teacher at the Orana Steiner School in Canberra, Australia told me that liked the Kindergartens best of all because of their outdoor classrooms. She described the use of natural materials, of paths avoiding sharpness, colours in the plantings, trees good for climbing, and trees good for bearing fruit. She emphasized the presence of living creatures, like the chickens in the yard. Then she hesitated, and I could see she was deciding whether to make her next point. A moment later, she added, "It's also the children. It's something about the children that invites the elements. Things grow better in the Kindergartens" (L. Walker, personal communication, February 3, 2005). In the framework of complexity and the Gaia hypothesis, the idea of children helping the plants grow is not such a far-fetched notion. Hiroko Hosoda (1998), a Japanese architect, makes a related claim. Hosoda described how the large camphor tree on a main street in a central part of the city of Sendai served for years as a symbolic centre of the community. In 1883, a school was built around the tree. During World War II, the school and the beloved camphor tree were destroyed by fire. A few years after the war, the school was rebuilt and in Hosoda's words, "the strange thing is that when the lively children came back, from the barely remaining stump, buds started to shoot. The camphor grew and once again became a great tree watching over the children and charming the inhabitants" (p. 23).

Another example of making a tree a centrepiece of a school can be found at the Shearwater Mullumbimby Steiner School, located a stone's throw from the most easterly edge of Australia. The school was designed around a white fig tree, which serves both as a symbolic and physical centre for the school. Before designing the master plan for the school, the white fig was inspected and found to be a relatively young tree of forty years, in good health, and expected to live for at least another two hundred years (K. Korobacz, personal communication, May 23, 2005). The tree makes a striking statement: like the Sendai tree and Kindergarten gardens, the fig tree flourishes and watches over the students of the school, guiding their movements and activities and, perhaps, thriving on the students as well.

When I tell people about the fig tree courtyard at Shearwater, I often encounter the response, "Well, that's fine and good in Australia where the weather cooperates. Try designing a school around a courtyard in Northern Ontario." Well, in fact, Toronto architect John Shaw did just that in the early 1970s when he designed the Central Algoma Secondary School in Desbarets, Ontario. Desbarets has a population of only 400 people, and so the high school draws its students from communities as far as fifty miles away: virtually every student travels by bus. The school was conceived as a fully equipped secondary school, replete with technological studies areas, art and music rooms, and home economics areas. It was built to replace three small high schools that could not possibly offer the same range of programs and facilities. Desbarets was chosen for several reasons, not the least of which was the incredible parcel of land upon which the school would ultimately be built—several hundred acres of open fields, swamp, and bush, with a quiet bay marking the boundary of the property. But the choice of location was not without controversy (Wilson, n.d.).

Desbarets was seen by some of the school trustees and the community as problematic because of the necessity for bussing. As well, nearby cottagers on the North Channel, flowing between Lake Superior and Lake Huron, were concerned about how a large school would deal with the treatment of sewage. So, drawing the students together to form a cohesive community was a major challenge.[19]

Figure 7. Courtyard at Central Algoma Secondary School
(photo by author)

One of the prominent architectural features, designed to create a place for the school community to gather, was a central courtyard. Like the school at Shearwater, this school was also designed around fig trees—six of them. Thirty years after being planted, five still thrive. In fact, they have grown so tall that they need to be trimmed back substantially at least once a year, so their abundant growth does not block too much of the natural light flowing into the inner courtyard. Unlike the courtyard in Australia, the Central Algoma courtyard is a covered one, although with the sun streaming in on the April morning when I made my visit to the school, I had no sense of being enclosed indoors. The courtyard is widely agreed upon as being the most successful feature of the school. Not surprisingly, it contains every element of the pattern *courtyards that live* identified by Christopher Alexander. Alexander describes a dead courtyard—we've all seen them in office buildings and schools—a perfectly squared-off area, encased in glass, often with only one entrance (often locked, in my experience), and filled with gravel and abstract sculptures. In contrast, he offers several features for creating courtyards that teem with life. One of those features is for the courtyard to have multiple

[19] In an interview on April 6, 2006, with former teacher Reno Palombri and principal Marcie Bell, I learned about the very extensive intramural games and sports system that was created to help form community in the school. This has been extraordinarily successful. The four intramural houses take part in all manner of traditional school sport—hockey, basketball and so on—as well as sports and activities that take advantage of the setting—ice fishing, winter survival expeditions, canoeing and the like. The intramural houses also play games—cards, crokinole, checkers, and chess. Over 50 activities are offered every semester.

access points: I counted eighteen different ways to enter the Central Algoma Secondary School (CASS) courtyard. Another feature of successful courtyards is that they lead to a larger open space: on one side of the CASS courtyard is the gymnasium, at the other, the cafeteria—two large open spaces, in fact. Several other patterns are contained in the CASS courtyard, such as *stair seats*. Six steps run along the entire length of one side of the courtyard, and students sit on those stairs between classes, talking with friends or reviewing their homework. Teachers gather in the courtyard too, and the administrative offices and staff room look over the courtyard from the second floor. In fact, this is a school that has no need for hallway patrol: the architecture provides so many natural surveillance possibilities that there is a sense people are looking out for one another: students are visible in all corners of the school (quite the contrast to the Columbine High School, which Tanner (2000) so severely criticized as a security nightmare).

Some of the natural surveillance at the school is accidental: built in 1972, CASS did not escape the vestiges of open concept planning. When walls were later erected to create separate classroom spaces, the result was that sets of three or four classrooms were linked as a chain of rooms. This means that students who need to leave the class to go to the toilet have to walk through two or three other classrooms to get there. While this might seem like a problem, the school has come to treat it as a welcome feature. As one teacher put it, "It means that we get to know all of the students, and that we all learn to be respectful of each other's classrooms." The presence of fig trees and the need to pass through one another's classrooms provide what philosopher Heesoon Bai (2003) calls relational moments.

Bai (2003) writes passionately about how people of cultures dominated by consumerism have committed untold acts of violence against others and against the planet. She says we must learn to balance extrinsic values with intrinsic ones, to replace control with harmony. We must understand how the "quality of our lives is reflected in the quality of our relational moments" (as cited in Patteson, 2004, p. 48). By way of example, Bai says that when we walk past a tree, we might only briefly register seeing it and continue on our way; if instead we stop in front of the tree, "gaze at it, and enter into a silent communion, having filled our consciousness entirely with the tree in all its sensuousness, then this is a profoundly different experience of seeing" (Bai, 2003). There are opportunities to enter into such communion with the fig trees at Central Algoma and Shearwater.

Providing a facility for learning to see in the way Bai has suggested is not a bad way to start thinking about a school, particularly in light of the issues raised by the Romanticists and complexivists. But what else should we consider in the process of designing schools in order to reflect the principles of complexity? Because complexity theory describes how collectives learn, it is self-evident that communities should be meaningfully involved in the design process. As Steven Bingler, then President of Concordia Architects and consultant to the U.S. Department of Education, derisively said, "Communities have become skeptical of the public hearing process. They have attended too many meetings where they reviewed some concept, gave their opinion, and then were ignored. They're called in after all the decisions have been made and are told, 'Here's where the school's going to be located, and here's a beautiful picture of it. Hope you like it.' At that point, who's going to stand up and say, 'I think we need four small schools instead of this one big school'?" (Bingler, 2002, ¶ 32).

I have met a handful of architects who speak the language of the Romanticists and complexivists and who cannot conceive of designing without community involvement. One such architect is Australian Paul Barnett, with whom I spoke in Canberra, Australia, several times over a period of a year, and whose work I described in the opening chapter. He describes his task as "bringing the spiritual impulse into matter." Indeed, his wonderfully eclectic background and interests make this approach the only possible eventuality. Other members of his design group share the same views. "After working here," Paul once joked, "they're not fit to work anywhere else" (P. Barnett, personal communication, February 18, 2005). When he decided not to become an industrial arts teacher, Barnett embarked on architectural training, studying Islamic architecture and tribal architecture—"anything where the relationship between the earth and cosmos brought some dimension of meaning to the people." His related interests include biodynamics and permaculture, and the influence of colour on human experiences in the Goethian sense.

Barnett helped design the much-acclaimed Resource Centre at the Orana Steiner School in Canberra. When I asked him why the Resource Centre had received so many architectural awards, he said he didn't know, tentatively suggesting that perhaps the awards recognized how the building was sited environmentally. One of the other members of his design group, architect Karin Gustavsson, suggested a completely different reason, claiming there was "more love in that building than in most school buildings" (K. Gustavsson, personal communication, March 23, 2005). According to Gustavsson, the love was in the detailing—including natural wood timbers, windows framed in various irregular shapes, as well as blue coloured glass in the clerestory windows. Barnett noted that the building was imbued with the passion of the teachers who had helped with the conception of the design. If the presence of children can help a tree or a garden grow, perhaps teachers and students can make a building come alive too.

Melbourne architect Gregory Burgess also thinks of buildings as living entities. When I asked him what buildings might teach, he suggested buildings were like people, with qualities of gesture and consciousness. Like people, buildings are greedy or modest, welcoming or aloof, and joyful or indifferent. Buildings make you feel very alive or half-dead.

Why is this so? American cultural critic and farmer Wendell Berry, believes that there are complex links among people, land, and community, stating that buildings must, in some way, respect and respond to the psychological, emotional, and physical needs of people, as well as to climate and land, to culture and history, and to the future. Berry said that in healthy and thriving cultures, these connections are complex, and further, that an overly industrial economy oversimplifies these complex connections, thereby making it difficult to see what the connections are or ought to be (Berry, 1981, 1983). For Berry, attempting to control what is essentially a decentralized and uncontrollable system inevitably leads to defeat and bewilderment. Burgess and the complexity theorists would agree. Embracing decentralized systems, acknowledging the relationship between shadow and light, creating redundancy and diversity, paying attention to human perception, and seeking beauty—these are the kinds of fundamental foundations we should be demanding for school design. Creating inviting settings where complex systems can emerge should be a central aim of school architecture.

Body
Taiko Drumming and Embodied Knowledge

In this chapter, I use the practice of Japanese Taiko drumming as a way of exploring the importance and largely unacknowledged primacy of embodied knowledge. One of the fundamental claims made throughout the book is that we learn with our bodies—by making artifacts with our hands and by moving our bodies through space. Another claim is that our most significant or authentic lifelong learning not only involves the body, but often also involves the arts and the natural world. One question explored in this chapter is whether schools can be built to allow more learning of this type. The value of apprenticeship learning is also discussed, and examples of architectural spaces supporting embodied learning—ranging from a dojo in Japan to performance spaces in American and German high schools—are described.

Lifelong Learning and School Architecture

When adults are asked to think of something they love to do, most people will identify a pursuit connected with the arts, the body, or the natural world. For many years, I have pondered how these three areas are linked. Why are these endeavours so important to our lifelong learning? To leading fulfilled lives? It is of note that these pursuits or hobbies are not undertaken lightly. Often a passion will be cultivated over many years, and while adults will say they take great pleasure in their learning, such learning is usually accompanied with a significant amount of struggle.

Playing the harp, stone carving, and ocean kayaking have the potential to fully engage the body, the intellect, the emotions, and the spirit. These kinds of activities connect us, in a fundamental way, with what it means to be human. The passion and seriousness people bring to such pursuits is precisely the passion required to nurture and sustain meaningful learning in schools—the kind of learning we do when no one is watching, when no one is evaluating us, and when the most important thing at stake is our own learning (whether we call it learning or not).

I am not alone in thinking that this kind of learning is possible in schools and in all subjects. Mathematicians and scientists who enjoy highly creative moments of inquiry—whether they are six or sixty years old—experience the same exhilaration from their accomplishments and discoveries as do artists and athletes. Mathematicians talk about the beauty of proofs and the grace of solutions, judgments involving an obvious aesthetic dimension. Goethe suggested that mathematicians can experience their work as "complete, transparent, comprehensive, pure, clear, graceful—even elegant" (Naydler, 1996, p. 68). Scientists also speak of beauty—and not only those scientists who would align themselves with the romantic notions of Goethe. I once heard a group of Canadian scientists describing the complexity of the forehead of an ant as revealed by a newly created microscope using synchrotron light; their description focused far more on the beauty of the ant than on the technical aspects of their findings.

This kind of learning resonates with Dewey's conceptions of children's learning: learning that includes elements of conversation, of inquiry, of artistic expression, of play. Many of the pursuits adults engage in as lifelong passions involve the creation of a product of some kind. Some passions fit obviously into this mode of learning—making pottery, composing music, or nurturing a garden. Others are less obvious, including the performance of music, where what is made disappears once the concert is over, at least in a physical sense, but where play is more prominently present, both in practice and in performance. And of course, the music does not disappear from the body of the performer. In fact, all art-making involves the body, even though some of the products of art-making may be more ephemeral than others. The ways in which people learn about their hobbies involve conversation, inquiry, and play in the most joyful sense of the word, spanning all of human development and learning.

Spontaneous learning has important lessons to teach about how to value the effects of learning. This valuing is of a qualitatively different type than the measurements we typically encounter in schools. The arts teach us how the products of our learning—the things we have made—ought to be measured by technical standards *and* by aesthetic standards—standards of beauty. With quiet force, my piano teacher once told me, "Of course every note must be correct, tempi must be chosen wisely and dynamic contrasts must be clear. But that alone is not enough to make music. It must be beautiful to be music." And so, I learned that having 90% of the notes in place was only a beginning and that even playing all of the notes right was not enough. The arts teach us about high expectations and beauty: about radiance. Learning involving the body (is there any other kind?) teaches us about other kinds of values, too—values of perseverance, precision, and even perfection. Transcendence. Not coincidentally, these characteristics also describe mindful encounters with the natural world.

When people are asked how they learn about the thing they love most, many will speak of learning from a mentor over a long period of time. Others seek out books on their subjects or search the Internet for resources. A number will say they learn from talking with a host of other people involved in similar pursuits, or in working side-by-side with a person engaged in the same activity. Most claim their learning involves long periods of solo work, punctuated by periods of intense self-reflection. The times for seeking guidance from others come most often when there is some kind of transition taking place in the learning. This approach to learning is like the project-based learning associated with the Reggio Emilia approach, where children are encouraged to pursue something of interest and are supported in their explorations by the teacher and the learning environment. With this kind of curriculum, Reggio Emilia schools are necessarily filled with atriums and studios where children are free to explore work in the arts, work involving the body, and in many cases, the natural world.

But most schools are not built like Reggio Emilia environments. So when adults are asked if they learned about their passion at school, very few say they did. For a very long time, I thought this was because teachers (and government curricula) failed to introduce the topics their students would later pursue with unmitigated energy when they reached adulthood. Not many schools include watercolour painting, Thai cooking, gardening, sailing, or playing the harp as part of the regular curriculum. But school buildings, too, are a determining factor. How can a teacher introduce Thai cooking in a school where the stoves have been removed to bring in computers? Or teach gardening in an inner-city school surrounded by seemingly impermeable concrete? Or teach sailing where there is no place to swim, let alone launch a boat? It strikes me that the schools we have built are not the best places for most forms of embodied and authentic learning.

Taiko Drumming: An Example of Meaningful Learning

Over the past few years, I have become engrossed by the Japanese-based art and practice of *taiko*. *Taiko* encapsulates some of the most pertinent and intriguing issues regarding learning for its own sake, and the places in which we do such learning.

Taiko is a form of ensemble drumming; the word *taiko* refers both to the drums and to the drumming practices. Some say *taiko* can lead to physical and spiritual connections between the drum and the player. *Taiko* integrates body and mind; it is a form of knowledge embodied through participation in socially and culturally prescribed systems of meaning (Powell, 2004). In North America, *taiko* is a growing artistic and political movement. One of the most influential American *taiko* groups, San Jose Taiko, is a forum for social action, cultural preservation, community development, and Asian-American identity (Uyechi, 1995). It was founded by two drummers in 1973, and for more than three decades it has nurtured the complementary goals of professional performance and community-based teaching, including public workshops and school-based visits and programs. Other *taiko* groups share similar goals and practices. When I was living in Australia, I had the privilege of taking lessons from members of TaikOz. At the time—and possibly still—TaikOz was Australia's only professional *taiko* drumming group. The teaching was extraordinarily engaging and effective (and I am not easy to impress when it comes to teaching). I was awed by the consummate musicianship of the people with whom I studied.

TaikOz is made up of a group of Australian musicians who have embraced and embellished Japanese *taiko* traditions. They perform pieces by Australian composers, including some by members of their own group. They also perform pieces by living Japanese composers, alongside traditional music that has been performed by Japanese *taiko* drummers for centuries. They describe their work as a synthesis of East and West, old and new. One of the primary goals of TaikOz is to provide professional performances, coupled with community outreach, although TaikOz has less of a political and more of a cultural focus than some of the North American *taiko* groups in this regard.

Ian Cleworth and Riley Lee founded TaikOz in 1997. The American-born Riley Lee is the *shakuhachi* (bamboo flute) player in TaikOz. He began playing the *shakuhachi* in 1971 with Chikuho Sakai, a master whose lineage traces back to the Zen Buddhist monks of the Edo period (c. 1603–1868) in Japan. A decade later, Lee became the first non-Japanese to attain the rank of *dai shihan* or Grand Master of the *shakuhachi*. Lee received his PhD in ethnomusicology from the University of Sydney in 1993, where he wrote a dissertation on the Zen repertoire of the *shakuhachi*. Since then, he has maintained an active scholarly career in addition to an astounding career of composition and performance, with concerts in Hawaii, New Mexico, Texas, California, England, Austria, Switzerland, Japan and throughout Australia, and appearances with major companies such as the Boston Symphony Orchestra. As the morning sun dawned on January 1, 2000, Riley Lee performed *shakuhachi* music on the roof of the Sydney Opera House. East meets West. Arts meets body meets natural world.

Ian Cleworth is the Australian-born artistic director for TaikOz. He began his *taiko* studies at the age of nineteen with the Japanese drum and flute master, Amano Sen of Yamanashi-ken. In addition to holding an honours degree in music from the University of Adelaide, he has continued his *taiko* studies in Japan over several decades, studying and playing with various masters and Japanese *taiko* groups. He played with Amano Sen's troupe for several years, and he returns frequently to perform in Japan. Ian has performed throughout North America, Europe, and Asia. He is involved in bringing TaikOz to school populations through performance and by developing programs to expose students and their teachers to *taiko*.

When I interviewed Ian Cleworth at the TaikOz *dojo* in Sydney, I wanted to explore his views of how people learn to drum and how the architectural spaces in which they learn affect their work. I also hoped he would tell me more about the work that TaikOz has undertaken in Australian schools, not only because of my abiding interest in how artists work with teachers and students in school settings, but also because I was sure issues of architecture would emerge in the conversation.

We met on a sultry Saturday afternoon at the *dojo* on Wattle Street, not far from Sydney's Darling Harbour. As I approached the large brick warehouse, I saw a number of young children skipping along the sidewalk, with *bachi* (drum sticks) in hand, filled with energy and joy as they emerged from their lessons.

The *dojo*, situated in an old warehouse, is not especially spacious, considering the size of some of the *odaiko*—the very large drums with heads over a meter in diameter. Along one wall the instruments are stored—*wadaiko* (Japanese drums) of various sizes and descriptions, and a marvelous and extensive assortment of hand-held instruments. Five hand-hewn timber posts run the length of the *dojo*, adjoining the equally heavy square beams running along the ceiling. At one end is an exposed brick wall, framing a massive mullioned window looking across to a wall of stone, about three meters away. We sat there for the interview, where a cool breeze wafted down the shaft from many meters above.

This room breathes. As old buildings of its kind often do, the room imbues a sense of time and timelessness; though not beautiful, the room has a richness and a history. I was drawn in and felt a sense of reverence, standing there on the old wooden floor, surrounded by *taiko* drums. Such reverence also comes with the *dojo*. Translated literally, *dojo* means "the place of the way." The *taiko dojo*, then, is the place of studying and learning *taiko*. As Ian reminded me, any space—anywhere—could serve as a *dojo*. What helps establish the old wool warehouse as a *taiko dojo* is the removal of shoes upon entering—a ritual denoting the space as unique and special. As Ian put it, "Removing your shoes affects the way you think and hopefully gives you a sense of purpose in your work here." Although Ian didn't mention them explicitly, other cultural and ritualistic practices associated with the *dojo* include bowing at the door and special ways of cleaning the studio space and caring for the instruments (Powell, 2004).

Ian explained that this particular *dojo* is not, as it turns out, a perfect architectural space for the study of *taiko*. The 10-foot ceilings would be better at double the height, and Ian lamented how the timber posts—while lovely—were a hindrance for large group ensembles and multiple instruments. The *dojo* is not soundproof, and so, during the day, lessons and practices take place with rugs under the drums to mute their body-shaking vibrations. But there is no limit to the sound musicians are permitted to produce at night, so the *taiko* are played with joyful abandon once the neighboring offices close for the day.

The fact that the *dojo* is not a perfect space points to an important issue: meaningful learning can occur in less than perfect settings. Many teachers pride themselves—and rightly so—in creating inspirational learning environments where physical settings are far from ideal. Perfect is not always possible. A colleague of mine was fond of saying, "Perfect is the enemy of good." In a tour of an elementary school I once attended with some other parents, one mother showed her evident disdain for two portable classrooms on the school campus—a campus that also boasts extraordinary buildings recognized by a number of architectural awards. The teacher giving the tour admitted that the portable buildings were not ideal, but also firmly and quietly said, "They keep the rain out." In creating our spaces for learning, we must first begin with what is fundamentally non-negotiable. In the case of the Sydney *dojo*, non-negotiable elements included securing a large affordable space with good storage, and where—at least some of the time—music could be made with abandon. And certainly one of the fundamental features of schools should be that the roofs don't leak. But surely we can do better than merely building schools with good roofs, especially if we are going to be spending billions upon billions of dollars, in the next decade alone, on new schools and school renovations, creating schools that will last for 50 years or more.

Taiko in Schools: Artist Roles and School Architecture

I asked Ian to describe the kinds of work TaikOz members bring to public schools. In the first year or two of their work with students and teachers, TaikOz hosted school groups during the day in the performing venue where they would later perform during the same evening. This meant that students were able to

hear and feel and view the drumming in the theatre setting, with a full complement of drums and the ambience of the performing space. However, Ian explained, this arrangement was impractical in the long term. Moving students, young children especially, to different locations is not a simple matter, especially when tight budgets make it hard to find funds for an extra bus or two (Belanger, 2005; Kraemer, 2003; Walsh, 2003). And so, TaikOz designed a

Figure 8. Teaching Taiko drumming (photo by author)

school program to take on the road in one van. This means that, instead of having a full set of drums and instruments, three musicians travel with just nine *taiko*, as well as a number of hand instruments such as *chappa* (small hand cymbals) and *atarigane* (a type of small gong). The sessions they offer are, by Ian's description, interactive. Students watch and listen, and are encouraged to respond to the music. Small groups of students play the *taiko* during the hour-long program. Like the performing repertoire for festivals and concert stages, the repertoire TaikOz brings to schools includes a mixture of works by Australian composers (founder Riley Lee, among them), pieces by living Japanese composers, and traditional Japanese *taiko* music. These choices reflect the commitment of TaikOz to cultivate an identity crossing cultural heritages and uniting centuries of old and living traditions.

These school performances typically take place in gymnasiums—adequate, but not perfect for *taiko*. Musicians from TaikOz have also performed in school assembly halls, and even in an outdoor shed, which was open on all sides but covered with a roof. When I asked why classrooms were not used, Ian observed—not surprisingly—that classrooms are "too small, both physically and acoustically." He also pointed out another serious roadblock: the *taiko* drums don't fit through most classroom doors.

There are, of course, schools that could readily house *taiko* sessions, including two remarkable German schools, one of which—the Evangelical Community School of Gelsenkirchen-Bismarck—I described in an earlier chapter. The Musikgymnasiums Schloß Belvedere bei Weimar (Music High School in Weimar) provides another example where performance spaces are ample and inviting (Curtis, 2003). There are North American schools that could accommodate an enterprise like *taiko* as well, particularly where a separate wing has been dedicated to the arts. The Noble High School in North Berwick, Maine, designed by Harriman Associates and completed in 2002, boasts a performing arts wing with separate teaching spaces for art, music, and applied technology, in addition to a 1,000-seat theatre (Bogle & Diamond, 2004). Schools like this one can accommodate much more than *taiko*: they would be dream schools for artists working in a wide range of media. Designing schools in this way is becoming increasingly important, as we learn more about the value of the work that artists and other members of the community bring to school environments.

In the mid-1990s, a group of educators and administrators in nine high-profile arts organizations throughout the United States gathered to discuss ways in which artists contribute to schools. The ensuing publication, *Creating Capacity*, delineates a continuum of artist involvement in educational settings, all of which have the capacity to engage students in artistic experiences, albeit with different levels of intensity (Gradel, 2001). On one end of the continuum, artists give performances or create exhibits for students and teachers without engaging the audiences in interactive learning experiences; an artist acting in this capacity is considered a "performing artist." Next in the continuum is the "interacting artist," where, in addition to performing and exhibiting, the artist engages audiences in pre-performance or post-performance discussions, interpreting the artistic work within an educational context. Progressing along the continuum, we find the "collaborating artist," who is more intensely engaged in the school setting, perhaps as an artist-in-residence, planning instructional and assessment strategies collaboratively with classroom teachers. Finally, on the opposite end of the continuum from the performing artist is the "master instructional artist," a person who is deeply involved with curricular planning and acts both as a leader in program design and as a mentor to other artists working in educational partnerships.

The kind of work Ian Cleworth described would fall in the second part of the continuum, for in their work with students and teachers, Ian and his TaikOz colleagues strive to engage the students in reflection and discussion but all short of collaborating with teachers or as artists-in-residence. I asked TaikOz members if there were plans to expand the school encounters—becoming collaborating artists in the continuum as identified by the American arts educators. TaikOz was contemplating this, but they also found it daunting to undertake such an expansion, given the resources required to develop curriculum materials or to engage in something as complex as an artist residency.

The physical space required for *taiko* is also a real challenge in schools. Ian described a high school in Sydney where TaikOz had considered setting up a residency. This school has a large gymnasium with high ceilings and attractive and effective halogen lighting; there are wooden floors and the gym has "everything but the soundproofing." As Ian was describing the space, he mused, "I suppose that's why we're thinking of doing the residency there." Makes sense. How could you set up a *taiko* residency in a place that couldn't support it architecturally? This example begs a central question of this chapter: what other kinds of teaching and learning—involving the body, the arts, and the natural world—are next to impossible in schools?

Embodied Learning in the Absence of Schools

Serious *taiko* instruction typically uses an apprenticeship model to bring new members into the performing troupe. Educators across cultures have recognized the long-lasting benefits of apprenticeships of many kinds. Inuit scholar, Louis-Jacques Dorais, described learning as taking place in any setting where the learner is watching, talking with, or imitating someone who is "really working." He translated the words of Taamusi Qumaq, an Inuit elder, who had this to say about the schools white people from the "south" have instituted in Canada's north: "A house is a school, it is run by Qallunaat [white people]. This [school] has people who are taught, many of them, who learn only through words. Also one person can be a school too, when one who is really working, who is trying to do something real, is looking at this person when (s)he is working" (as cited in Stairs, 1994, p. 67). In other words, for the Inuit, it is not the building (or house) that denotes learning, but the engagement with someone involved in real work.

Jean Lave and Etienne Wenger's work on situated cognition has been heralded for decades as an important way of learning for both adults and children. One of Lave and Wenger's (1991) well-known studies involved documenting women's knowledge of mathematics while they shopped for groceries. The women were able to perform complex calculations and estimations with great accuracy, but when asked to perform those same calculations outside the grocery store, they were unable to do so. This led to the notion of situated cognition, where certain ways of knowing are best demonstrated in the situations in which they naturally arise.

Despite the benefits of learning through apprenticeships in situated settings, these approaches are not commonly found in schools. There are isolated examples, such as the workplace learning programs some public high schools endorse (Munby, Hutchinson, & Chin, 2000), not unlike the work and farm placements students in Steiner high schools undertake, or volunteer opportunities for high school students, such as those created by the Canadian Katimavik wilderness program. Apprenticeship approaches can also be found where teachers have created Internet-based electronic writers-in-residence or electronic composers-in-residence programs (e.g., Beckstead, 1998), thereby eliminating the need for school buildings entirely. In all of these examples— workplace learning, volunteer placements, and electronic artists-in-residence— learning occurs outside school walls.

Do we even need schools as we know now them? British architect Cedric Price influenced architectural thought in the late 20th century in profound ways, though he built relatively little. His greatest influence was through his drawings and teaching, where he saw his role, as architect, to be one of asking the right questions. Price was famously known not for asking, "What kind of building do you want?" but for asking, "Do you really need a building"? (Banham, 1996)." This is a profound question. Adelaide architect and urban designer Robert Cheesman would agree with Price's stance.

For over four decades, Rob Cheesman has built an extraordinary career as an architect, master planner, and scholar. After graduating from Adelaide University, Cheesman moved to Canada, where he arrived in the midst of the major building boom of the mid-1960s. Working for the firm of Webb, Zerafa, and Menkes, he belonged to a team of architects, and he took part in designing landmark buildings in virtually every major city in Canada—buildings such as the Royal Bank of Canada in Vancouver, the Toronto Hilton, the Alberta Government Telephones (AGT) building and plaza in Edmonton, and the Standard Life building in Calgary.[20] Following this high-powered initiation into the profession, Cheesman completed a post-graduate degree in architecture at Cambridge University, where he engaged in mathematical and computer modeling of urban systems. This work inspired him to initiate a research group that would later conduct spatial analyses of all the British new towns established under the New Towns Act. Among his colleagues was the mathematician and architect Christopher Alexander, mastermind of *A Pattern Language* discussed in the previous chapter. Cheesman's (1986) resultant book demonstrated how 20th century planning was fixated on physical order to the detriment of economic, social, and environmental considerations. His theoretical work has led to urban design solutions for a number of projects with the aim of optimizing available space in institutions and campuses. In the years to follow, Cheesman established an environmental practice for the rejuvenation of green spaces in Adelaide, Melbourne, and Canberra. His building and planning designs—right back to his early days in Canada—have been recognized by an impressive array of awards.

When I met Rob Cheesman in his Adelaide office, he was in the thick of designing hospitals and other large institutions. Quite frankly, I was staggered to discover that his office of fifteen staff had just completed a round of hospital construction of over $250 million, and to hear about another series of projects of similar scope already well underway. Coupled with my amazement at the scope of his work was my surprise at finding someone with his experience involved in expansion for the Willunga Waldorf School—a school with just over 200 students, some 40 minutes outside Adelaide.

Cheesman was impressed by the deep sense of social responsibility and morality he observed in the students at the Willunga Waldorf School. He also admired the kinds of activities the children undertook—for example, woodworking, sewing and gardening. As we spoke, it became apparent he had always been interested in human activity. For him, the ways in which those

[20] Cheesman also worked for a year as a member of the seven-person project design team responsible for the extensive urban renewal proposals for the Toronto Waterfront—including the CN Tower. In our conversation he likened his time in Canada to being a field surgeon in a war—scarcely was one project off the drawing board, before another was begun.

activities are related to one another, on both social and environmental levels, hold the clues for architectural design. He said, "Let the architecture flow from the activities themselves."

Where did this orientation come from? Cheesman spent his formative years in a coastal fishing village in South Australia. From dusk until twilight, he and his friends explored the village, nearby farms, and the ocean.[21] When Cheesman later attended a posh boys' school in Adelaide, he continued to flourish in an environment where, in addition to traditional classes in mathematics and physics, other pursuits—such as two hours a week for woodworking—were equally valued. The boys learned to knit and to weave, and they helped tend the vegetable gardens and keep the bees. The headmaster gave weekly general lessons, with far-ranging topics. Cheesman described one lesson where the headmaster and the boys hopped on their bicycles and rode to all seven bridges spanning the Torrens River—bridges they then analyzed, sketched, and modelled. From what I could gather, these general lessons usually involved leaving the school grounds entirely.

Partly because of the nature of his early childhood experiences and formative years of schooling, Cheesman believes that school architecture is less important than access to engaging activities and immersion in deeply disciplinary and creative thinking (R. Cheesman, personal communication, May 25, 2005). He astutely observed that the Willunga's school architecture alone could not account for the prevalent sense of peacefulness found there; the peacefulness also stemmed from a combination of the curriculum, the learning opportunities, and the teachers themselves. For Cheesman, the character and ability of the teacher will always be the central factor, supported by an environmentally responsible and socially inviting campus. In other words, he considers issues of school architecture to be of lesser importance in achieving good educational outcomes. Students having access to *taiko* would be more important to him than having *taiko* in the schools.

Although I, too, value out-of-school learning, I believe we still need schools for students and teachers and other members of the community to meet, dwell, and learn. Some of the opportunities Cheesman described are simply not available to children coming from families with limited incomes: schools serve the important function of providing access to activities and occupations these students might not otherwise encounter. Despite the power of computers and their increasingly ubiquitous presence, neither apprenticeship programs nor computer-mediated instruction can take the place of school communities.

Indeed, I do not believe that computers should be at the forefront of learning, and most certainly not in the early years. While I cannot imagine working in a world without the many powerful forms of technology we now employ, it is learning to play, learning to think, learning to converse, and learning to inquire that should be at the forefront of education. Computers, like

---

[21] At the time of our interview, he was still an avid surfer and diver, and for fifteen years, had been a competitive rower. Cheesman's love of rowing manifests in coaching as well: in 2004 he coached a South Australian Masters' Team for the Australian Masters' titles.

other resources, are needed to support that learning, but the goal should not be about mastering the technology. In addition, learning to use a word processor or the Internet or a three-dimensional sketching program takes no time at all compared to learning to play a musical instrument. Some of the strongest supporters of computers as learning tools claim "important software applications are learned effortlessly by children" (Tapscott, 1997, p. 136). So why rush it, especially when so much research indicates the value of learning through the body and building sensory awareness (Healy, 1990)? Surely, the elementary years, at least, should feature learning about the physical world through the body. And surely children should partake in such learning with other children, providing both the redundancy and diversity required for complex understandings to emerge.

Connecting Mind and Body

The centrality of the body, of making things, and of the arts, is evident even in settings that seem far removed from such physical ways of knowing. My first visit to a video and computer game production studio occurred in California in the early 1990s, when I had a chance to spend time in the studios of Electronic Arts. There, I encountered a maze of sprawling, naturally lit, brightly coloured studio spaces. In this place where computer and video games were created and manufactured, more than half of the floor space was devoted to music and the arts. A typical music production studio had computers, sound systems, drum machines, and synthesisers lining the walls; in the centre of the room were acoustic instruments — a violin on a chair next to a music stand, alongside an old upright piano. The visual arts studios were similar. They contained sophisticated technological tools for still and animated graphics, but plastered all over the walls were sketches created by hand. Between scanners and mouse pads were pads of paper, pastels, watercolours, and pencil crayons. When I asked about the prevalence of so much "old" technology, the designers described how the computer-related technologies were only tools for supporting their artistic work. Designers, without exception, were quick to point out they were artists first, not computer technicians. Several artists commented on needing the physical immediacy of "old" instruments to think with, before they were able to fully take advantage of the technology before them. Most of the designers I interviewed there had learned to use the technological tools on site, apprenticing with others who were already familiar with the tools. Their training as artists and musicians was seen as something quite separate, something they couldn't have learned on the job but had been a part of their lives from their formative years (Upitis, 1999).

Taiko also provides an example of learning by apprenticing and learning through the body. This is abundantly obvious to a *taiko* master like Ian Cleworth. When I asked him about how people learn to drum, his immediate response was to say, "*Taiko* involves not just the ears in terms of listening to and perceiving music, but it involves the whole body. It is not just arms and sticks." Because of the fundamental importance of learning through the body, the approach TaikOz members take in their teaching is what Ian called a kinesthetic approach. This means that their teaching techniques highlight the visual, aural, and bodily knowledge as an integrated whole. The teacher, using a mirroring technique, repeats patterns and rhythms countless times; that is, the instructor faces the students and uses the right side of his or her body while the students use their left, and vice versa. There is more doing and watching and repeating than there is talking. TaikOz teachers do not use notation—not even notations developed by the Japanese (which I find much more intuitive than the Western notations for Japanese rhythm patterns and pieces). Their teaching techniques are designed to "foster memory—aural memory, body memory, muscle memory" (I. Cleworth, personal communication, March 12, 2005). This approach is in keeping with American educational researcher Kimberly Powell's (2004) experience of *taiko*, where she describes how drumming is taught through repetition, mimicry, and metaphor. She adds the paradoxical observation that drilling and other types of repetitive practices often result in a highly aesthetic quality of experience. Participants describe out-of-body feelings and of a spiritual unity with instruments, sounds, and other players.

As a beginning drummer, I have only once come anywhere near such unity. No doubt my *taiko* abilities have been hampered by Western classical training in music. In my first experience with a *taiko* teacher in Canada—a Canadian woman who had studied *taiko* in Japan—I had a great deal of difficulty remembering and producing the rhythms. I thought it would be easier if I could see them written in standard music notation. Of course, this strategy missed the point. Even after attempting to notate the rhythms, I only grasped them when I learned them in the traditional way—by watching and imitating. I made many mistakes at first, but I eventually developed the muscle memory to be able to produce the rhythms and movements without thinking—or, at least by thinking with my muscle memory rather than through a notational approach. This is not to say that *taiko* is "only" a physical undertaking. As Powell (2004) reminds us, the cardio-physical training needed for *taiko,* the musical drilling, the ongoing discussions about purposes of technique, and a grounding in the historical and cultural significance of *taiko* and its place in the contemporary context is all part of the larger picture, making for connections with, rather than dissociations of, physical experiences and other ways of knowing.

I have long suspected that my attempts to learn *taiko* are further hampered by my Northern European heritage, a suspicion confirmed during my conversation with Ian Cleworth. Cleworth unequivocally claimed that it is much harder for Westerners to learn *taiko*. He suggests the difficulty is partly cultural: some *taiko* movements and stances are based on Japanese ways of standing, sitting, bending, or walking. For example, *Miyake-daiko*, a form of *taiko* drumming that developed on the island of Miyake, is so named because it involves low, lunging stances like those movements used by the Miyake labourers to haul massive tree trunks down the steep mountain slopes as they pass the trunk down a long line, lunging from one side to the other.

It is possible that the difficulties Westerners encounter with *taiko* are partly due to educational factors as well. Traditional Japanese schooling—especially in the early years—focuses much more on physical learning than North American schooling. In Japanese schools, "young children are viewed as essentially and importantly physical" (Walsh, 2004, p. 97). As part of a study of five Japanese Kindergartens and daycares conducted in the late 1990s, American scholar Daniel Walsh found that the body was central to the cultural and educational narratives and that the Western mind-body distinction was never part of the Japanese view. To be what the Japanese term *genki*—which Walsh describes as an exuberant word meaning fit, strong, and physical—is highly valued. He describes how his own children became more physical during their time in Japan, partly because of the expectations set by their teachers, and partly because of the opportunities afforded by the designs of their schools, where swimming pools and large playgrounds were an inherent part of the school architecture. His children sat still less and exercised more because they spent at least as much time outdoors as in the classroom. They learned to be confident in their physical beings. There is evidence of young children everywhere experiencing *genki*, such as the four-year-old pictured here. But in some cultures, it lasts for a shorter period than in others. Certainly schooling should not contribute to the loss of *genki*, although I suspect it often does.

Figure 9. "Genki" (photo by author)

If it is the case that Westerners find it harder to learn *taiko* because of genetically encoded muscular intelligence (or lack thereof), combined with stark differences in early schooling experiences, then surely the best way to learn *taiko* is through the body: moving the body and engaging the most commanding of all instruments—the voice. The voice is prevalent in *taiko* practice, especially in maintaining *ki*, the sense of energy and unity associated with successful *taiko* playing (Powell, 2004). One way of maintaining *ki* is through *kiai*, the use of spoken syllables accompanying the drumming. In some cases, *kiai* are part of the composition itself, such as the loud "*so –re*" that is spoken in unison as part of a composition about a volcano. In other cases, the *kiai* are produced by individuals to help maintain energy, or to guide a fellow player back to the downbeat or structure of a song.

Here is another way the voice is intimately tied in with other parts of the body and with learning *taiko*. *Taiko* teachers often perform drills in four groups of eight, counting for the first round, in Japanese, *"ichi, ni, san, shi"* (1, 2, 3, 4), with the students chiming in with *"go, roku, shichi, hachi"* (5, 6, 7, 8) as they mirror the physical movements. For the second round, the teacher calls *"ni, ni, san, shi"* (2, 2, 3, 4), and again, students respond, *"go, roku, shichi, hachi"* (5, 6, 7, 8) while doing the movements. The third set then begins with *"san, ni, san, shi"* (3, 2, 3, 4), and the final set, *"shi, ni, san, shi"* (4, 2, 3, 4). Weeks after my sessions with TaikOz, I could easily recall *"go, roku, shichi, hachi"* (5, 6, 7, 8) but I couldn't remember, for the life of me, how to count "1, 2, 3, 4"—until I did one of the drills again, and could hear the numbers *"ichi, ni, san, shi"* singing in my head.

This experience brought to mind a striking experiment I once read about that was conducted with two groups of kittens raised mostly in the dark and exposed to light only under a particular set of conditions. In this experiment, the first group of kittens moved around freely but each kitten was harnessed to a carriage and basket containing another kitten, with the kittens in the baskets making up the second group. After a few weeks, both groups of kittens were released. The first group easily navigated the environment; however, the second group behaved as if they were blind—they repeatedly bumped into objects and fell over edges. Despite having seen the same environment as the first group of kittens and having moved through it while sitting in their respective baskets, the second group of kittens did not have the kinesthetic knowledge they needed to move competently through space (Held & Hein, as cited by Varela, Thompson, & Rosch, 1993). Now, I am not suggesting that our intelligence is scarcely more than that of a kitten learning to navigate through an environment. But this experiment provides strong evidence for how much of what we call intelligence is gained through physical learning.

Not long after my interview with Cleworth, I came across a book written in 1937 by British scientist Walter Cannon, titled *The Wisdom of the Body*. In it, he described what was known about regulatory systems in humans at that time, and about how humans had *learned* to maintain stable metabolic processes. He claimed that his use of the word "learned" was not unwarranted. He wrote, also, of the marvelous and beautiful adjustments of the human organism. In schools and in our culture generally, we ignore physical knowing at our peril. And what is the mind if not a physical entity? We have spent far too long, especially in schools, focusing on the body from the neck up—and designing schools to support such a fundamentally limited view of learning.

We are beginning to see a shift in emphasis from mind-only learning to other kinds of learning, but it is a slow shift. I attended a conference in 2005 with a keynote address delivered by a respected psychologist. After some promising comments about how the best pedagogies were marked by qualities of "connectedness" and social interaction, the speaker then said, "All learning happens in the mind." I beg to differ. So would the graduate students who had taken part in my educational psychology course titled *Psychological Foundations of Learning* at my home institution the previous year. This was a course I had not taught before, and I was grateful to inherit course outlines from colleagues who had previous experience with the course. I tried to follow their outlines, but for one session I couldn't resist adding the topic "Embodied Learning and the Arts." This session captivated the students, and they told me that it was the class they found most intellectually engaging. The next time I taught the course, I was brave enough to begin with the topic of embodied learning. Learning happens in the body *and* in the mind.

It is not just graduate students who find resonance with this topic. Students in North American elementary schools are aware of the importance of physical learning, too. Most parents and teachers know that if you ask elementary students what their favourite subject is at school, most will respond with "recess" or "gym." As part of a large-scale Canadian study on arts education, my colleagues and I asked thousands of students what subjects they liked best and what subjects they wanted more of in school (Smithrim & Upitis, 2004). Hands down, they wanted more time in gym: even 12-year-old girls, in the early stages of adolescence, preferred gym to every other subject. Next in line was visual art, followed by music, drama, and dance. Very few students sought more time in the so-called core subjects—science, math, language, and social studies. In contrast to 78% calling for more gym time, only 15% called for more time in the language arts. Why? Could it be that they perceived a fundamental shortfall in the system when it came to studies involving the body?

In the same research project, we compared students who were involved in the arts-based program, *Learning Through the Arts,* with students who had other special programs or were simply carrying on with the regular curriculum. In the *Learning Through the Arts* program, students learned about and applied a variety of art forms in the context of their other subjects—language, mathematics, science, and social studies. For example, in one unit, Grade 4 students learned about geometry through modern dance. After three years, students in the *Learning Through the Arts* schools performed better on the standardized test on arithmetic computation than their peers in the other schools, even though there were no differences in scores at the outset, and no other differences—such as household income—that could account for the results. We were interested in probing why this result was achieved and why it occurred in computation but not in other mathematics tests or in language scores. After surveying and interviewing thousands of parents, teachers, students, artists, and administrators, we concluded that the students in the *Learning Through the Arts* schools performed better at computation because they were more engaged in their learning—they were simply more awake at school. Parents, teachers, students, administrators, and artists commented on the importance of the arts in engaging children physically, claiming that as a result of the physical involvement, the students learned their lessons more deeply. They may be right.

Beyond Embodied Knowledge: Ritual and Spirituality

Thus far, my descriptions around the *taiko* example have focused on embodied knowing, learning through apprenticeships, architectural consider-ations, and cultural and educational views of embodied knowledge. But there is more.

In my conversation with Ian Cleworth, I was struck by his affection for a setting in which he had once practiced *taiko* in Japan. There is a small village in the Fukui Prefecture on the West coast of Japan named Ota-cho. In the mid-1980s, many villages of the magnitude of Ota-cho were granted funds to enhance their cultural facilities. The then-mayor of Ota-cho spent the allocated funds to build a complex that included a *taiko dojo*. In addition to the soundproof *dojo*, the U-shaped complex had a kitchen next to the *dojo*, beautiful baths, accommodation, and a restaurant. Next to the *dojo* was an outdoor stage, facing a large oval. A perfect *taiko dojo*. While Ian would admit to the possibilities of learning in almost any setting, he contemplated how Ota-cho's beautifully designed space, surrounded by mountains and trees, made it particularly conducive for study and reflection, and for transcending the physical to reach what might be thought of as spiritual knowing.

Study and reflection. Feelings of radiance, transcendence. Canadian scholar Brent Davis writes about the connection between embodied experiences and feelings of transcendence. He observes that most people can recall experiences where they lost track of time—when immersed in a good book or engaged in artistic activity or being swept up in a crowd (Davis, 2004). Davis contends that such experiences can also be cultivated through rhythmic and repetitive activity, suggesting the purpose of such activities or rituals is to "lift participants from their respective isolations into something greater than themselves" (p. 158).

This view is astonishingly similar to the perspective offered by bioevolutionary scholar Ellen Dissanayake (1988, 1998). Based on her anthropological work in Papua New Guinea and Sri Lanka, Dissanayake writes about how the arts are essential to human evolution and survival. She claims that we make the ordinary special through our rituals and so, too, make otherwise unbearable experiences bearable through the rituals we develop.

In addition to Dissanayake's anthropological work, there is mounting neurological evidence for the relationship between repetition and ritual and states of transcendence. For over 30 years, Eugene d'Aquili and his colleagues have been amassing evidence to show how ritual can lead to biological states of trance, opening a window for mystical and transcendental experiences (d'Aquili, Laughlin, & McManus, 1979; Newburg, d'Aquili, & Rause, 2001). In the 1979 book, *The Spectrum of Ritual: A Biogenetic Structural Analysis,* the authors examine the origin of human ritual through an evolutionary perspective and consider the neurophysiological mechanisms that might underlie the trance states associated with many human rituals.

But as Davis (2004) so aptly points out, it is one thing to demonstrate that experiences of transcendence are physiologically possible, and quite another to consider why they happen at all and why such experiences are more common than we might admit. Davis posits that there have always been transcendent unities by which people are made aware of their nature and of themselves. He says: "Human thoughts are not merely about the cosmos, they are parts of the cosmos—and so the universe changes when something as seemingly small and insignificant as thought changes. These convictions are at the core of emergent ecospiritual movements. The defining feature of ecospirituality is an attitude of respect and entanglement with all living forms. This sort of attitude is represented in almost every ancient spiritual tradition" (p. 159). Davis says that ecospirituality is as much about a recovery of an ancient understanding as it is about the emergence of a new one.

Earlier I described TaikOz co-founder Riley Lee's skill at playing the *shakuhachi*. The *shakuhachi* is an end-blown flute made of bamboo, with only a few holes. There no pads or keys as on a Western flute; but even with such a "simple" instrument, the range of sounds produced in the hands of a master is truly astonishing. Each *shakuhachi* begins, as Riley Lee so movingly puts it, "as a stalk of yellow-green bamboo swaying in the wind" (Lee, n.d., ¶ 1). *Madake,* the kind of bamboo used to make the *shakuhachi*, grows in abundant groves containing thousands of stalks of sizeable proportions: the *madake* will easily grow to 25 meters in height. Each stalk has its own clump of roots, connected by a network of runner routes. In this way, every stalk contributes to the nourishment of the entire eco-system. Small wonder that in the Edo period, making music with the *shakuhachi* was the primary meditative practice of a sect of Zen Buddhist monks. For the monks, the act of playing the *shakuhachi* relaxed the mind and body and aided their meditation and contemplation—just as Davis or Dissanayake would predict. The *shakuhachi* was a spiritual tool.

Spirituality rounds out the connection among the arts, the body, and the natural world, words I have repeated—drummed—many times in the previous pages. In Western settings, Davis (2004) says, the word spiritual is associated with the complete denial of the physical, the worldly. But in what he calls "ecospiritual discourses" (p. 159) matters of the spirit are, literally, matters of breathing. For *spiritus* is derived from the Latin word "breath." In this sense the spiritual can be thought of as a "constant physical connection to and material exchange with an animate world" (p. 159–160). This idea is well developed in non-Western cultures and in ancient conceptions of spirituality: historians and anthropologists have described these kinds of beliefs across cultures and across time. Perhaps it is time we breathed more of such spirit into our schools.

Value

Economic, Social, and Environmental Costs

In this chapter, I shift away from discussions of how we learn to a discussion of assessing what we have learned. In parallel, I deal with the difficult issue of how we attach costs to school buildings and to learning. The prevalent mode of attaching costs to a building, namely the value of the time and materials used in construction, is contrasted against a model that also takes into account the environmental costs in building and maintaining schools. The most prevalent model of measurement for student achievement—standardized testing—is discussed in terms of its political thrust as well as its inherent flaws. I close this chapter with a bridge to the final two chapters by evoking Rachel Carson's classic work on environmental damage caused by toxic chemicals, with the suggestion that if we lose sight of the effects of building on the planet and its resources, then the cost accounting for architecture or the standardized testing around educational attainment will be meaningless.

For centuries, a distinction has been made between schooling and learning in a deeper sense. Mark Twain is credited with saying that he never let schooling interfere with his education. Environmentalist David Orr writes how schooling has to do with the mastery of functions that can be measured by tests, while learning has to do with matters of judgment, "with living responsibly and artfully, which cannot be measured so easily" (Orr, 1992, p. xi). Such learning is not readily evaluated by standardized testing, but by an entirely different set of criteria—criteria involving truth, beauty, and goodness, so eloquently described by American psychologist Howard Gardner (1999) in *The Disciplined Mind: What All Students Should Understand.* Gardner emphasized the value of using vivid, dramatic narratives to capture children's imaginations and to develop a deeply felt understanding of truth (in Gardner's sense, an alchemy of science and folk wisdom), beauty (as found primarily in the arts and in nature), and goodness (issues of morality). Rather than filling the curriculum with a multitude of subjects and isolated facts, Gardner contended that students would be better served by studying a few topics deeply—topics such as evolution and the development of the species.

Standardized Educational Testing and Dual Forms of Accounting

The most pervasive ethos for assessing the value of schooling is through the completion of standardized tests to measure student achievement in the so-called core subject areas. Governments of most developed countries ask if students in schools are achieving at appropriate—and arbitrary—levels in mathematics and science. There are international comparisons made between students who are schooled in different countries (e.g., Trends in International Math and Science Studies, n.d.). The dominant public educational discourse is a highly limited and conservative one. The focus is on how governments (and principals and teachers) expect increases in achievement from one year to the next or in relation to one country or another. Rarely is there discussion about whether schooling has helped make students better human beings. One notable exception is the work of educator Alfie Kohn (1992) who has made considerable inroads in convincing teachers and parents of the limitations of this approach.

In accordance with colossal efforts to make teachers and students accountable for what is learned in school in limited and defined subject areas, attempts to regulate and standardize curricula have soared in every corner of elementary, secondary, and tertiary education. A standard school curriculum—including, for example, learning to factor quadratic equations—is simply absurd when we consider what a tiny amount of knowledge can be taught during the dozen or so years of mandatory schooling. Yet, how fiercely we hold on to that tiny amount, believing that if students don't learn the beginning and end dates of famous battles (as opposed to the complex social issues and long-standing cultural impact of those battles), they will emerge with an education disastrously incomplete.

Every education is incomplete. The job of schools is to educate students so they are disposed to learn throughout their lives, so that when they discover that they know less about the effects of World War II, for example, than they should, they will know how to pursue the topic, and moreover, wish to pursue it. We must also educate students to live in community, to find pleasure in their daily work and play, and to ensure they are awakened to the richness of human experiences and to the fragility of life. These goals are not new ones: for thousands of years philosophers have described such goals more eloquently than I have done. But no matter how these broad goals are described, students who emerge from their education with such achievements in place have an education of value. This view grows more pressing as our collective behaviours engender one global disaster after another.

The kinds of goals I have described are difficult to accomplish and to assess through the standardized curricula and tests that rule our institutions of learning. Put another way, the things easiest to measure are often also the least important. We can agree on the answers for simple sums and common spellings of words, but complex undertakings—such as taking part in a community project that provides hot soup for the homeless or composing a duet for flute and piano—are more difficult to quantify in terms of the learning that takes place. The measures we are witnessing at all levels of education focus on compliance; creative or divergent or pro-social or unexpected responses are a long way down on the agenda, if they are there at all. That is, most mainstream approaches to curriculum and its measurement are reductionist. Newtonian, one could say. Ultimately, the narrowing of curricula to those topics that are easiest to deliver and test only adds to the discontinuities associated with contemporary life, a time marked by increasingly fragmented interactions with one another and with the natural world (Everdell, 1997; Franklin, 1992; Lightman, 2005; Mumford, 1939, 1946, 1986).

Where did this emphasis on standardized assessments originate? While the approaches to such measurements in education have intensified over the past few decades, they have most certainly been present in our educational systems for well over a century. In 1939, Lewis Mumford offered this explanation:

> Merchants and money lenders have, of course, existed as a caste or functional group from almost the very beginning of civilization. Under capitalism, however, the interests, the preoccupations, and the habits of the merchant become universal ones. Every other social group is affected by the accountancy of numbers: timing, measuring, counting, labeling, ticketing; translating human gestures into mechanical movements and human desires into the calculus of price, the capitalist quantification of life creeps into every department. Education records this change no less than science: marks, examinations, annual inventories are its contributions to the new bureaucracy. (p. 136)

Having focused thus far on the flaws of standardized forms of assessment for learning—with their capitalist leanings—I should add that I fully understand that there is value in such measures. The very fact that conservative members of the public and conservative-leaning governments care so much about the results of such testing is not only because of capitalist concerns. The obsession is also there because schools, by their very nature, inspire energy and hope, hope for the world that our children's children will inherit and shape. Those of us with more progressivist leanings (in the Deweyan sense) are not always dismissive of standardized test results, either. I am just as interested as the next parent in knowing whether my children are "reading at grade level." Even though I value their development as civil, curious, active, healthy, and joyful human beings above all else, I also want them to be literate, in step with their peers. I have also made use of standardized tests in my research on arts education, recognizing the irony in doing so, just as there is irony in assessing patterns of school architecture in terms of achievement on standardized tests. While I do not believe achievement in mathematics and language tells us about the full value of an education rich in the arts, I also know I will have precious little chance of convincing politicians and educational policy makers about the importance of the arts if I am unable to demonstrate positive effects in the educational currency best recognized in our Western consumer-based societies: scores on tests of mathematics and language. Therefore, what I am arguing for is not to abandon such measures, but rather, to balance such measures other kinds: a dual form of accounting.

American philosopher and critic Wendell Berry (1983) contrasts internal accounting, which includes the costs and benefits only within the frame of capitalism and its concerns, with external accounting, which includes the value of the undertaking to the larger community. Berry insists that any accounting is incomplete if purely internal or purely external factors are considered; rather, he views these two types of accountability or valuing as complementary. The inspiring architects I have spoken with over the past decade would agree with Berry's view. While each of them has an overall vision of goals and dreams for school design—a form of external accounting—these visions are held, hand in hand, with the knowledge that internal accounting cannot be neglected. The same parallels can be drawn for inspiring educators.

We need to make a two-fold shift in our thinking. First, external accounting measures need to be brought more fully into our consciousness so the overall and long-term benefits of architectural design and educational outcomes are considered more broadly. Gardner's triptych of truth, beauty, and goodness is not a bad place to begin. Second, internal accounting measures should be broadened to include the less visible costs and values—an idea beautifully illustrated by the example of "waterharvesting" that I will describe later in this chapter when I move away from education to architecture.

Towards a Holistic and External Form of Educational Accounting

In addition to standardized test scores, many forms of measurement and research are already used to assess learning. While these methods do not receive the media attention accorded to the outcomes of standardized testing, they have a long history of development and use. In three of the schooling approaches threaded throughout this book—Reggio Emilia-inspired approaches to teaching, Waldorf schooling, and Montessori education—measures for assessing the nature of students' experiences and learning are not norm-referenced or standardized, but nonetheless tell us something significant about the value of the education these students receive.

In the Reggio Emilia approach, documentation is the key practice used by teachers to assess what is happening with students, and to guide curriculum decisions, professional reflections and study, and communication with parents. In an earlier chapter, I described the exhibit called *The One Hundred Languages of Children*, which showcases the ways children make meaning through a multitude of expressions—artistic, musical, bodily, verbal, and written, to name a few. By gathering samples of children's creations, describing the context in which they are generated, and comparing samples generated by different children or by the same child over time, Reggio Emilia teachers are able to assess children's learning and communicate the meaning of such assessments to others. Reggio Emilia teachers also use parent interviews and questionnaires to gather information as part of the documentation process (Fontanesi, Gialdini, Soncini, 1998). Howard Gardner (1999) describes this documentation process as steady, challenging, informative, and rewarding.

In addition to documentation, highly focused studies have been designed in collaboration with university researchers. For example, in the cities of Parma and Modena, researchers and teachers have studied the implications of attachment theory in the context of Reggio Emilia infant-toddler care (New, 2000). The kinds of techniques used to assess children's progress in Reggio Emilia schools are ones that encourage reflective practice on the part of teachers, and continual program evaluation and development for teachers. As Gardner noted, Reggio teachers are secure in their modes of operation: the methods and outcomes for the children provide their own rewards and value. Reggio teachers have spent decades fashioning a form of schooling that serves the entire community—teachers, parents, the physical setting, and, of course, the children. Gardner observes how the first lessons in Reggio schools come from the environment itself, an environment of beauty. Other lessons come from the relationships children form, where they are "part of a supportive extended family that is in constant communication and that seamlessly combines pleasure, responsibility, and learning" (Gardner, 1999, p. 90).

The Waldorf approach also uses documentation and observation to assess students' intellectual, social, emotional and physical development, although the approaches are generally less intense and systematic than in the Reggio Emilia schools. Testimonials of parents and graduates of Waldorf schools are an additional means of placing an overall value on the effects of a Waldorf education (Oppenheimer, 1999a). For many years, research on Waldorf schooling from people outside the school community was not welcomed—in part because much of the research used standardized testing tools. But in recent years, a growing number of Steiner educators have come to understand the importance of outside research in helping to paint a fuller picture of the experiences and accomplishments of their students (K. Smithrim, personal communication, May 14, 2003). A small number of studies suggest that Steiner graduates perform as well or better on standardized tests at the end of high school than their peers in other schools, but much research remains to be done on the effectiveness of Steiner schooling, both in terms of the mainstream measures of accountability and in terms of the measures more conducive to the Steiner approach (Oppenheimer, 1999a). Where the Reggio Emilia teachers have pursued documentation as a method of assessment that naturally complements their philosophy and approach, no doubt Steiner teachers could further develop their techniques in using narratives as an assessment tool to further depict the value of that particular approach, given the integral role that narrative plays in Steiner education.[22] I spoke earlier of how Gardner emphasized the value of

---

[22] There are growing numbers of Steiner teachers who, in their own graduate work, are using such methods to make public the various elements and benefits of Steiner education. For example,

narratives in capturing children's imaginations and in developing their understanding of nature, science, and morality, among other topics. Steiner teachers, too, have long recognized the positive values associated with such narratives.

Of the three approaches, Montessori schools have been most amenable to traditional empirical research on learning outcomes (Edwards, 2002). Numerous studies have demonstrated the effectiveness of the Montessori approach, particularly in the areas of reading and literacy, mathematics, and motivation (Chattin-Nichols, 1992; Clifford & Takacs, 1993; Haines, 2000; Loeffler, 1992; Miller & Bizzell, 1983). These studies have included a wide variety of assessment techniques, both quantitative and qualitative. Montessori teachers are trained to work with research mentors, to interpret research, and to frame research questions. Such willingness to embrace the culture of research has enabled Montessori educators to enter mainstream discourses around schooling. A measure of the awareness of the existence of Montessori schooling and of some of its principles can be taken from the number of parents who, with children approaching school-age, will ask one another if they are "sending their children to public school or to Montessori"—as if those were the only two alternatives.

Architectural Accounting: Internal and External Approaches

Thus far, I have explored some of the ways in which the value of education is assessed. What of the ways in which values and costs are attached to architecture?

To begin with, internal accountability in architecture has parallels with standardized testing in education with firmly held conventions growing from strong capitalist roots. The standard way of assessing the cost of a building is with the age-old formula of "time plus materials." That is, the cost of a building is determined by summing up the costs of the land, the price of the materials when they are purchased from the distributors, the design costs, and the wages paid to those who build the structure. These are important costs, to be sure, but they do not take into account the future operating costs of the structure or those things most difficult to measure: the environmental, social, and aesthetic impact of the structure. Nor do they take into account how the building makes people *feel* when they cross the threshold—how behaviors change, whether morale declines or improves. As in educational contexts, the money spent on time and materials is the easiest to measure and standardize, whereas the value of the aesthetic, psychological, and environmental aspects are the most difficult to assess, but in the long term, comprise an important part of the legacy of the building and are at the heart of each building's value.

Like their counterparts in education who are grappling with issues of measurement and value, some architects and planners have proposed other ways of measuring the cost and describing the value of our built environments—ways that resonate with what Mumford referred to as "a higher

Konrad Korobacz, one of the founding teachers of the Shearwater Mullumbimby Steiner School, pursued graduate work of this kind at the University of New England, NSW, Australia.

sense of human values" (Mumford, 1946, p. 136) or that contribute to external accountability in Berry's terms. Jonathan Block Friedman, Professor of Architecture at the New York Institute of Technology, is intrigued and inspired by Henry David Thoreau's attempt to live simply in the woods. In Thoreau's oft-quoted words: "I went to the woods because I wished to live deliberately, to front only the essential facts of life, and see if I could not learn what it had to teach, and not, when I came to die, discover that I had not lived" (Thoreau, 1886, p. 88).

Some readers will know that Thoreau (1886) built his enchanting, if meager, 10' x 15' cabin at Walden Pond over a period of roughly three months. The total cost of materials and labour that was not his own was $28.12 ½ — about three months' salary at that time. Of this $28, just over $8 was spent on boards, $3 on recycled windows, $4 or so on nails and other hardware, and $4 for a thousand recycled bricks; the remaining materials — timber, stones, and sand — he claimed from the land. After building the cabin, Thoreau had enough materials left to build a small wood shed, so in fact he actually built two structures for his $28.12 ½ and three months of work. Friedman developed a measure for assessing the cost of building based on Thoreau's example, resulting in a shelter for a lifetime at the expense of one year's rent.

When I heard Friedman (2005) describe his model, I was drawn to the idea that to truly assess the cost of a dwelling, we need to take into account how long the dwelling will be lived in and by how many people, in relation to the amount of time and money required to produce the dwelling. The resulting proportion, as Friedman put it, would "give an indication of the value of spirit in a particular culture, because clearly it is to a person's advantage to spend as little time as possible in erecting a shelter as there are many other things to do, especially in cultivating body, mind, spirit — which are endless and ever-rewarding human pursuits" (Case Study 3, ¶ 2). Friedman calculated a measure — which he calls "Thoreau's Number" — for the cabin on Walden Pond. Then he calculated the same measure for a typical suburban home for a family of four, where the family would be carrying a mortgage representing 10 years of work (a modest mortgage in some circles). Based on his calculations, Friedman contended that for every hour of free time enjoyed by the contemporary wage earner, Thoreau enjoyed two-and-a-half hours — which apparently gave him both time to dwell in the woods and to write a book about it.

In addition to his academic work, Friedman served as a senior planning consultant with Nassau County New York, the first major American suburb built after World War II. The County was filled with single-family tract houses, but even though it was one of the most populated parts of the United States, the county lacked many urban amenities, such as a central public library or park. By applying the notion of value as developed from Thoreau's example, Friedman and his colleagues proposed a plan for basic middle-density suburban settlement patterns called "Home for Generations." Dwellings were to be created in phases that would be "friendly to the minimal needs and economic resources of new young families, and that grow with the growing needs over time. In other words, these designs [sought] to show how architecture [could] help to minimize mortgage payments and maximize space when [it was] most urgently needed" (Friedman, 2005, Case Study 2). Combined with mindfulness of other factors such as universal access, minimum environmental impact, and maximum control over personal spaces, Friedman and his colleagues devised a scheme of phased construction for multi-generational family groups. Theirs is an intriguing scheme, one that caught the attention of the public as well as the governing executive of Nassau County. One wonders if more new schools could be constructed in such an embryonic fashion as well, distributing the very real construction costs over time and also securing the kind of time required for participatory design. Indeed, an example of this is the Evangelische Gesamtschule Gelsenkirchen-Bismarck (Evangelical Community School of Gelsenkirchen-Bismarck), arising out of Peter Hübner's architectural leadership and described in an earlier chapter. Because of funding issues, independent schools are often designed in this staged way, which can bring the added strength of a thoughtful, participatory, and evolutionary approach. As it turned out, the embryonic approach to designing the Evangelische Gesamtschule Gelsenkirchen-Bismarck meant that the construction costs could be distributed over time, and in the end the school was not any more expensive than other schools built in the area. When the retrofit of the adjoining high school took place in 2004, the work included adding an extensive set of solar panels along the south-facing roof. Those panels now generate enough electricity for the school with the excess being sold back to the grid (H. Lehmann, personal communication, February 21, 2009).

The approaches taken by Friedman and Hübner suggest that some of the most prevalent of our buildings—family dwellings and schools—need not cost as much in material terms as they currently do, that is, internal costs could be reduced. However, the idea of limiting material costs while designing more welcoming and environmentally sensitive schools is not an idea intuitively grasped by most people. More often than not, when I was working on this book, speaking enthusiastically about designing schools with natural lighting, ateliers, gardens, and pathways, I encountered the sentiment that designing schools in a different manner was all well and good, but it would never work if the costs of building were higher than present costs. And present costs are high indeed. School building is a booming industry: all the more reason to recognize that this is an ideal time to re-think our notions about school architecture. We are in the middle of a surge in school construction and renovation in North America, and in other Western countries as well, as schools built in the 1950s and 1960s to accommodate the baby boom are being retrofitted, and new schools are being built to accommodate the baby boom echo. An oft-quoted statistic from the United States General Accounting Office, published in 1995, suggests billions upon billions of dollars still need to be spent to upgrade existing schools (Baker, 1998). In 1999, more than $15 billion (U.S.) was invested in school construction in the United States (Tanner, 2000), and by 2006 this number had escalated to over $20 billion (Abramson, 2007). Untold numbers of students and teachers will feel the effects of these new buildings, and these effects will continue for 50 years as most schools enjoy at least a half-century of occupancy (Cobble, 2000; Honeyman, 1998). This begs yet another question: why are schools built to last for only 50 years? Surely we can do better with our current resources and knowledge.

Some accountants and architects have argued fiercely that if we were to calculate building costs in terms of the overall life of the building—whether that life is 50 years or more—then many of the so-called innovative features of school design I have discussed would lead to *lower* costs than those associated with the traditional boxes with classrooms attached to each side of a long corridor (Reicher, 2000). For example, researchers and architectural planners have demonstrated that the use of daylight in the context of a larger energy-efficient design is not only associated with higher levels of student performance but also can be effective in terms of long-term maintenance costs (Plympton, Conway, & Epstein, 2000; Reicher, 2000). Patricia Plympton, Susan Conway, and Kyra Epstein, researchers from the National Renewable Energy Laboratory in Washington, DC, suggested that design features that maximize the use of natural light should be regularly incorporated in school buildings to minimize building costs and to benefit students and teachers. These features include, first and foremost, orienting the building so that maximum light enters from the north and south faces, which is easier to control than from the other two faces (Plympton, Conway, & Epstein, 2000). Australian architect Glenn Murcutt encapsulates this notion with the lovely expression "tipping the roof to the sun" (R. Cheesman, personal communication, May 11, 2005).

Plympton and her colleagues also suggest using clerestory windows on the exposure that receives the most direct sunlight, with tall studio style windows on the classrooms that receive the least sun, so daylight can penetrate into all classrooms. They also encourage the practice of constructing sloping roofs for rainwater collection. Such design features are similar to those found in the more energy-conscious residential dwellings, and while residential dwellings are less likely to have elaborate energy management systems—for example, systems to control air circulation to correspond with occupancy levels or light-level sensors to adjust lighting—these additional features make schools healthy and inviting, and use less energy.

American architect Steven Bingler (2002) also made the point that good school design need not cost more. Just after former American President George W. Bush passed down the 2002 budget eliminating funding for smaller schools, Bingler showed how smaller, more flexible schools can be less expensive than larger ones. He pointed to land costs alone, observing that a 12-acre school site in Los Angeles would cost around $40 million, whereas in the inner city, less expensive 2- or 3- or 4-acre sites are more readily available, and the money saved on land could be re-directed to the school buildings themselves, with less costly and more satisfying end results. Bingler was also quick to point out that if student performance is considered in the costing, then smaller schools almost always come out ahead, particularly if dropout rates for larger American schools are factored in. When Bingler was interviewed, the cost of educating a student averaged just under $6,000 a year. But as he said, students who drop out and end up in jail cost society an average of $20,000 to $35,000 a year—figures that don't show up in the calculations because they come from the criminal justice budget.

When I visited the Tarremah School in Kingston, Tasmania—a delightful cluster of buildings, housing students from Kindergarten through to Grade 8—I was silently thinking that while the school was unquestionably inviting, it had probably been expensive to build. After all, this school had separate stand-alone structures for each grade, each with their own entrance areas and their own gardens. There were a number of additional buildings too, including an administrative building and a library. When I spoke with James Morrison, one of the school architects, I was surprised to find out that the construction costs were below the government grants for building schools in Tasmania. I had to ask him twice to be sure I heard him correctly the first time. Why were costs lower? He offered two compelling reasons. First, by making separate buildings, virtually all of the space was classified as teaching space, thereby generating the maximum amount of government grant money (as opposed to corridors, for example, which generate less government revenue). Second, construction costs were reduced because parents contributed to the finishing work. Paradoxically, one suspects that while construction costs were reduced, the external benefits—to the larger community—were enhanced. I encountered similar situations at other schools where both material and labour costs were minimized through good design. There are, of course, instances where the opposite is true—despite best efforts, there are buildings that are designed well, involve volunteer community labour, and still come in at three times the projected costs, consequently curtailing a good deal of future campus development. But those are the exceptions when community labour is involved. It doesn't have to cost more to build better schools.

Towards a Long View of Building Costs and Values

Lifetime Accounting: Balancing Aesthetic and Expeditious Thinking

We have already seen that there is more to costs and accounting than the initial capital investment to build. In most cases, the lifetime of a structure has associated costs that far exceed those of the original building. I have claimed that there are instances when the initial capital investment is relatively high, but arguably worth the investment when compared to the lifetime value of a structure and to the lifetime value to members of the community who inhabit the structure. Amory Lovins, Director of Research at the Rocky Mountain Institute in Snowmass, Colorado, gives a convincing example of this. The Rocky Mountain Institute, a 4000-square-foot structure, is more than 99% passive-solar heated. With very high levels of insulation (e.g., R-40 walls [where most houses have R-20 at best], an R-60 roof, and R-5.3 windows), the building is warm in the winter and cool in the summer. By using compact-fluorescent light bulbs, Lovins estimates that *each* bulb in the building adds a ton less of carbon dioxide to the atmosphere than would the equivalent incandescent bulb. As he says, "Saved energy doesn't pollute, run out, get cut off or hurt anyone" (Lovins, 1991, p. 4). The energy savings will pay for the entire building in 40 years—a fraction of its expected lifespan. For Lovins, beauty and efficiency go hand in hand: if it's not efficient it's not beautiful (Hawken, Lovins, & Lovins, 1999). And the figures that Lovins quotes are based on a climate where the temperature can drop to - 47° F (-44° C).

In the opening chapter, I gave an example of a school refurbishment project that Paul Barnett's design group in Canberra, Australia, was responsible for developing and completing, where expeditious thinking was the aim of the clients. I talked about how a project with a quarter million dollar price tag was bogged down over a $12.00 piece of glass. Sometimes those extra amounts are, of course, more than $12.00. In general, Barnett estimates that with a few extra weeks of time and a mere $2,000 on a school renovation costing $200,000—a scant 1%—he can provide finishing touches that would make a merely safe and functional structure into a truly inviting space. But in our conversation, Barnett lamented that such a commitment is difficult to secure, especially when there is resistance by project managers and educational administrators. And for most public or state schools, the new buildings and renovations to existing buildings are intimately tied to the funding cycle dictated by the financial and academic years. As Barnett so succinctly put it, "There's an indisputable and tight process. The school district has resolved that they need two classrooms added to an existing school: here are the proposals, here is the money, build it now because we need the classrooms in time for the first day of school" (P. Barnett, personal communication, March 10, 2005).

Barnett spoke of how school renovations and building are often accompanied by an administrative push to open the buildings "next week," while the builders and the tradespeople require a few more weeks to do their jobs well rather than just quickly. He spoke of how contracts, with liquidated damage clauses, penalize people if they take too long to complete projects. He well understands how architects and project managers who want to do something a little different—which is bound to take a little more time—need first to gain the respect of those they are serving. They need to demonstrate that they can manage the costs and the time frames before they can think about the aesthetic elements—elements that ultimately contribute to the external value of the school.

Certainly, there is a place for both aesthetic and expeditious forms of thinking. Despite his fondness for thinking that involves the aesthetic and the organic, critic Lewis Mumford (1946) described how these forms of thinking are less expeditious than more mechanical thinking, which is akin to Berry's (1983) internal valuing. Mumford claimed that there are times when purely mechanical responses are required, particularly in answer to pressing situations. I laugh every time I read these words of Mumford: "If someone must be rescued from a burning house, only an idiot would think of asking first how he got there or how [recently] the fire underwriters had [inspected] the wiring" (p. 149). Burning houses are not the time for aesthetic or reflective thought: clearly, the appropriate mechanical response to a burning house is to *get out*.

In our conversation about aesthetic and expeditious approaches to building, Barnett lamented that it is often difficult to gain the respect of one's clients to the point that aesthetic forms of thinking can emerge in something of an organic fashion. He talked about the history of Australian school architecture, where in the 1970s and 1980s, school architects were, in his view, rightly "accused of being prima donnas and designing monuments to themselves. Roofs leaked, [schools] took too long [to build], they cost too much, and [architects] didn't listen to what clients wanted. Architects of my generation have spent a lot of time redressing that image." Melbourne-based architect Gregory Burgess, too, talked about how architecture can be a profession of ego and fashion, with the result that "many important public buildings and precincts loudly proclaim individualism and iconic celebrity" (Burgess, 2004, p. 98). Peter Kollar (1960) had the same thing to say. In an article in *Architecture Australia* published in 1960, Kollar quoted Goethe's words, "The deed is all—the fame is nothing." He continued with the observation: "This [attention to the deed] is the first and perhaps the most difficult thing to perform in our field of activity, when the cult of individuality has reached unprecedented levels in our times" (p. 100). But when the notion of architect as demi-God falls away, the ground shifts. Barnett's group is actively sought out by clients who are looking for a thoughtful artistic or environmental response, and these clients are ready to provide the extra time needed for such responses.

Creativity in the Trades

With creative and artistic responses to architectural challenges comes yet another value: artistic responses often require tradespeople to demonstrate more of their specialized skills. Paul Barnett visibly grimaced as he noted how companies secure jobs by providing the lowest bid by "squeezing the contractors"—underpaying those who labour to create the buildings we inhabit. As we were having this conversation, I was thinking how even the language reflects this hierarchy: in the building industry, those people who stack the bricks and plumb the toilets belong to what are known as the "*sub*-trades." What a difference there is between being viewed as a member of a sub-trade and being viewed as an artisan. An artisan is involved in a creative act and leaves the marks of the maker behind. In 2008, I began working with a contractor on a new straw bale building project, a project with a scope too large for me to build or even coordinate on my own. He, too, holds the "sub-trades" in high regard, and his language reflects this esteem: he calls them not "trades" but "disciplines," and he engages his colleagues in what he terms "creative thinking and discussions." I enjoyed the process of working with this contractor and his colleagues immensely, along with the hundreds of volunteers who helped raise the bales. And I love the building we jointly created.[23]

Barnett, too, claimed that when objects and structures are built with the right materials and where skilled people interact with one another with respectful engagement, the buildings are loved more. He continued, "There are lots of old buildings that are still loved, not because they're works of art but because they were built with care. They are valued in the community because they've become important places to gather and take part in social and cultural events" (P. Barnett, personal communication, April 6, 2005). It is tough to put a price tag on

---

[23] The building I refer to is the lodge for Wintergreen Studios (wintergreenstudios.com), an off-grid education and retreat centre in the Frontenac Arch Biosphere Reserve in South-eastern Ontario.

that kind of value in capitalist terms, but it's exactly the price tag I put on the buildings I have a hand in designing and building.

French architect Lucien Kroll also spoke about this tension between the work normally associated with the sub-trades and the work of the craftsman [*sic*], claiming that the work of the craftsman is "flexible, decentralized, [and] ecological" (Kroll, 1986, p. 25). Kroll suggested that craftsmen or artisans are likely to work on a small scale with the result that they cannot work fast enough to remain solvent in the face of what he calls "hard industry" (p. 25). No wonder Barnett says that it is easier to make an impact with small buildings—buildings of a human scale, a scale that matches the work of the artisan rather than what Kroll calls the "mindless drudgery" (p. 25) associated with larger, more industrial building styles.

While there are exceptions, many of the buildings Gregory Burgess designs are also modest in scale. Kim Dovey, Professor of Architecture at the University of Melbourne, is an unabashed fan of Burgess, describing his work as "a celebration of everyday life … an affirmation of the art of architecture as the art of dwelling… a radical architecture that catches the public imagination" (Dovey, 2004, p. 101). The one regret Dovey expresses about the work of Burgess is that his efforts have been concentrated almost exclusively on small-scale buildings. But Dovey's observation begs the question: would something be lost if the scale of his works were to change, if Burgess were no longer interested in designing buildings as seemingly insignificant as Kindergartens?

The Intersection of Architectural Costs and Educational Values

In the late 1990s remodeling of the Apollo Elementary School in Issaquah, Washington issues of cost and value of both education and architecture came clearly into focus (Muir, 2001). When the school's standardized test scores dropped to the lowest in District #411, with fewer than half of the ten-year-olds passing the reading test, the school was provoked into new ways of thinking. Only a few years after receiving the lowest scores in the District, the school was identified as one of Washington State's most improved schools, with scores well above the average. What motivated this rapid reversal? First, there was a colossal effort by staff and parents to address curricular issues, to set high expectations for the students, and to increase the intensity of the collaborations between the community and the school. At the same time, the school was physically remodeled. That process featured many of the elements of participatory design, with a three-year planning period involving teachers, parents, engineers, architects, and every one of the 600 students in the school. The physical results contained many features that would support learning as characterized by complexity theory. For example, because the new hallways were designed to be much wider than in conventional schools, there were places where children—and ideas—could interact in informal ways. Skylights were incorporated in many rooms, allowing daylight to enter, and an intimate interior courtyard created a welcoming green space for unexpected encounters.

The cost of labour and materials for this renovation was substantial: over $7 million (U.S.). But in terms of the value of the work—by internal and external measures—the investment appears to have been a good one. Test scores improved. And while the true value of the renovation are not reflected in the improvements in test scores alone, there would certainly be good reason to question whether the renovations had any positive effect if the scores had remained the same or decreased. Teachers and principals point to other measures too, of course, painting a fuller picture of the true value of the renovation—including the pride that students, staff, and parents express in describing the school, the substantial decreases in incidents of vandalism, and a sense of purposeful intent radiating throughout the school (Muir, 2001).

Environmental Costs of Building Schools

The Apollo Elementary School example illustrates how internal and external measures of accountability interact, and how some of the principles of complexity can be seen in operation as a result of architectural design. But the example does not address other costs, such as the loss of creative skills in the trades, as already examined. Nor does it address the kinds of costs French architect Lucien Kroll (1986) identified in the context of subsidized housing where he argued that the costs of the salaries of the housing officers, the bureaucrats, ministers, statisticians and accountants, among others, ought to be considered in assessing the cost and value of a building. Moreover, it does not address another major and ever more crucial concern: the environmental impact of construction, including depleted natural resources, pollutants associated with building, and the long-term maintenance of energy greedy buildings.

In looking at environmental costs, both aesthetic and expeditious thinking come into play once again. In one of our interviews, Paul Barnett gave a simple but illustrative example of this notion. One of the goals of his design group is to use environmentally sensitive timber finishes. This means, for example, using an oiled finish that, at the time of construction, takes longer to apply than a polyurethane finish. However, unlike the oiled finish, the polyurethane finish needs to be stripped and re-applied when it is damaged, to say nothing of the environmental harm of producing and applying such a finish in the first place.

The discussion of what kind of finish to use on windowsills not only illustrates the tension between aesthetic and expeditious thinking, but also is part of a growing trend in construction to choose environmentally respectful materials. James Morrison, the architect who, along with Yvette Breytenbach, designed many of the buildings of the Tarremah School near Hobart, Tasmania, is scrupulous in his attention to the kinds of materials used in school buildings (J. Morrison, personal communication, April 20, 2005). His basic construction materials are mud brick and local timbers. Whenever possible, Morrison and Breytenbach also use plantation-grown eucalypt; native to the area, the tree grows quickly, and plantation growth ensures that the timbers are not from old forest growth. They use environmentally friendly paints and finishes, and like Paul Barnett, prefer to use natural oils whenever possible in treating the wood.

For insulation, Morrison and Breytenbach have chosen to use a fibre that combines an acrylic material with sheep's wool—again, a product that is at least partially homegrown. What I found particularly interesting was their use of a product called Macrocarpa timber for the structure and cladding. Macrocarpa trees are non-native to Tasmania and are considered weeds. By using Macrocarpa, Morrison and Breytenbach have effectively chosen to use a weed as a resource. This is an easily replenished resource, producing low ozone levels (Haslett, n. d.). It has a warm texture, not at all institutional in feel. Liz Hamilton, from the Department of Natural Resources and Environment of the State of Victoria, Australia, also describes the appearance of this wood most favourably, describing it as "lustrous" (Hamilton, 2000). Since using these materials has

Figure 10. Natural and local materials, Tarremah School, Hobart, Australia (photo by author)

resulted in a school that costs less than the average school, these materials are valuable in many ways, both easily measured and less directly valued.

A full discussion of sustainable building—and all of the implications that stem from it—is well beyond the scope of this book. But the work of Morrison and Breytenbach and others like them—such as the designers and builders of the "green" Kindergarten building at the Lake Champlain Waldorf School in Vermont—encapsulate some of the key features of sustainable building: there is a focus on energy reduction, on use of local materials, and an avoidance of toxic substances. Many of these projects also involve volunteer labour as in the case of Tarremah and Lake Champlain, where parents and teachers were involved in the actual construction. And better yet, schools that use sustainable building principles of one form or another become buildings that teach: as American architect Peter Gisolfi put it in 2008, the educational facility itself becomes a learning tool.

Competing Dialogues on Sustainability

Carol Boyle (2004), a New Zealand researcher with the International Centre for Sustainability Engineering and Research, says that most of the focus for so-called "green buildings" has been on energy conservation, both in terms of construction and operation as well as the use of recycled and native materials. Less attention has been paid to issues such as water consumption. But Boyle observes that the issue of sustainable buildings is complicated by architectural design trends, which can be short term in nature: long-term planning is required for sustainability. She contends that the environmental impact of the construction itself is high, especially in light of the extraordinary number of buildings projected for construction over the next half-century. She argues that significant impacts from construction are overlooked because many measures for assessing sustainability center only on embodied energy concerns. Boyle has therefore developed much broader tools for measuring the oft-conflicting ideologies associated with so-called "green buildings," tools that assess depletion of resources, proximity of resources, waste produced in the construction process, energy efficiency, as well as the actual materials used in the building process.

British scholar Simon Guy identified five competing discourses around "green buildings."[24] I will describe two of these five discourses to illustrate how the aims of "green building" can be conflicting. The first of these green discourses, which Guy calls *ecological*, is driven by sustainability as the emblematic issue (Guy, 1997). In this discourse, the overarching image is of buildings as polluters, the inherent risk in design and building is planetary survival, the rhetoric is ethical, the design strategies focus on reducing the footprint, the urban scale is one of de-centralization (ideally cars would be banned), and the success of buildings based on this ecological discourse is to be measured in holistic ways. Contrast this to the green discourse Guy calls *community*, which holds democracy as the emblematic issue. In this discourse, the overarching image of buildings is of homes or dwellings, the major risk of poor design is the alienation of the individual, the rhetoric is societal, the design strategies focus on the creation of identity, the urban scale is one of centralization where trips between locations are to be minimized (whether in private automobiles or other forms of transport), and social cohesion is the prominent criterion for evaluating the success of the buildings. The other discourses Guy detailed are those of *smart* (as in buildings that are responsive, with the use of hi-tech devices, so that energy needs are minimized), *aesthetic* (where the use of organic and recycled elements are emphasized and the success of the buildings is evaluated in terms of "truth to nature"), and *comfort* (where the cultural life of the inhabitants is seen as paramount, where the rhetoric is scientific and medical, and where the design strategy focuses on creating a "living" building). Throughout this book, I have referred to a number of Guy's

---

[24] I remember being shocked at how loosely the term "green" was applied at a national trade show that I attended in 2004 where various building materials were being displayed by their manufacturers. One form of insulation, for example, while "green" in the sense that it did not emit noxious fumes once installed in the building, involved the use of any number of toxic chemicals in the manufacturing process. When I questioned the exhibitor about this, he shrugged and said what you needed to do to be "green" at the convention was to check off that box upon registration.

discourses, although primarily those of the ecological, community, and aesthetic. I now provide an example that encapsulates the aesthetic and ecological discourses.

Waterharvesting: Childhood Play and Sustainable Water Technology

Regardless of the green stance that one might take as described in the previous section, it has been argued that the choice of building materials ought to be an act of purposeful intent (Ford, 2007). Education should also be about acts of purposeful intent—like engaging in conversation, in inquiry, and in play. What follows is a story of play and exploration with extraordinary implications for the way we value buildings and the landscapes around them, for the way we value resources that we treat as if they were infinite; and for the way that what is hidden can be made visible.

Paul Totterdell is a landscape artist and designer of sustainable water systems. I first set eyes on Paul at the Orana School in Canberra, Australia, where he was digging a trench around a garden. We fell into conversation, and it was then that I learned about the genesis of Paul's successful "water-harvesting" designs. When Paul was a boy, he and his family would often travel to the Great Dividing Range in Kosciusko National Park. He and his brothers would play freely while their father, a professional photographer, captured the flora of the park on film. One year, while exploring the hidden valley surrounding Blue Lake above the headwaters of the Snowy River, Totterdell fell through a thin heath membrane into a surprising underground world. His brothers were not far behind, and the three of them, having fallen into the tunnel, were entranced by the underground landscape before them. In a written account, Totterdell described it this way: "The roof was heath, the walls clay with a floor of rocks and pebbles. The tunnel ran north up into the mountain branching and twisting, becoming narrow and choked with branches. It ran south down towards the stream becoming broader with side tunnels entering from both sides. Water mysteriously appeared, running for a way and then just as mysteriously disappeared again, remerging further downhill in pools and bogs" (Totterdell, 2004, p. 1). Some time later, he recognized that he had been witness to an "amazing and unexpected natural drainage system" (p. 1). From this childhood experience—an experience of exploration and play in the most Deweyan sense—his life's vocation developed.

When he returned to the site some years later, he was astonished by the presence of the water in the melting snow. His attention was constantly drawn to water— it seemed to turn up in the most unexpected places. He also noticed that after a rainfall, mud and dust discoloured the water where the rain had shed off disturbed areas of soil. Once this discoloured water entered the underground creek bed—which he knew from his boyhood experience was lined with large sections of rubble—it emerged downstream "clean and clear again as if by magic" (Totterdell, 2004, p. 2). It occurred to Totterdell that this natural filtering function could serve as a model for natural drainage for urban and rural built landscapes. He spent the next decade developing a landscape drainage system reflecting these natural principles, a system called water-harvesting.

The landscapes that Totterdell and his colleagues design involve the use of submerged biofilters made up of rocks, stones, gravels, sands, and soils, which mimic the naturally occurring underground dry creek beds he first observed at Blue Lake as a child.[25] These biofilters hold back, filter, and recycle excess water, nutrients, organic wastes and pollutants produced from the built environment surrounding the constructed landscape. The system dries out and aerates in dry weather, providing a balance of aerobic and anaerobic conditions. These landscapes provide a barrier to the buildup of pathogens, and they provide moisture and nutrients for plant growth. Plant growth in these waterharvested landscapes can be up to twice the normal rate expected for landscapes not fitted with the waterharvesting system.

In the past century, the first task of land developers and engineers when preparing new land for new buildings was to bypass natural drainage features and replace them with pipes, channels and tanks. Totterdell pointed out that this approach deprives the water cycle of a critical and effective filtering action — that which is provided by the earth itself (Totterdell, n.d.). Put another way, most grey water and stormwater collection systems are bio-exclusive rather than bio-inclusive. Collected waters are excluded from the landscape and treated in sealed engineered units before being released into the environment, an approach that has been promoted as the only safe way to deal with liquid waste. But this kind of thinking must change if conclusions in reports such as *The Value of Water*, an inquiry by the Australian Parliament into Australia's uses of urban water, are correct (Allison, 2002). The report concludes that Australians' use of water is unsustainable. But there is no sense of the urgency and seriousness regarding the matter. The same conclusions have been reached in other countries: managing water demand is a key issue for discussion at international conferences on water, such as the one held in Stockholm in August, 2005, attended by water experts from around the world (International Development Research Centre, n.d.). Canadians are very much implicated in this environmental crisis: we are the world's second largest consumers of water *per capita*, and are responsible for using the most energy, *per capita*, in the world (Organization for Economic Co-operation and Development, 2008), a significant portion of which is associated with our water consumption. If water is being used in unsustainable quantities — which it is — then bio-exclusive methods of dealing with greywater are unsustainable as well.

Totterdell's waterharvesting approach is bio-inclusive because the landscape itself acts as the treatment system. During one of my conversations with Totterdell, we talked of the science of complex and dynamic systems. Natural underground creek beds are a complex system: they vary greatly in terms of size

---

[25] Clearwater Environmental Design (CED) designs and manages sustainable development projects based on waterharvesting and recycling principles. Paul Totterdell, along with Terry Brittliffe, serve as the two directors of the company, with offices in Canberra and Perth. See http://www.iobbnet.org/news/kenneth/whsheet-0604.pdf for further information.

and make-up, but share certain fundamental features. The emergence of new creek beds and the changes in existing creek beds are evidence of how the system is dynamic—and "learns" if one adopts a Gaian view of the earth. We mused as to whether the waterharvesting landscapes—with creek beds physically created by Totterdell—could also evolve over time so that new creek beds would be formed, just as in the natural world. It remains an interesting empirical question.

Totterdell is quick to provide figures—hard dollar figures—that make it difficult to argue against the waterharvesting system on any level. I was not surprised to find that the system could be installed at a lower overall cost than conventional landscaping because it relies on clever design and labour rather than a labyrinth of manufactured pipes and pumps. And while I was also convinced that the system would benefit the environment in countless ways, there was a moment while the garden at Orana School was being constructed— long before the plantings in the months to come—that illustrated most powerfully, for me, the full value of the approach.

When I first met Paul working in the Orana School garden, the waterharvesting system was in the very beginning stages of construction in the large landscape oval of the high school campus. For several weeks, landscapers and students were busy digging large and narrow trenches into the hard earth. Soon, more familiar aboveground landscaping features were added; for instance, an interlocking brick pathway, in what Paul called a "lazy S" shape, was laid. This particular shape was fashioned so that the entire landscape would be wheelchair accessible—not just around the outside borders of the garden, but through the garden itself. Great boulders were used to build retaining walls for the various levels of the garden. Three months later, nearly all of the underground creek beds had been covered, and they were already doing their work. What impressed me most as I walked through the landscape was the emergence of spontaneous growth. The breezes had carried seedlings that had taken root in soil where the creek beds flowed under the ground. This was in utter contrast to the neighboring patches of barren earth at the edge of the landscaped garden, patches of earth so hard and dry that I could barely scrape a few grains of sandy soil from the surface. In that moment, the invisible work underneath the ground was rendered visible to me. It is an image I will never forget.

The Ultimate Accounting

Some readers will recall the book written by marine biologist Rachel Carson, titled *Silent Spring*, in which she warned of the dangers of toxic chemicals to all living things. In this case, Carson's work at rendering the invisible visible was not the joyful underground work of Totterdell's waterharvesting, but rather, the invisible harm of chemical build up. The book opens with a chilling view of the future. Carson (1962) crafted a fable about the death of a once lively and prosperous town. Animals—fish, chickens, sheep, birds, pigs, and cattle—had died. Children had not survived the winter. Apple trees, vegetation, and crops—

all had died. And each death described in the so-called fable was based on an event that had already happened, in some community, by 1960. Part of the fable goes like this:

> There was a strange stillness. The birds—where had they gone? ... It was a spring without voices. On the mornings that had once throbbed with the dawn chorus of robins, catbirds, doves, jays, wrens, and scores of other bird voices there was now no sound; only silence lay over the fields and woods and marsh. ... No witchcraft, no enemy action had silenced the rebirth of new life in this stricken world. The people had done it themselves. (p. 2–3)

When we calculate the cost of our schools, we would do well to remember that nothing will really matter if we awaken to a silent spring. Thinking in ways that ensure that we do not find ourselves facing a spring without sound—by designing curricula that encourage creative thinking and promote thoughtful citizenry, by building schools that take internal and external costs to heart—these are the things we must value the most.

Nature

School Architecture and Sustainability

Throughout this chapter, I make the unabashed claim that schools and their surrounding grounds must teach students about the increasing fragility of the natural world and about our collective responsibilities to heal the planet. The importance of school gardens is highlighted, including a detailed description of the Edible Schoolyard, a garden located at an inner city school in Berkeley, California. Other examples of sustainable and ecologically mindful buildings and gardens are described, such as the Ecological Studies Center at Oberlin College, Ohio, and the Seabird Island Community School in British Columbia. The intellectual, physical, and social benefits that students experience in these exemplary settings are outlined.

I have always loved forests. I grew up with trees in my backyard, the same towering Douglas firs that surrounded the elementary school I attended over forty years ago. At the bottom of the school playground, there was a gully where I spent endless hours crouched down by the creek, learning about the animals and insects and plants that thrived there. The school was built around an inner courtyard, accessible from the library that bordered one of the walls of the courtyard. The courtyard was fully visible from the other sides as well, through large windows flanking the hallways around the courtyard. My childhood memory was of courtyard trees growing so tall that they popped out over the top of the school. When I returned to the school decades later, I expected to be disappointed. But to this day, the branches of a robust and glorious Douglas fir tree still reach well above the roof of the modest school.

On weekends and in the summer months, our family traveled into the interior of British Columbia. I can still summon up the extraordinary sense of peace and belonging I felt when walking along the trails through those old growth trees. Rainforests hold me captive too. Whenever I travel anywhere near a rainforest, I will detour several hours just to feel the warm dampness wrap around me, marvel at the greenness of the ferns, and breathe the moist air (even though I know that I have used precious fossil fuels in the process. I am principled, but by no means pure).

We now live in a part of Ontario with mixed growth forests; I love these forests best of all. On our two-hundred-acre wilderness plot of land there are birches, white pines, sugar maples, hemlocks, oaks, ironwoods, cedars, and beech trees. The forest teems with life. Since it was last logged over a century ago, very little has disturbed the evolution of the forest. We have built three small cabins on the land, but there is no road. No electricity. Many of the materials for the cabins came directly from the forest; the rest of the materials — often salvaged or reclaimed — were hiked in on a trail that passes through the woods, across beaver dams, past granite outcrops, and over small streams and marshes, until it opens up onto a small lake where the cabins stand. We fashioned the cabins almost entirely by hand, using simple hand tools — a hammer, a square, a pry bar, a measuring tape, and Japanese saws.

When I am hiking the trails, two hundred acres seems like a big piece of land to me. I love those surroundings more than any other place on earth, and I hope it will all still be there for the children of our children's children. Our neighbour is an environmentalist, and it was largely due to his efforts that the land in our immediate area was designated as a United Nations Biosphere in 2004, giving us some measure of protection against development in the surrounding areas, which could be — shall we say — less than sustainable.

I have read statistics that tell me that by the time this day is over, human activity will add almost 20 million tons of carbon to the atmosphere (Sawin, 2005) and that we will eliminate up to 140 species of plant and animal life in rainforests alone (Raintree Information, 2007; Ryan, 1992). By conservative estimates, one child dies of hunger every five seconds (Black, Morris, & Boyce, 2003). Each year, we destroy 17 million hectares of tropical rainforests — an area larger than Switzerland (Rainforest Information, 1991). Numbers like these leave me with an overwhelming sense of sadness and helplessness. Nevertheless, these numbers remain incomprehensible. Somehow, they do not affect me personally for very long. I carry on, day after day, as if nothing is wrong, as if nothing has changed. I am shocked when there is another oil spill in the Atlantic or when I hear of a water crisis in a developing nation or even in our own country. But I am ashamed to admit that the shock doesn't last.

The reports on deforestation stay with me in a way the other news does not. In 2001, the United Nations reported how tropical countries alone would lose 15 million hectares of forests a year to agriculture and logging.[26] That's over 41,000 hectares a day, or just over 100,000 acres. At that rate it would only take about three minutes to wipe out my land, land that provides a habitat for deer and a

---

[26] A subsequent report issued in 2003 indicated that the Amazon deforestation rates had increased by 40% since 2001. See Deforestation of Amazon is on the rise, *UN Wire*, 26 June 2003, Retrieved June 24, 2004, from http://www.worldwatch.org/features/timeline/tlitems/14.htm

few black bears, squirrels, loons, lake trout, spiders, black rat snakes, beavers, field mice, woodpeckers, grouse, great blue herons, black flies and mosquitoes, moths and butterflies. Three minutes.

Because I can begin to understand what it would mean to lose our small parcel of land—and by understand, I mean emotionally and spiritually, first and foremost—I make decisions to steward that tiny dot on the planet. I have learned, partly through schooling, but mostly through experiences with the land itself, what it means to live on such a piece of land. I work to preserve the land because of my love for it.

Place-based Education and School Architecture

Students who are fortunate enough to be schooled in places where the natural environment is one of their teachers may, as I did, also learn to know and love the land around them and come to steward the land in ecologically meaningful ways; statistics alone are not likely to have a lasting impact on their actions. From this understanding of how students learn deeply about the natural environment comes a growing movement called place-based education. The discussion of place-based education is a burgeoning one. Perhaps because of the recent proliferation of writing on place-based education, there is a lack of agreement within the field about what "place-based" means, with some holding the view that place is a socially constructed phenomenon while others maintain the importance of physical geographies in the development of a sense of place. In this book, I emphasize the physicality of place, although it is clear that social interactions within and beyond those physical spaces are of importance to establishing a sense of place as well. That being said, with increasing concerns about disruptions to the environment caused by fundamentally unsustainable practices, scholars in many fields have turned to an examination of indigenous ecologically sensitive traditions, whether they refer to them as "place-based" or not. These fields include (a) environmental studies (Ellen, Parkes, & Bicker, 2000), (b) environmental philosophy and eco-justice (Bowers, 1995, 2001; Bruun & Kalland, 1995; Glasson, Frykholm, Mhango, & Phiri, 2006), (c) ecofeminism (Gradle, 2007; Kronlid, 2003; Riley-Taylor, 2002), (d) artistic and aesthetic practices (Broudy, 1972/1994; Leuthold, 1998; Matsunobu, 2007), and (e) education more generally (Miller, 1996; Nakagawa, 2000). Architects and scholars studying built environments have also engaged in this discussion. American environmentalist and architectural critic David Orr (1992, 1999) claims that education for sustainability must connect knowledge of subject disciplines with knowledge of place and with the hands and heart.

Shearwater Mullumbimby Steiner School

At the Shearwater Mullumbimby Steiner School, located at the edge of a rainforest near the northern border of New South Wales, Australia, students learn a great deal about the land through place-based educational practices.

The Shearwater School was founded in 1993, with a mere 37 students. The first classes were held in the home of one of the founding teachers. Within half a year, the enrolment had almost doubled, land was purchased, and the first buildings were erected. This remarkable growth has continued, with the same speed and abundance as the growth in the remnant rainforests that skirt the edges of the school property. When I visited the school in 2005, there were over 500 students in Kindergarten through to the end of secondary school. Konrad Korobacz was one of the two founding teachers and now serves as an administrator for the school. He understands well the notion of *genus loci,* and

for him there is no question that the phenomenal growth of the Shearwater School is partly attributable to place.

Shearwater is located in an area where powerful geographies converge: the winds sweep from the most easterly point of the Australian coast-line that is only a few miles away, and the school sits in a valley where two mountain ranges meet on the volcanic soil, marking something of the tur-

Figure 11. Shearwater Mullumbimby Steiner School (photo by author)

bulence of the past. But the strength of Shearwater is more than just the good fortune of being located in such a place. For Korobacz, geography of place also entails acknowledging the inter-connected relationship of human beings to the planet and understanding how human development is a basis for a spiritually based education. For the teachers at Shearwater, place acts as a stimulus for lesson content, too. Curriculum is fashioned by taking into account language, race, and culture, as well as Australia's unique weather, geology, flora and fauna, and its indigenous population and their relationship to place (Korobacz, 2005).

Nature is not an afterthought in this school: it is the guiding consideration. The name of the school is itself a tribute to its place. "Shearwater" refers to the graceful seabird that follows a magnificent migratory path around the Asia-Pacific region and beyond. "Shearwater" also identifies the school geographically in the Asia-Pacific region, to which Australia has become culturally and economically connected. "Mullumbimby" identifies the school locally, acknowledging the Aboriginal presence before the arrival of the Europeans. For the school's founders, "Steiner" points to the Steiner-based curriculum and philosophy, and also identifies the school with European culture and spirituality (K. Korobacz, personal communication, May 22, 2005).

From the very first years of the school's operation, sewage and grey water has been treated within the school grounds. This is accomplished by means of a reed bed through which the wastewater flows. I was impressed by the sheer beauty of the bed. When I was there in May, the reeds were healthy and tall, and ready to be harvested. During the harvest, which occurs twice a year, the reeds are cut back and composted for use on the other gardens on the school's grounds. The reeds grow under a flat enclosure, an impressive timber structure with a translucent roof, which was built by one of the Grade 11 classes. The whole enterprise is functional and beautiful. It turns out that sewage treatment does not have to be ugly or unpleasant. Imagine that.

There are other ways in which the Shearwater School pays homage to its geographical location. When I visited in 2005, the students, teachers, and parents had been involved in an eight-year rainforest re-generation project along the bed of the creek. After clearing out the non-native plants that were introduced when the original rainforests were cut down, over 5,000 native trees were planted in their place. These trees were thriving. In an earlier chapter, I wrote about the white fig tree that serves as a physical and symbolic centre of this school. David Jacobson, one of Shear-water's architects, calls the tree a symbolic generator because it serves to unite the school and to remind the community of how the school

Figure 12. Reed bed for grey water treatment at the Shearwater Mullumbimby Steiner School (photo by author)

seeks to embody its environment with its curriculum (D. Jacobson, personal communication, June 14, 2005). When I asked Jacobson to say more about the process of how the school was planned, he emphasized how much attention was given to the development of the master plan before any of the permanent buildings were erected. He credited the school's founders for their commitment to a core theme: the study of place. He also observed that no one had seriously challenged the design that arose from the core theme, such as placing the rooms for cultural activities at the heart of the school surrounding the fig tree and making outdoor spaces as important as indoor ones. No doubt this unity of vision was another reason for the rapid and smooth growth of the school's edifices, population, and community.

The symbiotic relationship between the indoor and outdoor spaces was evident even as I conversed with Konrad Korobacz in his office. As we spoke, I was aware of the soothing sounds produced by a small waterfall, audible through the open window. This waterfall is part of the creek that runs under the school buildings. A series of pavilion-type buildings, constructed from locally produced timber, were built by local tradespeople; the individual buildings rest on concrete pillars and are joined by an intricate system of covered verandahs and walkways. And so, as the students move from one building to another, they walk along over the creek, past the white fig or the reed bed, with the rainforest visible beyond. The natural world is ever present.

The kinds of activities I witnessed the students undertake at Shearwater reminded me of Thoreau's (1886) discussion of life at Walden Pond. David Orr (1992) characterizes Thoreau's approach as "an antidote to the idea that education is a passive, indoor activity occurring between the ages of six and twenty-one" (p. 125-126). In Orr's view, Thoreau's Walden experience is an example how personhood, pedagogy, and place can be united. Orr claimed that Thoreau's genius was in allowing himself to be shaped by Walden, suggesting that it was not Thoreau who wrote Walden, but in a very real sense, Walden that wrote Thoreau. Orr then makes the sobering observation that place has no particular standing in contemporary education. Many people in the world's most consumer-driven countries are what Orr calls *deplaced*. The architectural expressions of deplacement are ubiquitous shopping malls, apartments, neon-lit strip malls, inter-state freeways, and glass and steel office towers—and, I might add, schools. None of these architectural expressions encourages a sense of connection or responsibility or belonging.

Seabird Island Community School

The notion of place as a significant aspect of education is understood and honoured by Aboriginal peoples the world over. Seabird Island, on the Fraser River delta and surrounded by distant and majestic mountains on all sides, is near the town of Agassiz, about 120 kilometres east of Vancouver, British Columbia. The island is a traditional home for the Sto:ló Nation: the people of the river. The school there is known as the Seabird Island Community School. On the carved wooden sign at the entrance, these words appear: *Lalme Iwesawtexw*. When Gracie Kelly, programs coordinator for the Seabird Island Band, gave me a tour of the school, she suggested that a close translation of the words on the wooden sign is "house teaching rooms" (G. Kelly, personal communication, July 6, 2005). Like the Inuit people of Canada's far north described earlier, the Sto:ló also do not have a word for "school." Rather, schooling occurs in a house or dwelling filled with the kinds of rooms required for teaching. The rooms are not named by number (e.g., Room 1B) or function either (e.g., Computer Room), but are adorned by signs like *SP' OQ' ES* (Bald Eagle).

One of the most important teaching rooms in *Lalme Iwesawtexw* is the kitchen. It is located in the very heart of the school, immediately adjacent to the front entrance. The kitchen serves as a site for home economics classes, to be sure, but it also provides food for students throughout the school day, and regularly occurring community events are hosted there as well. At the time of my visit, Gracie Kelly spoke of a major feast scheduled to take place at the school at the end of July. As she was describing the plans for the feast, I thought about how the end of July is a time when many other North American schools lie dormant or are boarded up to prevent vandalism.

During the course of our conversation, Gracie Kelly revealed that were it not for the generous gift of land offered by Sto:ló elder Mary Charles, the school would never have been built. A likeness of Mary Charles hangs in key places in the school—in the gym and in the entranceway—places where one might expect to see a picture of a British king or queen.

In my interview with the school's architect, John Patkau, he acknowledged the pivotal role played by another Vancouver-based architect, Marie-Odile Marceau, in the realization of the school. At the time, she was an employee of Indian and Northern Affairs and had been charged with the task of commissioning the design for ten new schools for First Nations people. Marceau sought out young architectural firms that believed deeply in the notion of schools as teachers and had already demonstrated an understanding of how culture, community, and curriculum might shape children's development and sense of place. These firms were then invited to submit designs for the ten schools, of which the Seabird Island Community School was one. The successful bid by Patkau Architects for the Seabird Island project was based in part on their

Figure 13. Seabird Island School with roofline mimicking the mountains beyond (photo by James Dow, courtesy of Patkau Architects)

understanding of how the school was intended to be much more than a building for the Kindergarten through Grade 12 students who would attend there. They were also selected because of their belief in the importance of a consensus-based, consultative design process—and surely, also, because of the stunning sense of form they had already demonstrated in other projects.[27] Since John Patkau and Patricia Patkau established Patkau Architects in 1978, they have become known

---

[27] See the Patkau Architects website at http://www.patkau.ca

for their imaginative designs "in dialogue with the landscape" and have been described as "among Canada's most acclaimed architects" (Cook, 2005).

But Gracie Kelly's deeply evident love for the school comes not from the fact that acclaimed architects designed the school. Like other types of love, her love arises from a blend of reasons—what the school does for the community, the ways the landscape is acknowledged, and because of the subtle forms Patkau Architects envisioned and designed. As we approached the building, she said that if I looked closely, I might see one of the figures—a salmon or an eagle— embedded in the shapes of the building. I learned later in my conversation with John Patkau that his objective was to encapsulate the Aboriginal belief of "life in inanimate objects," and to do so through the form of the building itself rather than with "some clichéd expression of aboriginal beliefs" (J. Patkau, personal communication, July 7, 2005). In this he succeeded.

That the Seabird Island School evokes a sense of place has not escaped the attention of others who have written about the school. Seabird Island is showcased in casebooks on school architecture and has been described in a number of published accounts (e.g., Bradley, 1998; Cantley, 1992; Dudek, 2002; Fisher, 1995; LeCuyer, 1992). The design has been recognized by several awards, including the Canadian Architect Award of Excellence (1989) and the Governor General's Medal for Architecture (1992).

The sense of place comes, in part, from the location of the school, for it is linked with other public spaces including community buildings, a village common space, outdoor play areas, and Seabird Island itself. Patkau Architects created a school that mimics the shapes of the mountains beyond with its considerable spatial complexity (Dudek, 2002). Both the interior and exterior are reflective of the Aboriginal peoples of the Pacific Northwest: traditional post-and-beam construction was used and entryways are adorned with Aboriginal carvings. The structure of the porch along the south side is evocative of the racks used to dry the salmon the Sto:ló have traditionally harvested—not far from the school, there are salmon drying racks still in use.

Members of the community band did much more than play a consultative role in the design of the school: the band members constructed the school as well. To the delight of Patkau, the community "took complete ownership of the school and the architect faded into the background" (J. Patkau, personal communication, July 7, 2005). The community constructed their school building well within the budget set by the federal government, with a result "vastly more ambitious" than the original plan.

When I asked Patkau what the community had learned from the Seabird Island Community School, he readily suggested several possibilities, not the least of which was that young men learned valuable building skills and enjoyed the products of their labour. He said the school continues to teach its inhabitants about imagination, because the building is neither "predictable nor formulaic," but offers multiple ways of creating spaces—rooms, Gracie Kelly would say— for learning. Finally, Patkau contended that the building reinforces both the value and means of expressing one's culture through daily activities—such as the preparation of food in the very center of the school, which takes place year-round.

Strawberry Vale Elementary School

Another school designed by Patkau Architects, also featured in many published accounts, is Strawberry Vale Elementary School (Curtis, 2003; Dudek, 2002). It, too, is a much-lauded design; in 1995 it received the Progressive Architecture Award, and in 2002 it received a Governor General's Medal in Architecture. Strawberry Vale is located in a semi-rural area called Saanich, just outside Victoria, British Columbia. Once again, the sense of place and the presence of the natural world are paramount. The school is set in a neighborhood of single-family homes, and on the south edge of the school grounds there is a park with mature Garry oak trees and granite rock outcroppings. The school faces this southern orientation, "symbolically turning its back on the city. All classrooms look out towards the woods and distant hills" (Dudek, 2002, p. 141). All of the classrooms were constructed on-grade, allowing direct and easy access to the outdoors, in the manner Hertzberger (1969) strongly endorsed so many decades ago. The design also ensures that every classroom is wheelchair accessible to the outdoors—a much more pleasing arrangement than creating one or two designated wheelchair accessible entrances for the entire school. In fact, the design of Strawberry Vale approaches what Australian landscape architect Fiona Robbé and others refer to as universal design, where outdoor areas are accessible to students and teachers or caregivers who encompass a full range of ages and abilities. But by accessible, Robbé means much more than wheelchair accessibility. In fact, she is quick to point out that very few children with a disability use wheelchairs: in Australia these children represent 2.3% of the population (F. Robbé, personal communication, February 11, 2006). In Robbé's view, spaces must be much more than physically accessible, they must be socially and intellectually accessible as well. This is particularly true for children who have various intellectual challenges and sensory impairments. For Robbé, outdoor activities and spaces must provide the social message of "equal welcome," not segregation. For this to occur, several conditions must be in place, including such features as the sensory richness in surfaces and textures and the smooth ground level changes embedded in the indoor-to-outdoor transitions at Strawberry Vale School.

The school design also optimizes natural light with the use of clerestory and roof windows. Local timbers were selected as the primary building materials, with the addition of steel beams as required in order to avoid the use of first-growth timber (Curtis, 2003). In addition to these features, the hydrology of the site forms a major aspect of both the design and the curriculum (Dudek, 2002). Rainwater from the wall and roof surfaces is collected in concrete trenches below the roof overhangs, and this water is discharged into an open watercourse, creating a shallow marsh. When I visited the school, it was raining, and the teacher who was showing me the building was visibly pleased that I would see the irrigation system in operation. Children have planted and monitored the growth of native cattail grasses and bulrushes, and, year after year, they learn about the birds that come to nest in the marsh as a result of the native plantings. The classrooms themselves are grouped in pods, and the spaces between the classroom pods and other facilities have created small-scale informal gathering places for "extend[ing] the educational and social curriculum" (Dudek, 2002, p. 142).

But despite all of these fine features, in the words of John Patkau, Strawberry Vale is "not a success story." With a supreme sense of irony, marked also by deep sadness, he observed that while Strawberry Vale was even more architecturally successful than Seabird Island, because of its "terrible history" the project was ultimately less successful than it might otherwise have been.

I had visited Strawberry Vale School a couple of days before meeting with Patkau, and based on the published accounts, I expected brilliance. What I encountered was a school that felt more dead than alive, a school shrouded not only by the lack of life July can bring, but also by a sense of discord and unease. I was struck by the dichotomous views expressed by the teachers whom I interviewed. Some told me that Strawberry Vale Elementary School was a great place to teach because each classroom faced south and opened to the outdoors; because they could so easily teach about natural systems; because there were nooks and crannies where students could gather; because the light was warm and plentiful; and because the classroom acoustics were so thoughtfully designed — that is, as long as the teacher stood at the intended "front" of the classroom. But, they also pointed out many problems with the school. Some teachers had difficulties with their knees and joints after teaching for many years in a building with concrete floors. Other problems were blamed on the construction, such as leaks in the walls, half-installed systems for regulating the air, and difficulties with upkeep. One teacher ruefully commented, "The maintenance people hate it—one guy said he should have brought in his bulldozer to fix it." Yet another teacher talked about difficulties in staging artistic productions in a gym with neither a stage nor a way of blocking out the abundant natural light.

During my conversation with John Patkau I learned something about the history of the school and started to make sense of my troubled impression of the facilities. Partway through the construction process when, as Patkau put it, "conservatism hit the world," officials in the British Columbia Ministry of Education caught wind of the Strawberry Vale project and chose to make an example of the school as an unnecessarily extravagant public building. Patkau assured me that the school was designed within the provincial budget allotted for new schools; however, he said, because the building "looked expensive," it was assumed to be so—which, not coincidentally, was one of the phenomena cited by American architect William Bradley (1998) as a detriment to innovative school design. As Patkau described it, the remainder of the project was doomed: "There was a sinister atmosphere driving the building process. It was evil. Plans were compromised." Policies were set in place to cut school building budgets across the province of British Columbia—including limiting windows to 10% of the surface area—and "the disaster unfolded over the entire province." A contributor to the magazine *Canadian Architect* observed that the eye-catching design "attracted the derision of the provincial Ministry of Education and became a public symbol of wasted taxpayer money" (Weder, as cited in Gislason, 2009, p. 46). In Patkau's darkly comic view, this was a Ministry of Education that well understood that buildings have the capacity to teach. He told me about the views of the officials responsible for the decisions about Strawberry Vale and for school construction in general. These officials felt that schools—as the first public buildings encountered by most children—must be "mean and nasty to demonstrate our fiscal prudence" (J. Patkau, personal communication, July 7, 2005).

Patkau's description of the unfolding of the school's construction was hinted at in various newspaper accounts in 2002, when Patkau Architects won a Governor General's Medal in Architecture for Strawberry Vale. The Vancouver-based newspaper *The Province* called the school "much-panned" (Patkau School Lauded, 2002), while the *Victoria Times Colonist* used a similar phrase, saying "some critics once panned [Strawberry Vale] for having an excessive structure" (Unique Saanich School, 2002). In an earlier article appearing in the *Vancouver Sun,* four years before Patkau Architects won the Governor General's Medal, columnist Robin Ward wrote how the school was singled out by the provincial government as an example of money wasted, with the Education Minister being quoted as telling school boards to "tell your architect friends to stay at home" (Ward, 1998, C4). I noted the irony in Maria Cook's observation of how the 2002 Governor General's award winners had displayed excellence in the design of Strawberry Vale in spite of modest budgets. Despite these recent vindications, Patkau told me his architectural firm was crushed by the experience, and they are only now beginning to recover from the public blows to their reputation— and to their core beliefs about learning and schooling. Well over a decade has passed since the controversy. Patkau Architects has not designed a school since.

Belonging: Social Cohesion, Beauty, Regional Surveys, and Manual Activity

As the events that unfolded around Strawberry Vale so poignantly illustrate, place and people are inextricably linked. Over a century ago, Dewey suggested that schools should be thought of as "embryonic communities," with activities in schools "reflecting the occupations of life of the larger society" (Dewey, 1900/1956, p. 29). Put another way, the social environment also defines an essential aspect of place. Even with designs that are architecturally successful by some standards—like Strawberry Vale—if social coherence and community support are lacking, the result will not be a happy one.

The importance of social coherence runs even deeper. As environmentalists, philosophers, economists, and scientists have all argued, environmental degradation is a crisis that has arisen with remarkable speed and has occurred simultaneously with the loss of a sense of citizenship. The destruction of the environment and the loss of community are mutually reinforcing trends (Berry, T., 1988, 1996; Berry, W., 1981, 1983; Capra, 1996, 2005; Carson, 1962; Lovelock, 1987; Margulis & Sagan, 1997; Orr, 1992; Putnam, 2000; Ward & Dubos, 1972). The problems we are now experiencing with energy and resources, climate change, water shortages, lack of biological resilience, and international security issues, signify, above all else, a crisis of community and spirit. I read an account by mathematics educator Nel Noddings—in an international handbook on arts education, of all places—where she says that the school curriculum for teenagers misses the mark. Noddings (2007) says schools need to teach teenagers to develop a love of place and nature, to make a commitment to their homes as a work of art, to become devoted to the process of raising children, to continually reflect on how their characters are developing, to learn to enjoy the delights of a rich social life, and to find work that they really like. To be sure, these lessons are easier to learn in some schools than in others.

Beauty is part of the equation as well. James Lovelock, one of the originators of the Gaia hypothesis, speculated about how beauty might be an essential element linking human behaviour with the natural world. Lovelock (1987) wondered if the instincts that recognize beauty are also those that recognize fitness in the sense of biological survival. While he acknowledged that it would be exceedingly difficult to "test experimentally the notion that the instinct to associate fitness with beauty favours survival … it might be worth a try" (p. 143). After reminding his readers how the capacity to reduce entropy is itself a measure of life, Lovelock continued, "Let us set beauty as equal to such a measure of life. Then it could follow that beauty also is associated with lowered entropy, reduced uncertainty, and less vagueness. … It might even be that the Platonic absolute of beauty does mean something and can be measured against that unattainable state of certainty about the nature of life itself" (p. 143–144).

In reading the essays of the philosopher and architecture critic Lewis Mumford, I once again encountered the notion that place and pedagogy should be united through community engagement. Further, Mumford offered a way for students to think about fitness as described by Lovelock. In an essay titled *The Social Responsibilities of Teachers*, Mumford (1946) suggested that students should be involved in *regional surveys*, based on an idea proposed by Patrick Geddes in Edinburgh in the 1890s and which can be traced back to the ideas of Froebel and Rousseau (Wilson, 1969). By regional survey, Mumford meant that students should learn about their communities and regions by learning as much as possible about the places in which they lived, coming to deeply understand the networks of relationships formed by the physical geography and human community of the region, a notion expressed by recent proponents of place-based education as well (Stedman, 2003). In the epilogue to *Gaia: A New Look at Life on Earth*, Lovelock (1987) wrote about how his own feeling for natural things developed as a result of the many walks he took with his father, a man who was, in Lovelock's words, "an excellent and enthusiastic gardener and also a very gentle man. I remember him rescuing wasps from drowning after they had blundered into the water butt. He would say, 'They are there for a purpose, you know', and then explain to me how they controlled the aphids on his plum trees and how they were surely due some of the crops as a reward" (p. 141). His father never explained why he believed that everything in the world was there for a purpose, but Lovelock surmised how a mixture of "instinct, observation, and tribal wisdom" (p. 144) would have led to such beliefs. Lovelock, then, was involved with a regional survey of his own as a boy. The Gaia hypothesis must have emerged—at least in part—from the teachings of his father.

Mumford did not regard the regional survey as something to add to an already overburdened curriculum (this, in 1946—what would Mumford think of the curriculum now?). Rather, he viewed the regional survey as an approach that would serve as the "backbone of a drastically revised method of study, in which every aspect of the sciences and the arts is ecologically related from the bottom up, in which they connect directly and constantly in the student's experience of his [*sic*] region and his community" (Mumford, 1946, p. 151–152). Mumford's idea of the regional survey involved knowing as well as acting, thereby breaking down what he called the "disabling breach between facts and values" (p. 153).

The regional survey can also mend the even more disabling breach between nature and human society. In his discussion of the pedagogy of place, Orr identifies several overarching reasons for the importance of this kind of study. The first has been alluded to already, namely, in order to undertake a regional survey approach, thinking must be combined with direct action—action of the sort the students and school community have undertaken at the Shearwater Mullumbimby Steiner School. Action can be both physical and social. Orr is vehement in asserting that students need to do more than comprehend; they also need to act. Orr suggests that "if the place also includes natural areas, forests, streams, and agricultural lands, the opportunities for environmental learning multiply accordingly", as do the opportunities for social and political action (Orr, 1992, p. 129).

I return now to discuss another kind of action—manual activities. Some of the great educational philosophers of the 19th and 20th centuries—Alfred North Whitehead, Johann Pestalozzi, Lewis Mumford, Maria Montessori, Rudolf Steiner, John Dewey—considered the so-called manual or practical skills as essential to the development of good thinking. In *Aims of Education*, Alfred North Whitehead (1929) described the essential reciprocity between thinking and manual creative activity, saying that knowledge loses its abstractness when it is applied to solving tangible and direct problems in specific places. Dewey (1900/1956) expressed a similar view about the links between education, nature, manual activity, and social cohesion:

> We cannot overlook the importance for educational purposes of the close and intimate acquaintance got with nature at first hand, with real things and materials, with the actual processes of their manipulation, and the knowledge of their social necessities and uses. In all this there was continual training of observation, of ingenuity, of constructive imagination, of logical thought, and of the sense of reality acquired through first-hand contact with actualities. The educative forces of the domestic spinning and weaving, of the sawmill, the gristmill, the cooper shop, and the blacksmith forge, were continuously operative. (p. 11)

These types of activities belong in the Steiner and Montessori curricula as well. In Steiner schools around the world, six-year-old children learn to spin wool and to knit with wooden needles they have fashioned by hand. As the first-grade teacher at one Steiner school said: "It's not about churning out a whole generation of children who will make knitted hats for a living. It's about engaging their hands in this tricky little task so they develop dexterity for other kinds of tasks and enjoy the satisfaction of having created something beautiful by hand." But knitting is not a task universally regarded as important for Grade

1 students. In some circles, the idea of sending a child to school to learn to knit is met with undisguised scorn and ridicule.

When did we lose admiration and respect for working with our hands? These kinds of activities were once commonplace, and although some of the practices were highly gendered—which led to another set of problems and limitations—there was nevertheless a time when men and women and children could spin and weave, sew clothes, grow crops, cook and preserve food, build shelters, and decorate their homes with artifacts crafted by hand. And while the work was often hard, there was pleasure in doing it well. Mumford (1946) argued that it was during the Renaissance that the "daily discipline of manual effort" involved in humanistic and cultural activities of the kinds I have described was eroded by the growing view that educated persons did not work with their hands. He suggested that "the inability to work with one's hands became a point of pride among the educated classes" (p. 156). This view persists. Some of the most educated people I know—if one measures education by university attainments—are proud that they "never cook or clean." What a twisted view of education we have spun.

The current ethos of schooling reflects the changes that came with the Renaissance—school is now most often characterized as a place to learn about facts and figures (not about cooking or gardening), a characterization visibly reflected in the obsession with achievement results on language and mathematics measures (Gardner, 1999). But a foundational claim for this book is that "manual" activities—activities requiring the engagement of hands and the body—ought to be *central* to schooling. For this to happen, the built and natural environments must provide affordances[28] for such learning to take place, so that knowledge—like the statistic that 41,000 hectares of rainforest will be destroyed by the end of this day—is not about memorizing abstract facts but about building understanding through physical, intellectual, and emotional engagement. The notion of affordances is central to the ecological approach to perception and learning described by psychologist Eleanor Gibson and her colleague Anne Pick (2000), building on the earlier work of James Gibson.[29] An "affordance" refers to the fit between the animal's capabilities and the environmental supports or obstacles; thus, a path leading to a destination can contain affordances that support the journey, such as a smooth terrain, or that create obstacles, such as unexpected objects directly in the way of the journeyer.

---

[28] This concept of affordances frequently appears in landscape designer Robin Moore's writing, where he claims that both the content and form of outdoor spaces can be managed to afford many positive opportunities, leading to the possibility of spaces evolving into unique and sacred places.

[29] Readers familiar with the work of James and Eleanor Gibson will know that these two psychologists made extraordinary contributions to our theories of perceptual development. After James Gibson's death in 1979, Eleanor Gibson continued to expand the earlier notions of ecologically based theories of perception, culminating in a work published in 2000 by Eleanor Gibson and Anne Pick. Eleanor Gibson died in 2002 at the age of 92.

Curriculum theorists also point to the importance of the built and natural environments in learning about place through practical activity. A well-received series of curriculum materials, developed to support the learning of the core curriculum subjects through a study of place, was produced in the United Kingdom in the mid-1990s (Keaney, 1993; Rhydderch-Evans, 1993; Thomas, 1993). Science activities on the school ground, for example, involved various comparisons between mowed grass and indigenous long grass, bird surveys, insect and pond studies, weather statistics, waste management, and the study of materials used in the construction of the school building itself (Thomas, 1993). Similar curriculum approaches have been developed in North America, some of which are based on observations of children's spontaneous play (Burriss & Boyd, 2005). Another approach has involved examining how outdoor environments contribute to students' physical and social growth. Early childhood educators have demonstrated how children who are not involved in play will suffer developmentally—a loss that is not only physical, but also intellectual and social (Adams, 1991; Brett, Moore, & Provenzo, 1993; Moore & Wong, 1997; Stine, 1997).

There is convincing evidence that play is equally essential in the years of pre- and early adolescence (Wood, 2005). One striking feature of all of the accounts I have described—whether nursery schools, playgrounds, or adolescent play areas—is that scholars and practitioners alike emphasize the importance of providing landscapes that are, in some sense, unfinished (Frost, 1992) or rough (Moore & Cosco, n.d.). Pristinely tailored landscapes and playgrounds leave little scope for imaginative play. American educator and children's play advocate Joe Frost went so far as to say that the most meaningful play settings for learning—such as construction areas containing scrap lumber and tools, and natural areas with indigenous plantings and animal habitats—are often not supported by adults.

Another aspect of untailored or rough landscapes is that they contain what landscape architect Robin Moore and his colleagues describe as "all manner of loose parts"—petals from flowers, pebbles, decaying leaves, and so on (Cosco & Moore, 1999). Play areas should be smellable, holdable, pickable, and tasteable. It is through nature's loose parts, Moore argues, that children learn about science—and how to climb and maneuver about. Moore provides striking evidence gathered from a play area at California's Bay Area Discovery Museum (R. Moore, personal communication, February 9, 2006). The Bay Area Discovery Museum, located on just over seven acres at the foot of the north tower of the Golden Gate Bridge, offers a multitude of indoor and outdoor activities for exploring art, media, science, and the environment. There are theatre programs, school programs, cultural festivals, and summer camps—a cornucopia of vibrant offerings for children and their families. It came as a surprise to the museum's exhibit designers that Moore found that children made most frequent use of the *least* refined play areas and materials available—the loose parts. He tells a lovely story of how a simple gravel pit and an old boat fostered more play and exploration of cause and effect than the most sophisticated (and expensive) so-called interactive exhibits. If it is the case, as Moore suggests, that scientific play develops spontaneously and deeply in outdoor settings with loose parts, then the potential for the kind of engagement called for by Orr, Dewey, Mumford and others is greater in schools where natural settings are enhanced, where the curriculum supports Mumford's regional survey approach, and where relationships within the school and community are nurtured. Talking with Robin Moore reminded me of my earlier conversation with Annie Ball on the beach in Tasmania. For her, too, the loose parts were paramount—whether they might be the sand, shells, creatures, driftwood, and the ocean itself, or the twigs, plants, stones, and leaves in the Kindergarten yard.

As if the links between thinking and doing contained in the study of place were not reason enough for place to be central to schooling, Orr (1992) offers an additional reason for the importance of the study of place: it counteracts the detrimental effects of overspecialization, what he calls a "terminal disease of contemporary civilization" (p. 129). Orr argues that places are such complex sites of diversity that they cannot be understood fully from the vantage point of any single specialization. Rather, what is needed is a wide understanding of how the various elements defining a place are interrelated—here again, the language of complexity is invoked. Mumford (1946) offered words to similar effect when he suggested that "instead of overstressing subject matter and forgetting relationships, we must stress orientation, and make it possible for the student to find his [sic] way from any given starting point to every other relevant part of human experience" (p. 212).

The study of place re-engages people with community and educates people in the art of living well in the region they call home (Orr, 1992). Orr contrasts this state of engaged living to the deplaced occupant described earlier—the occupant who lives in the indoor worlds of office buildings, shopping malls, automobiles, apartments, and suburban houses. Alan Lightman (2005) uses a different language to describe the same sense of deplacement, suggesting that most people in Western societies live lives filled with "a sense of urgency, a vague fear of not keeping up with the world" (p. 186). With this sense of urgency comes a sense of loss—loss of time to "waste," loss of silence, loss of some part of one's inner self. Lightman attributes this sense of loss not to the built environment but to the pervasiveness of technology of all kinds— computers, yes, but also microwaves, televisions, and mobile telephones— making us what he calls "prisoners of the wired world." This notion of deplacement is also related to conversation, a critical ingredient in thinking about school architecture. According to Lightman, conversations with nature must necessarily be governed by cycles of the day and night and the seasons, as well as the larger rhythms of evolutionary time. But the human sense of time is increasingly frenetic, driven by clocks and computers.

The notion of being a deplaced occupant or a prisoner of the wired world is as much an attitude of mind as it is about developing a sense of place in the deeper sense I have described. When I first traveled to Italy over thirty years ago, I was delighted by the question posed to me by Italians who spoke English as a second (or third or fourth) language. The question was: "Where are you living?" They were not asking about my permanent place of residence; rather, they meant where was I residing while in Venice? I was struck by the contrast of the phrase "Where are you staying?" to "Where are you living?", for one can live in a place even if the stay is a temporary one, just as one can be deplaced in a permanent home. Urban dwellers, too, can have a clear sense of place and connection, if they dwell in places where residents can meet informally, where energy needs are reduced by appropriate design, where car traffic is kept to a minimum, and where gardens thrive.

In contrast to the deplaced *occupant*, the *inhabitant*—rural or urban—dwells in an intimate, organic, and mutually nurturing relationship with a place (Illich, 1984). Students who dwell in schools like Shearwater or Seabird Island have an undoubtedly rich relationship with the place. That relationship is partly due to the place itself, but it is also due to the curriculum and to the communities forming the core of each of those schools.

Pedagogy of Place and Ecological Footprints

Pedagogy of place helps students understand the notion of the ecological footprint. Architects use the term *footprint* to describe the space a building occupies, and the notion of the ecological footprint is a related one. By some estimates, the city of London, England, requires productive land 125 times the size of the productive land of the United Kingdom to support its inhabitants, yet London houses less than 15% of the country's population. American author Thomas Friedman (2008) writes that in 1800, London was the world's largest city with a population of one million people. There are now over 300 cities that top the million inhabitants mark, with the number of megacities—ten million people or more—expected to reach 26 by the year 2015. Friedman says, "These exploding populations are rapidly overwhelming infrastructure in these megacities—nineteen million people in Mumbai alone—as well as driving loss of arable land, deforestation, overfishing, water shortages, and air and water pollution" (p. 28).

At this rate of population growth and resource depletion, we will soon need at least three planets to sustain the inhabitants of the earth. Cities, as author and film-maker Herbert Girardet (2003) argues, must begin to remodel their functions based on natural ecosystems—systems with a circular metabolism, where each individual output is also an input that renews the environment of which it is a part. This is in stark opposition to the linear metabolism present in our ever-expanding cities, where consumption without renewal is the norm. Australian architects Paul Downton and Rob Cheesman would agree. It is telling that both of these architects live in urban environments and yet their own footprints are relatively small: they have learned to tread lightly upon the earth, a notion popularized by American environmentalist Steven van Matre two decades ago (1990). Downton and Cheesman both acknowledge that cities have the capacity to reduce their footprints by many orders of magnitude—and that they must.

Karen Malone (2001) is the Australian Director of the UNESCO-MOST Growing Up in Cities (GUIC) project. GUIC, based on the pioneering work of American Kevin Lynch (1977), was designed to give young people a voice in the planning and creation of their local urban environments. A guiding principle for

Lynch—one that remains at the forefront for Malone—is that children and youth should be able to express ideas about their environments and contribute to substantial changes in their local neighbourhoods (Lynch, 1977). A few years ago, I heard Malone speak at an international gathering of architects. There, she made the riveting observation that the future is "undeniably urban" (K. Malone, personal communication, February 9, 2006). Of course it is. Nezar AlSayyad (2004) is an urban historian as well as a practicing architect with projects in the United States and in Egypt. When I met him, he was serving as Chair of Middle Eastern Studies at the University of California at Berkeley. He said the same thing as Malone. In his words: "urbanism will always be a vibrant arena" (N. AlSayyad, personal communication, February 9, 2006). But how can urban environments, and in particular, school environments be made to be *more* vibrant for children? And with that vibrancy, create a smaller ecological footprint? For it is one thing to situate a school on the edge of an ancient rainforest; it is quite another to build a school in the middle of a sprawling suburban carpark. How can schools be fashioned to enable students and teachers to meet their educational needs in deeply challenging and joyful ways, without damaging the natural world or endangering the living conditions of other people by disproportionate consumption?

Barbara Schreiner lives in Canberra, Australia. On her small suburban plot of land, she grows far more food than she needs to sustain herself. Schreiner trained first as an architect in Sydney. In her early professional work in architecture, she was attracted to working with architects and other professionals who were interested in patterns of human behaviour, and how those patterns interacted with the built environment. Not long after graduating, Barbara was invited to join a research group at the University of California at Berkeley where these questions were being explored. One work that emerged from this research group was the already discussed book *A Pattern Language* by Christopher Alexander and his colleagues. But it was not her work with Alexander's research group that changed her life most profoundly during her time at Berkeley. Rather, it was a deceptively simple encounter with the bulb of a daffodil.

During one of many conversations we had in Canberra, Schreiner described how she still remembers standing in the garden of the Berkeley woman who handed her the bulb. As she took the bulb, she was immediately fascinated by what she described as the brown papery layers, the conical tip, and the untidy end. Somehow, the bulb seemed to her to be imbued with confidence and certainty. Schreiner planted the bulb and watched with wonder as the green shoot first appeared, followed some time later by the precise structure of the yellow flower. This was an astonishing and life-shaping event: a metamorphosis, for the bulb, yes, but more profoundly a metamorphosis for her (B. Schreiner, personal communication, April 11, 2005).

The flowering of the daffodil was the pivotal event that would shape her next few years of formal education and future work and passions. She left Berkeley, and after spending six months as a gardener in England, soon thereafter moved to New Zealand where she studied horticulture and botany at Christchurch. Since then she has been growing her own food. She gives loving attention to the plants she grows and is part of a local social network that is satisfying and full. Schreiner spoke repeatedly about community, celebrating the interdependence of the respective communities of which she is a part. She spoke of connections, of patterns—the language of complexity—saying that the greatest problem to be overcome is the "separated society," where people are alienated from the sources of the goods they consume. As she said this, we were sitting at a café at the local university. She asked me if I knew where the table came from. The chairs? The cup I was drinking from? Predictably and regrettably, I did not. These questions put an even deeper and more troubling spin on Orr's notion of displacement.

When I asked Barbara Schreiner what she thought was the most important thing to teach children, she answered, "They need to grow their own food." Having students grow their own food means more than producing the food they need to eat: it means learning to recycle on site, learning about native trees and plants, and learning about the social capital of the neighborhood in which schools are located. When Schreiner teaches courses on backyard gardening, she asks her participants to take a ten-minute walk around the neighborhood to identify resources that might help with their gardening venture—what she calls the community side of permaculture. Discarded grass clippings from a neighbour's freshly mowed lawn, for example, are the kind of resource Schreiner is looking for. Schreiner takes Mumford's regional survey beyond exploration: it is regional living, regional commitment that encapsulates the circular metabolism that Giradet (2003) claimed city dwellers must embody. A recent embodiment of this phenomenon—growing one's own food in urban settings—is beautifully described and illustrated by Fritz Haeg (2007) in the book *Edible Estates: Attack on the Front Lawn.* In addition to a number of inspiring examples from across the United States and in England, Haeg reminds us not only of the benefits of growing our own food, but the catastrophic consequences of cultivating lawns over food. For instance, homeowners use up to ten times more chemical pesticides per acre on their lawns than do farmers who still use pesticides on their crops. And lawns in the United States alone consume an average of 270 billion gallons of water *per week*—enough to water over 80 million acres of organic vegetables. And to top that, Americans spend over $750 million a year on grass seed and more than $25 billion on do-it-yourself lawn and garden care. Imagine if that money was spent on do-it-yourself vegetable gardens instead.

Ecological Triumphs: Uniting Head, Heart, and Hands

Environmentalist David Orr has written how education for sustainability will, by necessity, connect disciplines as well as various aspects of human knowing: knowledge of the intellect, the hands, and the heart. This connectivity is echoed, with almost the same words, in the Waldorf motto of "schooling for the head, heart and hands." What are the architectural implications of educating for sustainability? Orr (1999) provides us with a compelling answer to this question.

Joseph Adam Lewis Environmental Center

In the early 1990s, the Environmental Studies program at Oberlin College, Ohio, where Orr worked, outgrew its space. Orr (1999) recognized an opportunity to design a building that would embody the principles he had espoused for decades. He began by organizing a forum consisting of a class of twenty-five students and a dozen architects who would meet over the course of two semesters to develop the core ideas for dealing with the problem. They asked, first, whether there was a need to build anything at all. Once they determined that new facilities were indeed required, they drew up a list of criteria that would to apply to the 14,000 square foot facility. The list included a building that would (a) generate more electricity than it would consume, (b) discharge no wastewater, (c) use no materials known to be carcinogenic, (d) use materials grown or manufactured sustainably, (e) be landscaped to promote biological diversity, (f) meet the requirements of full-cost accounting, and (g) promote ecological competence and mindfulness of place. In Orr's words, the building would cause "no ugliness, human or ecological, somewhere else or at some later time" (p. 142).

The then College president opposed the project, but with a new president arriving in 1995, the project went forward, albeit under rather restricting conditions imposed by the College trustees. The design team was assembled, and it included graduates of the class originally involved in the planning stages, as well as scientists, engineers, and architects. The architectural firm of William McDonough and Partners, based in Charlottesville, Virginia, was intimately involved with the process. It was a fine choice—in fact, perhaps an inevitable one. William McDonough and his colleagues are far more deeply committed to green building than most firms can even imagine. They have built an international profile based on the notion that design requires a future-oriented stance, recognizing that every design decision affects "lives that are continents and generations apart."[30] Their 30-person firm practices environmentally intelligent design strategies, drawing inspiration from living systems and processes. As they put it, their approach celebrates nature's abundances: daylight, fresh air, diversity, and life.

McDonough's result is surely one of the most outstanding examples of ecologically based architecture in North American universities: the Joseph Adam Lewis Environmental Center opened in January of 2000 (Oberlin College, 2005). Classes in a variety of disciplines are held there, including conservation biology, environment and society, sustainable architecture, ecological design, environmental education, physical geology, and solar energy. It would seem like a good place for courses on literature, politics, sociology, and sculpture as well. In addition to the features of the building described earlier, landscaping included the restoration of a small wetland and forest, as well as the planting of

---

[30] The quotation was retrieved April 11, 2006, from
http://www.collinswood.com/FrontPageResources/WilliamMcDonough/FPMcDonough.html. For a full sense of the extraordinary work that William McDonough + Partners have undertaken, see http://www.mcdonoughpartners.com/.

gardens and orchards. According to Orr (1999), the building "was designed and built to instruct its users in the arts of ecological competence and the possibilities of ecological design applied to buildings, energy systems, wastewater, landscapes, and technology" (p. 146). When I visited the Center in the fall of 2009, I was impressed by this teaching function of the building. It was, of course, implicit in the design of the buildings and grounds. But the teaching was also explicit: interactive displays all through the two floors of the building invited visitors to learn about the building, and about energy efficient buildings in general. The other striking thing for me was that I found the building more beautiful than I had expected from the photographs that I had seen prior to my visit. Perhaps it was because the architectural photographs depicted the building as soon as it was completed. In the interim, the building has had time to blend into its setting, take on the life of its inhabitants.

We will erect more buildings in the first half of the 21st century than we have built throughout all of recorded history. Orr (1999) cautions that if these new buildings are erected "inefficiently and carelessly, we will cast a long ecological shadow on the human future. If we fail to pay the full environmental costs of development, the resulting ecological and human damage will be very large" (p. 147). Orr concludes that education—more than any other institution—has a "moral stake in the health, beauty, and integrity of the world our students will inherit" (p. 147).

The Edible Schoolyard

To be sure, the Joseph Adam Lewis Environmental Center at Oberlin College is inspiring. But it's a daunting example as well because of its very scope and because of the considerable political and financial obstacles that had to be overcome in order for the building to be erected. The same ends can begin to be met on a more modest scale. Just as Mumford (1946) described the regional survey as beginning with the world of the infant, so too are there important learning environments that begin at home. The most obvious of these is the humble garden.

The most striking example of a school garden that I have come across is the Edible Schoolyard at the Martin Luther King Middle School in Berkeley, California. When the garden was started in 1995, the school cafeteria had been closed and students were buying packaged food from a shed at the end of the parking lot. The garden, founded by chef and author Alice Waters and former school principal Neil Smith, is a one-acre spread of bountiful organic produce, located on the site of the former cracked asphalt parking lot. Students and teachers grow an enormous variety of crops—far too many to list. A small sampling of these crops include fruit such as blackberries, ground cherries, blackcurrants, hazelnuts, figs, kiwi, mulberries, grapes, gooseberries, and raspberries. The children also grow run-of-the-mill vegetables—like corn—in addition to edible bamboo, scarlet runner beans, hibiscus, jasmine, passionflower, chayote, mint, gourds, tomatoes, asparagus, chives, peas, pole beans, and bush beans, onions, leeks, peppers, basil, broccoli, and collard greens. And there are olive trees, citrus fruit trees, and apple trees. Eggs are produced by the garden's Araucana and Rhode Island Red chickens. All of this — and more — on one urban acre.

Alice Waters credits the enlightened leadership of the principal in making what might have been simply a well-intentioned fantasy into a thriving reality. She wrote, "He understood that a new school garden and a renovated cafeteria and lunchroom meant more than just the beautification of school grounds. He understood that these were the central elements of a revolution in both the lunch program and the entire school curriculum." The Edible Schoolyard is not a small-scale operation. Close to a thousand students attend the school, and every one of them is involved with the Edible Schoolyard.

The process of developing the Edible Schoolyard began with a design symposium involving teachers, parents, chefs, administrators, business people, students, landscape artists, and other design professionals to dream up a school garden. While the first-year plantings of fenugreek, crimson clover, oats, and vetch were growing throughout the acre and cleansing the soil, the former school cafeteria, built in the 1930s, was refurbished to become a kitchen classroom. The latter was relocated in 2001 after an earthquake retrofit, and the new kitchen classroom is now located in an old bungalow directly adjacent to the garden. In designing the new kitchen classroom — which also serves as a gathering place for such events as family writing nights — redwood drawers and cabinets from the original kitchen were recycled. For reasons like these, the new kitchen won a design award from the International Design Magazine in 2002.

Together, these two learning environments — the garden and the kitchen classroom — provide a setting for students to grow, harvest, and prepare seasonal produce. As a result, they learn about principles of ecological literacy, too. Fritjof Capra, Peter Buckley and Zenobia Barlow established the Center for Ecoliteracy in Berkeley, California in the same year the Edible Schoolyard garden was first planted. The Center helps students and teachers recognize the intricate patterns and networks involved in school garden production. Not surprisingly, we once again encounter the notions of complexity: the garden is a site for learning about networks, interdependence, diversity, complexity, nested systems, cycles, energy, resources, succession, co-evolution, self-organization, flexibility, stability. The garden serves, as Capra (1996) would say, for learning about nothing less than the web of life.

And what, exactly, do students at the Martin Luther King Jr. Middle School learn through the Edible Schoolyard? In 2003, J. Michael Murphy, a researcher associated with the Center for Ecoliteracy, conducted a study on the effects of the Edible Schoolyard garden-based curriculum. Qualitative and quantitative data were derived from surveys and interviews with students, teachers, parents, and administrators as well as from school grades, test scores and attendance records. Fifty 11-year-old children from the Martin Luther King Jr. Middle School were compared with 50 students in a control school; as well, 64 teachers from the two schools took part in the study. Over the course of a school year, the academic achievement scores in mathematics and science for students involved in the school garden program showed significantly greater gains than the scores of students in the control school. Predictably, the students involved in the garden-based program also made greater gains in understanding ecological cycles and showed an improved understanding of sustainable agriculture. Teachers involved in the garden-based program rated their school as more conducive to learning than the teachers in the control school, and they ranked compassion for living things as one of their top three teaching priorities. This latter finding is of particular importance, as other studies also demonstrate how teachers' understanding of nature-knowledge-culture systems directly influence their teaching (Glasson, Frykholm, Mhango, & Phiri, 2006). The importance to children's learning of adults who model sound environmental practices is not a new notion: decades ago, Bandura and Walters (1963) demonstrated how modeling and imitation foster moral development. This moral development applies equally in the field of environmental ethics. When adult conservationists were questioned about the childhood experiences that shaped their views of the environment, two influences emerged—free hours spent outdoors with plants and animals, and an adult who modeled attentiveness and respect for wild things (Tanner, 1980).

In addition to the intellectual and moral benefits of place-based education, there is some evidence for physical and social gains related to outdoor environments. In the garden-based program described above, Murphy (2003) also found that significant psychosocial gains were made by the students in the garden-based program as compared to those students in the control school. Early childhood educators have also demonstrated how children who are not involved in play in natural environments will suffer developmentally—a loss that is not only physical, but also intellectual and social (Adams, 1991; Brett, Moore, & Provenzo, 1993; Moore & Wong, 1997; Stine, 1997). Moore and Cosco (n.d.) refer to a Swedish study by Patrik Grehn comparing two groups of children. One group attended a typical Swedish nursery school; the other children attended a school with an "outdoors-in-all-weathers" approach where a wild garden was the primary outdoor space. The children at the outdoors nursery were more physically advanced, were sick less often, found it easier to remain on task, and demonstrated more diversity in their play in the affective, imaginative, and creative domains.

The Edible Schoolyard is a striking example of a highly urban environment where students engage with place-based education, receiving various academic and psychosocial benefits (Murphy, 2003). In addition to these benefits, Murphy found that the students who made the greatest gains in understanding fundamental principles of ecology also developed more healthy eating practices, as evidenced by the numbers of daily servings of fruits and vegetables they consumed. This is in keeping with the findings of Moore and Wong (1997) with the Environmental Yard project at the Washington School, also located in Berkeley. Moore and Wong claimed that one of the major educational outcomes for students was to develop skills in growing, buying, and preparing food. They describe a range of related activities—reading and writing recipes, cooking and eating, and investigating aspect of nutritional science and health—all of which were encompassed in formal classroom investigations as well through the informal investigations conducted by students. The Environmental Yard project also included studies of climate, where students documented daily weather changes, linking their local climate to the region and beyond (Moore & Wong, 1997).

Other School Garden Programs

Other schools in California have followed the lead of The Edible School Yard, such as the Marin Academy, a college preparatory school for 400 students and just over 50 faculty members. When a major construction project for a new kitchen and dining facility had been planned and approved, a group of students, teachers, and administrators reviewed the design and determined that it was not sustainable. The head of the school, Bodie Brizendine, supported the redesign, and has since claimed that the redesign reverberated throughout the curriculum, student life and governance leading to what she called a change of consciousness around issues of sustainability. The aforementioned Center for Ecoliteracy played a major role in guiding the discussions and subsequent changes (Stone, 2007).

The Center for Ecoliteracy also sponsors a state-wide program called *Rethinking School Lunch.* Alice Waters writes about the role that public schools can play in restoring the rituals of the table to children's lives:

> Public education has the required democratic reach. In addition, it desperately needs a curriculum that offers alternatives to the fast-food messages that saturate our contemporary culture. These messages tell us that food is cheap and abundant; that abundance is permanent; that resources are infinite; that it is okay to waste; that standardization is more important than quality; and that speed is a virtue above all others. (Waters, 2003).

While there have always been pockets of interest in school gardens, as evidenced by the work of Frank and Clarice Gale in the United States (Gale & Gale, 1975, 1982, 1984), the efforts of Lucas and Mountfield (1995) in England, and the projects of Cox, McMaster, and Obuch (1990) in Australia, the idea of a school garden as a site for learning is gaining fresh momentum. For example, in England a program called *Growing Schools* (n.d.) was launched around the turn of the millennium to transform barren playgrounds into gardens and green spaces. By 2007, 12,000 schools were involved in the program. The aims of the program include enhancing the learning of the national curriculum, as well inspiring young pupils to gain a deeper understanding of the natural world and supporting healthy, regional eating. If the findings regarding the Edible Schoolyard as described by Murphy (2003) occur in these other gardens as well, then the pupils tending the gardens will have a much better chance of developing lifelong habits of stewardship of natural habitats than those students whose schooling does not include systematic and deep contact with the natural world.

Becoming Both Architect and Gardener

E.B. White, American children's author and essayist, wrote pessimistically about the future of humanity because our approach to nature is "to beat it into submission," adding that we might stand a "better chance of survival if we accommodated ourselves to this planet and viewed it appreciatively instead of skeptically and dictatorially" (as cited in Carson, 1962, p. vii). The students who tend school gardens learn that it is not possible to beat nature into submission, at least not in the long term. As Rachel Carson (1962) observed, in nature, nothing exists alone. The students of the Edible Schoolyard learn this lesson, too. Like Henry David Thoreau (1886), who said he came to love the rows of beans he planted at Walden Pond, these students, too, come to love the plants they grow, and, perhaps, develop lifelong patterns of stewardship for natural habitats. Steiner schools and Montessori schools, among others, practice approaches to learning based on participation involving gardens and other kinds of manual activities that Dewey and Mumford and Whitehead endorsed.

The same year that Lewis Mumford wrote about the regional survey, architect Warren Holmes—an unknown practitioner from Lansing, Michigan—waxed poetic about the virtues of the rural school, speaking first about the importance of community projects as the center of learning activities. These projects included putting up the winter's supply of fruit and vegetables, and activity that makes for "an atmosphere of practicality and reality that not only adds zest to the work of pupils and teachers but endows the school building with a certain character irrespective of its style of architecture" (Holmes, 1946, p. 68). Holmes talked about school gardens, patches of woods, and fields of growing crops as essential to the landscape and life of the school.

Massachusetts architect Malcolm Wells (1982, 1992) would agree; in fact, he goes further. Wells claims that the work of most architects expresses nothing less than contempt for the earth's central resource: plants. He boldly claims that architects are a "major threat to life on earth" and laments that criticisms extended to architects' work tend to be merely visual—"the buildings look bad, the paving is ugly." Wells (1992) concludes—time and again—that the architect and gardener must become one. Wells is perhaps best known for his 1982 book, *Gentle Architecture*, in which he makes the case for underground buildings—where plants thrive above ground and where humans dwell below in comfort and fully aware of their natural surroundings. I must confess that the first time I thought about earth-sheltered buildings, all I could imagine were dank, dull, and dark interiors. Further study of underground buildings—or buildings that nestle into the hollow of a hill—changed my mind. I visited spaces that were warm, alluring, and bright. And if the assertions that Wells makes are correct, these dwellings are also less prone to being ravaged by disasters than their above-ground counterparts.

I have come across two underground schools—The Wildwood School in Aspen, Colorado and Riverheights School in Brandon, Manitoba. Judging from the award the Wildwood School received in the spring of 2005, the school does much more than burrow into the hollow of a hill. The Green Tree Business Award was presented to the Wildwood School in recognition of its organic and vegetarian food choices for students, alternative transportation choices, water conservation measures, exemplary recycling of standard items and hazardous materials, awareness of chemical hazards, environmental programs—and yes—for being a "green" building. This school is for children from three to six years of age. Imagine what stewards those youngsters will become.

The other underground school I am aware of—ironically called Riverheights—is less successful. As I was in the final stages of writing this book, one of my doctoral students, who had once been a music teacher at Riverheights, was conducting research on the architecture of the school. Most of the teachers she interviewed lamented that the school is far too dark (there is only one skylight in the library) and that it is, in fact, a cold, dank, and uninviting environment (J. Brook, personal communication, April 3, 2009).

Over a half-century ago, philosopher Lewis Mumford (1946) wrote that humans had conquered the physical world, overemphasizing what he called "mechanical invention" for the sake of expansion and pillaging the resources of the planet in the process. He wrote: "If civilization is not to perish, the habits of expansion must give way to a belief in the need for balance, intensive cultivation, stability. The watchword for the new age is not conquest but cultivation: not more power but more life" (p. 141). Nearly fifty years later, David Orr (1992), scholar and environmentalist, said practically the same thing when he observed how modern education was "designed to further the conquest of nature and the industrialization of the planet," producing unbalanced, underdimensioned people tailored to fit the modern economy" (p. x). He contended that education must now serve a different agenda, "one designed to heal, connect, liberate, empower, create, and celebrate" (p. x).

Plus ça change, plus c'est la même chose. If education is to serve the agenda that the likes of Mumford and Orr propose, then the natural environments forming the outdoor classrooms of our schools—both urban and rural—must support the agenda as well, so that teachers can, in turn, do their work with the students. Everything I have read about energy consumption, water use, and global warming tells me that we do not have the privilege of another fifty years to think about these issues—especially if we come up with the same conclusions. Never has there been a greater need for urban ecology and school gardens.

In the opening chapter, I observed how several powerful models of schooling were born of a wish to educate children so they would become contributing members of a peaceful society. To a considerable extent, these values have been shared in mainstream education as well. As theologian Thomas Berry (1996) says, students generally have a strongly developed moral sense about suicide, homicide, and genocide. But he also observes how relatively trivial human rights now prevail over urgent rights of natural systems, particularly with our legal systems that foster human rights above all else. Consequently, we have "no moral sense of biocide or geocide, the killing of the life systems themselves and even the killing of the Earth" (p. 1). It behooves us to shape schools to develop these moral purposes. Paying attention to place-based sensibilities—becoming both architects and gardeners in the process— seems a natural way to begin.

Dwellings
Places to Live and Learn

In this concluding chapter, I make the case that schools should be places in which to dwell, and that it is in our best dwellings that we are also best able to learn. The resultant implications for the scale of our schools, for the furniture, light, and colours that surround students and teachers, and for the ways in which buildings and their grounds might evoke warmth and stimulate curiosity, providing places for play and inquiry are discussed. I revisit the importance of involvement in school design and building by parents and teachers and students, with a focus on how physical engagement in the building process affects those who dwell there.

I was recently reminded that educational philosopher John Dewey not only had much to say about the learning that takes place in schools, but also, about the learning that takes place in the home. He identified the traditional work of the home—domestic work, gardening, and carpentry—as having the potential to engage children in the most important learning of all: learning to live a satisfying life. In Dewey's view, the ideal home would find a child learning through the family's social interactions, through household occupations and tasks, and by tending the garden and exploring surrounding fields and forests. Dewey (1900/1956) also acknowledged many of these activities take place in the most meager of homes, albeit in a more haphazard manner. This final chapter is about dwellings: places where learning might take place in the Deweyan sense of learning in the home.

Humble School Buildings: A Feeling of Home

By dwellings, I refer not only to homes, but also, to schools and campuses with the potential to function as home-like environments. And just as Dewey claimed that learning happens in the most meager of homes, learning—good learning—can happen in the most meager of school settings. Time and time again, as I was interviewing people for this book or reading accounts of outstanding moments in people's educations, I was reminded that some of these golden instances occurred in the most humble of teaching spaces—or outside of schools entirely.

Over the past few decades, no small number of teachers have talked about how they used community venues for school events when their own schools could not accommodate them. Almost all of these teachers saw the use of community spaces as an opportunity for their students to bring their work to the broader community and experience some of the fine facilities their cities had to offer. Certainly that's the way it was for me and for my colleagues when we were staging school musicals with the students from Hennigan School at the MIT theatre in Boston. In a similar vein, Australian architect and gardener Barbara Schreiner spoke to me of how her children benefited from attending a local state high school. There, each of her children blossomed, learning about their own capabilities and the strengths of others. This learning occurred in what she described as "primitive buildings of *the* most unimaginative and insensitive kind" (B. Schreiner, personal communication, April 8, 2005). In a convocation address, architect Gregory Burgess (2005) spoke fondly of the "old battered army hut under those swaying palm trees [where] we proved that architecture with a capital 'A' was not a prerequisite for holding a vital, creative, and enjoyable education" (p. 1). The lovely Mumbulla Steiner School in Bega, New South Wales, Australia, started out as a cinder-block commercial laundry building—it was not only humble, but as far as I could glean from the archival photographs, truly ugly. However, as one of the Mumbulla teachers observed, "There's something home-like and comfortable about our school. It got its soul as it went along" (R. Alves, personal communication, April 12, 2005).

Some of the buildings at the Mt. Barker Waldorf School outside of Adelaide had equally humble beginnings. While the school now boasts a number of purpose-built structures, including an extraordinary gymnasium that was still under construction when I visited in 2005, some of the less sensational buildings had a lasting impact on me as well. The first three buildings the school acquired, over a quarter century ago, were transportable wooden buildings constructed for Florence Nightingale to use as makeshift hospital buildings in the Crimean War. The war ended before the buildings reached Crimea, so they were "shipped to the colonies"—to South Australia, as it turns out, where a quarantine station was being established on Torrens Island. The quarantine station closed just as the Mt. Barker School was established, and so the school bought the three wooden buildings—which look more like quaint cottages straight out of southern Ontario than school portables—and installed them on the school grounds. One of these wooden transportable buildings is now a multi-purpose building; another serves as a Kindergarten. These buildings will not be transported again.

These buildings are surrounded by beautiful verandahs, designed by John Whisson, a secondary teacher at Mt. Barker, and built by John and a group of dedicated parents. The expansive gardens that surround the verandahs make it apparent that the buildings have been there for years and that they have settled and grown into their surroundings. When I asked one of the founding teachers at Mt. Barker to identify the buildings she liked best, these wooden dwellings were among them. "I have a soft spot for those old buildings," she said, "It is an attachment that grows over time."

Figure 14. Mt. Barker Kindergarten (photo by author)

Another example of a blended school, where there are both "found" and purpose-built components, is The Upper Valley Waldorf School. Set in one of the most picturesque parts of Vermont, not far from Quechee Falls, the school sits on a bluff overlooking the village below. But except for the four Kindergarten classrooms, this is not a purpose-built Steiner school. The main building is the old village public school, a modest single-storey building with large windows facing the natural light. The school is trimmed with hardwood throughout, even more beautiful with the patina of age than it would have been when it was first installed in the 1920s. The new village school, barely visible in the distance, is certainly more spacious. But it is—fundamentally—a box. Alex Keats, the administrator at Upper Valley, ruefully commented how the new school is described as "neo-penitentiary" by one of the local architects (A. Keats, personal communication, November 9, 2005).

Perhaps all of these examples of humble learning environments—while not architecturally inspiring—can be seen to share several features: they are buildings with longevity and history, the teachers who have worked in them are committed and passionate, students and parents have contributed to beautifying the spaces as much as possible, and the buildings offer a sheltered place to learn in cohesive communities. Of course students can learn joyfully in humble places like these, especially if there are other conditions present to support their learning. Indeed, in a vernacular sort of way, buildings like these *can* be viewed as architecturally inspiring because they have provided a place for schooling and for learning in a deeper sense—like a residence that is more than a house, but a home. As Mary Catherine Bateson (1990) says, homes provide a great deal more than physical shelter: "You keep a house, but you make a home" (p. 118). She contends that society's homeless lack far more than shelter: homelessness brings with it "a breakdown of social ties and supports of all kinds" (p. 119). So too do schools that have not achieved a home-like feel.

Fostering Social Cohesion Through Architecture

If one thinks about Bateson's definition of the home—a place that includes social ties and supports of all kinds—then any work people do to create "homes" for learning or living can be thought of as architectural. Here is a case in point. Earlier I described the Tarremah School and the work of the South African school architects, James Morrison and Yvette Breytenbach. James and Yvette graduated with architecture degrees from the University of Cape Town and the University of Witwatersrand, respectively, in the mid-1980s. Because of her interest in how built environments interact with social aspects of human behaviour, Yvette subsequently obtained another degree in the Social Sciences (Y. Breytenbach, personal communication, June 17, 2005). In the late 1980s, the two were involved in a form of community architecture where no actual buildings were designed or built. As members of an anti-apartheid development action community group they became deeply committed to working with people living in rudimentary squatter camps around the edges of South African cities. Some of these people had lived there for as long as thirty years and were being threatened with a mandatory move to government-supplied housing. James and Yvette worked with their colleagues to create legal cases for the residents to remain in their communities, using social, environmental, and ethical arguments. As James cheerfully observed, when he and Yvette eventually settled in Hobart, Tasmania, they were perfectly suited to help create a school in an under-resourced community. Like the South African squatter communities, the Hobart community had members with an abundance of energy, talent, and willingness to provide labour as the school grew. The result, not surprisingly, was a school with both the layout and feel of a small village. Each classroom at the Tarremah School is housed in a separate building, and each building has its own arrival space and outdoor area: the school is a collection of linked dwellings.

I am convinced that the work of Morrison and Breytenbach in South Africa was architectural, just as I am sure that Dewey was right that even in the most meager of homes important learning happens. As the examples show, learning can happen in the most meager of classrooms as well. But surely, better and less meager dwellings make for better learning and better living. We have an unprecedented opportunity to shape schools that will last through the present century and beyond. To make do with meager, when magnificent is possible, is not only shortsighted, but irresponsible.

Humane Architecture: Light, Colour, Sound, and Furniture

Lewis Mumford more than once claimed that a formative influence on his architectural views came from his many walks through the congested, dark, and foul tenements of New York's Lower East Side. Mumford observed that "the absence of space, order, intelligent design, even sunlight and fresh air—the sense of all of the human qualities were missing—taught [him], by contrast, what to demand in every work of humane architecture" (Mumford, 1975, p. 149).

Humane architecture ought to be a fundamental feature of school design. In the opening chapter, I wrote about the links between crime, schools, and architecture. I quoted Wente's (2004) characterization of large high schools— "the most dysfunctional institutions yet devised by the developed world" (p. 142). Wente provocatively wrote that large schools "deaden the souls, confine the bodies and bludgeon the spirits of the inmates. They incarcerate young people in their prime and trap them into the cruel hierarchies of adolescent society. Their intellectual climate is unspeakably banal, and their life lessons are all wrong. ... The best thing you can say for high schools is that they keep the inmates off the streets. ... We need to make them small and intimate again. We need to make them places where teachers actually know who the kids are and have the time to teach them deeply" (p. 142–143). It is the notion of how architecture creates such intimacy that forms the focus of this section of the chapter. I now examine four architectural features that have the potential to contribute to intimate and humane architecture: light, colour, sound, and furniture.

Light

What makes for a good school dwelling, one that allows for the kinds of human relationships that Wente and others have called for? As Mumford suggested, some fundamental issues have to do with maintenance and good light. A poorly lit school—even if it is small—will not make for an intimate place of learning. Abundant research demonstrates that students are more likely to achieve high levels of academic performance if the schools they attend are well maintained, meet safety standards, and are kept clean. Students in schools with leaking roofs, broken windows, missing toilet stalls, and dark classrooms don't fare so well (Berner, 1992; Boss, 2001; Kolleeny, 2003; Lezotte & Passalacqua, 1978; Peters, 2003). This should come as no revelation.

Nor should we be surprised by research that demonstrates how the use of daylight and warm colours can be conducive to learning. Goethe and Steiner knew this. So did Montessori and MacMillan. For nearly a hundred years, engineers, architects, psychologists, and educators have examined the associations between lighting and color with learning, with health and physiology, and with behavior, forming the same conclusions as Goethe did so long ago (Dudek, 2000; Hathaway, 1995; Luckiesh & Moss, 1940; Muir, 2001; Rice, 1953; Rittner-Heir, 2002; Romney, 1975; Sherman, 2001; Tanner, 2000).

Some of the aforementioned studies on lighting have been highly controlled and longitudinal in nature, such as the research of Matthew Luckiesh and Frank

Moss (1940), carried out in Joplin, Missouri. In this study, students' achievement scores were compared over a three-year period. Students were assigned to one of four north-facing classrooms: two experimental classrooms—with better lighting—and two control classrooms with inferior light. Students were matched at the beginning of the study in terms of socio-economic status and school achievement. At the end of the three-year period, the gains in achievement for the students in the experimental rooms with the better lighting, which included a combination of artificial and natural light, were significantly higher than those for the students in the two poorly lit control rooms.

A study carried out some thirty years later used a similar experimental design, this time reporting on the experiences of sixth-grade students in Albuquerque, New Mexico (Romney, 1975). In this case, students in windowless classrooms were compared with students in classrooms with windows. As with the previous experiment, the students who took part were matched in terms of socio-economic status and in terms of all other architectural aspects of the two classrooms, right down to the vinyl-asbestos flooring, ventilation (or lack thereof) and acoustic ceiling tiles. The relationship between student performance on rote and conceptual learning tasks and the window/windowless environments was ambiguous. However, students in the windowless environments were found to be more likely to be bored and to display aggressive behaviour.

When I first read about these studies, I wondered whether these kinds of experiments could still be carried out, given the stringent ethical criteria now in place for conducting research on human subjects. As I mused further, I was deeply disturbed when I realized that these sorts of "experiments" have been carried out for years in schools that were—and continue to be—poorly lit. It's just that the results are rarely measured or reported because we do not think of our everyday normalized practices as "experiments."

More recent research on the effects of lighting has taken the approach of comparing test scores across school districts, such as the study described by Patricia Plympton and her colleagues, where the achievement of 21,000 students in three school districts in California, Washington, and Colorado was analyzed (Plympton, Conway, & Epstein, 2000). After controlling for the usual sets of factors—such as family income and education levels—researchers found that where natural light was used, students outperformed their peers. A related Canadian study demonstrated how students in full-spectrum lit classrooms were less likely to be absent from school than their peers (Hathaway, 1995).

There are detrimental physiological effects from poor lighting as well. One of the most comprehensive studies I have encountered was undertaken in Sweden, where it was shown that students who were in classrooms that lacked both natural and artificial daylight demonstrated a marked delay in the annual rise of cortisol, a hormone associated with stress reduction. This delay, by as much as two months in children in the windowless classrooms, caused the authors to conclude that environments lacking adequate illumination resulted in severe disturbances in the chronobiological system regulation of the production of hormones (Küller & Lindsten, 1992). Based on physiological and observational data, the authors also concluded that children with the lowest cortisol levels in December were more likely to experience illness. Seasonal factors also had an impact on body growth. In addition, researchers measured diurnal ranges of cortisol and found that students with high levels of morning cortisol were inclined to be more sociable than their peers, while students with overall moderate values of cortisol were more able to concentrate on their individual schoolwork.

The authors concluded that working and living in classrooms without daylight upset a basic chronobiological rhythm, and this change in rhythm influenced students' abilities to concentrate and socialize. It also had an impact on body growth and overall health. What a high price to pay for windowless classrooms. Members of the Swedish government and the school board were so taken with the results of this study that they provided funds to install windows for the two windowless classrooms used in the study. It's too bad the results of the American research in the 1930s didn't engender the same outcome at the policy level, not only for the so-called "control" classrooms used in the studies, but for all the other classrooms built and maintained in the same way for the remainder of the century.

Colour

Long after Goethe's prescient observations on colour were made in the late 18th and early 19th centuries, results as dramatic as the experiments with lighting have been found with experiments on colour. Again, I am struck by how some of this research was carried out long ago, and yet, the work remains either unknown or ignored. I will describe just one study to make the point.

In 1953, Arthur Rice published what is now an oft-quoted report on the effects of colour on students' emotional responses and achievement. Like other studies of this era, the research employed both experimental and control conditions. Researchers from the John Hopkins University conducted a two-year study—financed by a paint manufacturer—involving three elementary schools and three junior high schools in Baltimore.[31] The three elementary schools catered to students from similar backgrounds, and more to the point, all three schools were in desperate need of painting. Neither teachers nor students were aware of the study. For the first year of the study—the pre-painting period— records were kept of achievement and attitudes towards school: there were no differences among students in the three schools. In the second year, one school was painted in the conventional colour of the time period, the all-too-familiar light green (or "school green" as it is not so affectionately called in some educational circles). Another school was decorated with paint colours chosen by the manufacturer, with bright primary colours featured in the Kindergarten, and a variety of single colour schemes in the later grades, such as blue walls in the classrooms with sunlit exposures. After the classrooms had been painted for a

---

[31] According to Rice, Wendell R. Garner, then Director of the Psychological Laboratory of The Johns Hopkins University Institute for Cooperative Research, along with his colleagues, Hudson Bond and Randolph Hanes, conducted the study. I could not locate a document by Garner and his colleagues detailing their findings.

year, the children in the two painted schools performed better on all motor, social, and cognitive measures taken, with the children in the brightly painted Kindergarten benefiting most by a paint scheme creating a "playroom away from home" (Rice, 1953, p. v.) In the junior high school experiment, similarly conceived, students were asked their impressions of the classroom environments. A number of the students' comments are reproduced in the Rice paper, such as, "Last year [before the painting occurred] the school looked like a jail. That's how it felt. Now it looks like a home and feels somewhat like one" (p. vi).

Sound

Yet another set of studies has focused on the detrimental effects of noise in the learning environment, and the findings suggest that too much noise or distracting sound undermines achievement and leads to discomfort (Boss, 2001; Chan, 1980; Tanner & Langford, 2003). Niven Stines, a recording engineer at the School of Music at the Australian National University, has thought a great deal about how sound affects workplace and learning environments. He made two striking points during our conversation. First, sound is given relatively little consideration when schools and other learning environments are designed. Second, current building practices resulting in particular acoustical conditions make it difficult to concentrate in schools (N. Stines, personal communication, March 31, 2005). These practices cause increased levels of stress for students and teachers and can be easily avoided. Stines gave some appalling examples. For instance, some building engineers believe that a steady hissing sound, introduced through the air-conditioning units, is *less* distracting than the regular sounds of the environment. It seems to me that this notion is just as misguided as one that windowless classrooms increase concentration because of a lack of distractions from the outdoors.

The abiding beliefs about noise are largely an outcome of a view held in the 1970s, during which time many presently functioning university and school buildings were constructed. At the time, it was felt that environmental control could "meet all the physical, physiological, and psychological requirements of the occupants." The artificially created and synthetic environment proposed by engineers of the day was described as "superior to the natural one. No exterior atmosphere is comparable to an air-conditioned and humidity-controlled room" (Doelle, 1972, p. 3). As Stines was speaking, I thought about how my shoulders relax and the tension leaves my body when the hiss of my office's air conditioner is shut off after regular working hours.

Countless studies have determined that classroom acoustics require further attention. High levels of background noise in classrooms compromise children's ability to interpret speech; limit the effectiveness of assistive technologies for students with hearing difficulties, and cause additional difficulties for students for whom the language of instruction is not their mother tongue. In many studies, heating, ventilating, and air-conditioning units have been identified as the primary culprits for contributing to poor classroom acoustics.[32]

Like many other people who have been thoughtful about school design, Niven Stines believes that appropriate building treatments for sound need not be expensive; certainly, no more expensive than some of the treatments now used. There are expensive solutions, of course, such as using a soft surface on corridor walls to absorb sounds; but soft surfaces are expensive to install and require more frequent replacement than the overly durable surfaces most often encountered in schools. Less expensive methods, such as using textured concrete or installing acoustic ceiling tiles can be equally effective. The latter treatment is especially important for transportable classrooms where the acoustical environments are often particularly troublesome.

Joanne Valentine and her colleagues (n.d.) conducted a comprehensive study in New Zealand on the effects of modifying the ceiling construction on classroom noise. Through the use of teacher surveys, speech perception tests, daily recordings of noise levels in classrooms, and measurements of reverberation time and clarity, the researchers identified a dozen classrooms considered either "good" or "poor" in acoustic terms. After adding acoustic ceiling tiles to rooms considered acoustically poor, the measurements were repeated. Not surprisingly, both teachers and students were enthusiastic about the improvements. The improved classrooms resulted in lower levels of frustration, better ability to hear what was being said, and more on-task work. The improvements also made it easier for students to work in small groups—an essential feature of learning in a complex system.

German-born composer and sound ecologist Hildegard Westerkamp lived in British Columbia for decades. When she was teaching courses in acoustics at Simon Fraser University, she met Canadian composer and educator R. Murray Schafer. Westerkamp joined Schafer's World Soundscape Project, an extraordinary undertaking through which Schafer and his colleagues have drawn attention to how sonic landscapes affect all manner of human interactions. Much of his work highlights the negative effects of technologically produced sound, particularly on city dwellers (Schafer, 1977). Westerkamp (1980) is a pointed critic of poorly designed acoustical environments. She concluded that students in newly built schools and universities all over North America study with artificial lighting in rooms without windows, breathe recycled air, and find themselves in isolation from the often very beautiful, still surroundings in which these buildings are located. A shocking example described by Westerkamp is the Museum of Anthropology in Vancouver. The Museum is set on a breathtaking site on the campus of the University of British Columbia, overlooking the Georgia Strait and the mountains of the North Shore. Surrounded by trees, the museum has been fitted with a complex air-conditioning system. As a result, ambient sound levels—*after* visiting hours when the building is empty—can be greater than the levels measured *outside* the building. When Westerkamp conducted her tests and wrote about the museum

---

[32] A list of such studies is available at http://www.access-board.gov/ABNEW/acoustic/acoustic.htm.

in the early 1980s, only one of the galleries met the noise criteria recommended for museums, libraries, and other spaces for study.

In the remodeling of the Apollo Elementary School in Issaquah, Washington, one of the most welcomed changes was to install carpet throughout the school (Muir, 2001). Students and teachers alike favoured the change: they liked the warm and calming colour scheme, they liked being able to work on the floor, and they also liked that the carpet cut down the noise in the learning environment. One teacher described the former open-air (uncarpeted) corridor as being "as cold and windy as a Boeing test tunnel" (Muir, 2001, p. 3). When these corridors were enclosed and carpeted, not only was the vastness of the corridor reduced, thereby decreasing the feelings of isolation students experienced, but also, the new interior walls provide the additional benefit of display space for student artwork.

Furniture

We should not underestimate the importance of appropriate furniture (Bullock & Foster-Harrison, 1997). Early in the 20th century, Dewey wrote how he spent hour upon hour looking for suitable furniture for students. He finally encountered a dealer who said, "I am afraid we have not what you want. You want something at which the children may work; these are all for listening" (Dewey, 1900/1956, p. 31). A hundred years later, the issue of furniture remains problematic. A few years ago, one of my graduate students was researching the factors influencing academically at-risk young women in their final years of high school. Many of the predictable factors emerged, including parental support, attitudes of teachers, and influences of peers (Grover, 2004). But one of the unexpected findings was the extent to which these young women talked about how much the furniture in the school mattered to them. As my graduate student observed, with evident puzzlement: "Here I was expecting to hear about how a caring teacher made a difference to their academic attainments, and all they wanted to talk about was how much they hated the furniture" (S. Grover, personal communication, November 25, 2004.)

When I use the term appropriate furniture, I am speaking about more than furniture suitably sized for students in various stages of physical development. The psychological and emotional fit of the furniture is equally important as noted by Australian architects Mark Baxter and David Jacobson. They have designed many schools and community centres, as well as offices, cafés, residences and wineries. Some years ago, they designed the Oyster Bar on the Sydney Harbour, right next to the Sydney Opera House—an alluring stopping place for refreshment and conversation that, as near as I can tell, is busy every hour of the day and evening, year round. I suspect the choice of furniture— chairs that look as if you could sit in them for hours—has something to do with its appeal. Every time I had the pleasure of walking by, I felt pulled to the spot. Baxter and Jacobson are also known for their designs of Steiner schools. Much of their work can be seen throughout Australia, including the Shearwater School at Mullumbimby and some of the buildings of Mt. Barker. I asked them what messages they would most want to relay to the architects and education officials involved in school design. For Jacobson, the most fundamental message would be this one: every aspect of architecture affects children: every choice of form, colour, and volume, for example, has physiological and psychological consequences (D. Jacobson, personal communication, June 14, 2005). The same goes for other objects besides furniture; aesthetics are as important as function. Baxter added that when schools are created artistically, vandalism is a rare occurrence, reminding me of Steiner's belief that there is no point in creating laws for society if the buildings do not support those laws (M. Baxter, personal communication, June 14, 2005).

Students' Views on Humane Architecture

What happens when we ask students about the places in which they would like to learn? If furniture is important to students, as it appears to be, what do they have to say about other aspects of the schools they inhabit? Do they speak in the same terms as Jacobson and Baxter, Mumford and Morrison?

In a six-year European study carried out by Christian Rittelmeyer (1992), several hundred students from Lower Saxony and Baden-Württemberg were interviewed. As a result, Rittelmeyer made the following conclusions: schools feel inviting, attractive, and healthy to students only if they convey warmth, if there is a lack of constriction, and if buildings feel balanced. Regarding balance, Rittelmeyer concluded that monotonous box structures produced the impression of "architectonic rigidity, lifelessness and tedium" (p. 2). Conversely, if the students' sense of balance was "excessively irritated" by a preponderance of, for example, oblique lines and structures, then the experience was one of anxiety, threat, or chaos. When the form of the building was balanced with a combination of oblique lines along with verticals and horizontals, then students interpreted the space as being lively and exhilarating. Students used terms like "cold," "lacking in character," or "uncongenial" to describe buildings without balance. Rittelmeyer surmised that school vandalism is a form of counter-attack to what he calls the "architectonic attack" of buildings that are either excessively rigid or off-balance.

In the first chapter, I quoted some the words of a young adolescent boy named Arthur in describing his school environment (Coles, 1969). Many other adolescent students in the study conducted by American psychiatrist Robert Coles also expressed sadness and even horror about a school architecture that was anything but humane. Their descriptions focus on light, on furniture, on sound, on colour—giving student voice to the research studies cited earlier. Arthur's younger sister, Margie, had this to say about furniture and light:

> I'll tell you one thing; I'd tear this building down. There's nothing to do but that. Then, if I could build a new school, I'd make it pleasant-like. I'd get rid of all the desks, every one of them. … We could open and close the windows and they wouldn't be stuck like now. …And they could have some places, some big sofas maybe, where if you didn't feel too good, you could lie down, or you could just sit in them sometimes, and you'd be more comfortable. (p. 48)

And Arthur offered the following comment, beginning again with a discussion of furniture:

> I'd like comfortable chairs, like ones that had cushions so your back doesn't hurt and your bottom either... I'd like a sink, where you could get some water to drink, and you wouldn't have to ask the teacher to go down the hall, and half the time she says no...We could have our books in a bookcase, and we wouldn't have to sit in the same place all the time. And most of all, really most of all, a window in the roof so you could just look up and see the sky and the clouds and the sun and when the rain falls you could see it falling and you'd like it better, being in school. (p. 49–51)

Children from impoverished homes were not the only ones wishing for schools to be more dwelling-like. Susan lived with her family in a single-family home in a middle-class neighborhood and attended a relatively new school. She mused about what a home-like school atmosphere would entail, including comments about scale, light, sound:

> If I could build a school, I'd make the school warm and small and not big and too hot one minute and you're shivering the next. I'd have a lot of little schools. I'd have every home-room a school, separate from the rest...And it's too dark in school; way too dark. And once you're inside, you never see the outside until the big bell rings and you can leave...A lot of the time, I think, if they put on the radio, like we have at home it would be better than not hearing anything but yourself and the clock. [The teacher's] chair squeaks a lot...they should get rid of that chair. And they shouldn't have us go to the bathroom way down the hall...and the lunchroom, it's too big and everyone gets lost in it...we could have little sun-rooms, with plants in them, and we could go and eat there, a few of us in each one, and it would be cozy. (p. 52)

Margie suggested that her old school simply needed to be torn down and replaced with a garden, a place to play, and a building that paid homage to her leaders and heroes:

> I think the best thing to do is tear down the old school and let it be a place for us to play, the land. Then we could build another one...outside it would have statues of our people, black leaders, like I saw in the news they had someplace, in front of some building. And you could walk right in the building without steps, and it would be good inside. They'd have a garden, with rocks and water and flowers ... and they'd have a map of the world on the walls, all around everywhere, and you could stand and see all the continents and the oceans. (p. 55)

The comments made by the students in Coles study could have been made—and indeed were made—by students describing their schools in 2009. The call for comfortable spaces—for sofas or couches—rings loudly from students in Iceland, in Minnesota, in Germany, and in southeastern Ontario (Davis et al., 2009; Gislason, 2009; Peterson & Upitis, 2009; Upitis et al., in press). In fact, many of the elements that I have described thus far—including good light and ventilation, appropriate furniture, and the need for green spaces— were recognized as crucial school features by the first American Commissioner of Education, Henry Barnard (1848), in his classic work on school architecture written over 150 years ago. Why have these sentiments not been heeded? Equally, why have students' views not been heard? For a century and a half, we have built schools that lack good light, good furniture, balance, inviting entryways, and green spaces.

Dewey's Utopian Schools: Places to Dwell

In the early 1930s, Dewey imagined what he called the "utopian" school. He began the discussion with physical space, only later turning to issues of pedagogy (Uline, 1997). He made a plea for large grounds, gardens, and greenhouses. He described the need for "open-air" interiors, a variety of workspaces, and access to books—all of which would help create the feeling of a "well-furnished home." Dewey was "not shy about emphasizing beauty and comfort and excitement" (p. 196). Nor were the children interviewed by Robert Coles nearly a half-century ago.

Bruce Jilk, former chair of the American Institute of Architects Committee on Architecture for Education, has embraced the teachings of Dewey and created a series of design principles to help architects and designers create innovative learning environments. These principles include the identification of (a) unique elements of the school or site, (b) learning expectations, (c) forms of learning likely to take place at the school, and (d) ways of blending the school and community life (Jilk, Copa, & Pease, 1992). One environment resulting from this series of design principles is the Minnesota School of Environmental Studies, located on the grounds of the Minnesota Zoological Gardens (Boss, 2001; Bingler, 2002). In that school, hundreds of Grades 11 and 12 students pursue various interdisciplinary projects with the kinds of inquiry that Dewey must have envisaged.

In a similar vein, the Edible Schoolyard in Berkeley, California, is a place where interdisciplinary projects are inevitably pursued. The garden is a central school feature—described as the hearth—of the once-derelict Martin Luther King Middle School in Berkeley, California, and offers students opportunities for conversation, inquiry, and the culinary arts at their finest. The idea of both these schools is not to teach children about zoology or horticulture alone, but to provide settings for exploration. In turn, these settings create possibilities for learning things unanticipated by student and teacher alike. As in any complex learning system, it is the expansion of the possible, the growth of community, and the patterns that connect the various interrelationships that are at the heart of these learning environments. These dwelling places, filled with growing and living things, should be present in every learning environment. Schools lacking lively outdoor spaces are not dwelling places. Classrooms without plants are not dwelling places. Schools without animals are not dwelling places, either.

Anne Meek (1995b), editor of the book *Designing Spaces for Learning*, addresses the complementary notions of dwelling and deep meaning. She writes:

> It's not easy for people to attach deep meaning—a sense of belonging, affection, and loyalty—to the index of leading economic indicators. But it *is* easy, in fact, inevitable, to attach deep meaning to the school where you first trudged up the steps to make friends and meet teachers; where, perhaps, you ... tried out for the senior play;

understood the beauty of algebra or the chemistry of cooking; or began to see the connections between the Elizabethan origins of the settlers of your state and the language of your family. ... For these reasons, the school as a place is a fertile ground for the creation of deep meaning and, therefore, of symbolic importance in the hearts and minds of people. (p. vi)

Deep meaning is attached by many of us to our early experiences of schooling. Sometimes such meaning and the memories it engenders are less than ideal. I find it not the least bit surprising that British architect Mark Dudek would devote a substantial portion of his professional life on the study of school architecture, given his early schooling experiences. In *Architecture of Schools: The New Learning Environments*, Dudek (2002) recalled his first schooling experience in a temporary wooden hut built after World War II. The huts were noisy, filled with unpleasant smells from a nearby kitchen, and the playground areas were hard. Dudek further described how the chaotic environment and sense of impermanence of these huts offered a stark contrast to the "relative order of [his] home environment" (p. ix). Contrast these huts to the new purpose-built school that Dudek attended from the age of seven years onwards: the new school had spacious classrooms and large windows that opened and provided views of the nearby playing fields. Dudek concluded that the bright new school with its surrounding green spaces had a direct effect on his academic performance, and his health improved in equal measure—what he identified as the effects of a "truly therapeutic environment" (p. ix). While Dudek acknowledged that the teachers must also have been responsible for his new sense of well-being, it was the architectural qualities and the ordered rituals associated with those qualities that fixed within him a measure of his own value.

For some, the smells of schools are remembered most. When I asked an Australian teacher what she remembered of her early days of schooling, the first thing she described was the smell of the eucalyptus trees—a distinctive and strong smell if there ever was one, especially after a rainstorm. This Australian teacher also talked about the smell of the soil. Her teacher was a gardener, and the students came to be gardeners too, growing food for the classroom table.

Rina Naranjo Swentzell, a member of the Santa Carla Pueblo nation, is an architect and scholar.[33] She describes her first place of learning as the fields and hills that surrounded her community in Santa Carla Pueblo, New Mexico (Swentzell, 1992, 1998). Swentzell provides a vivid description of pushing her barefoot toes through the mud, becoming aware of how the colour of the mud, the earth, and her toes, were all the same. Along with other children, she "learned an intimacy with the plants, rabbits, rocks and clouds. We belonged" (1992, p. 8). Contrast this with her first experiences in the Bureau of Indian Affairs School at Santa Clara Pueblo, where the fenced-in school with its straight walls was designed to keep out the animals and the community elders, and where all large rocks, trees and shrubs were scraped away. Students were told

---

[33] Rina Swentzell's daughter, Roxanne Swentzell is a celebrated potter and her younger sister, Nora Naranjo-Morse, is a sculptor and poet. Swentzell serves as an architectural and educational consultant to museums, including Santa Fe's Institute of American Indian Arts and the Smithsonian.

"when to play, read, add, subtract, eat, sleep and talk. The school was part of a world that embraced time, assignments, divisions, specialized buildings, artificial playgrounds and passive learning. It was authoritative, hierarchical and non-sensual" (1992, p. 8). Hardly a place to dwell. Or to learn.

A Community Sensibility

Dwellings for learning go beyond good lighting and ventilation, appropriate furniture, and green spaces. Dwelling places are for the young and old, for work and play, for assembly, for sport, for festivals and political meetings (Schnebli, 1998). The notion that community is central to dwelling—just as community is central to natural abundance—comes up in much of the contemporary literature on school architecture and is one that is gaining momentum. For example, a collection of cases published in 2007 features recently built school facilities selected not only for their successful learning environments and uses of natural light and ventilation, but also for their community use (Canizares & Fajardo, 2007).

What underlies the push for schools to serve as community meeting places and the concomitant push to include family resource centres, human services, cafés, and sports centres in the same campuses is much more than an economic incentive to build more efficiently. By integrating community resources, the community itself becomes more integrated. American architect Steven Bingler (2002) observed that, a hundred years ago, more attention was paid to the role of the school in the community. As he wrote: "The auditorium was a neighborhood auditorium, the gymnasium was a neighborhood gymnasium. Schools were connected to neighborhoods, not to cities or regions" (p. 14). It is time we return to having schools play this kind of local community focus.

A community approach is not limited to schools in rural areas or schools with relatively small student populations. Indeed, there are examples where large urban high schools have dealt with the issue of scale and community building by creating a series of clusters or pods within a single geographic site. American architect Isaac Williams, and now professor at the University of Maryland, worked extensively on school design with Prakash Nair and Randall Fielding, international school design consultants (Nair & Fielding, 2005; Nair, Fielding, & Lackney, 2010). Williams has gone so far as to argue that it is only by creating communities within a larger community that large high schools—that is, schools with up to 4,000 students—can ever expect to achieve success (I. Williams, personal communication, February 16, 2009). I have often wondered if the success of the Noble High School in North Berwick, Maine, even though it is large, owes something to a design that divides the 1,500 students of the school into 15 "learning communities." The school also serves as the community centre for three towns, housing a health care centre, a day care centre, an adult education centre, and one of the largest performing arts centres in the region. Similarly, Hübner's Evangelische Gesamtschule Gelsenkirchen-Bismarck (Evangelical Community School of Gelsenkirchen-Bismarck) was conceived of as more than a school: this large campus was modelled after a small village, with clusters of classrooms around a central "street" or "pedestrian spine," and with many parts of the school open to the outside community. This is just the sort of thing the late Canadian urban critic and connoisseur Jane Jacobs (1961/1984) recommended to rejuvenate urban life. Perhaps such an approach to scale can work for rejuvenating large urban schools as well.

Campus

When we think of the word *school*, many of us will picture a single building, probably made of red brick and surrounded by parking lots and maybe an open playing field. *Campus* is something entirely different (Gisolfi, 2004).

A campus is more than a group of buildings. Rather, there are relationships among the buildings, among the indoor and outdoor spaces. On an appealing campus, the overall appearance of the buildings is often unified in some way. Some thoughtful school architects urge that when schools are expanded, the idea of campus should be invoked, rather than invoking the model of a cargo train, where boxes of classrooms are attached to the original school wherever land is available (Gisolfi, 2004). When schools are considered as campuses, an extraordinary richness emerges in the spaces between the buildings, a notion discussed at length in an earlier chapter. This, in turn, leads to the kinds of social relationships that support learning and community, as people move from one space to another.

The Orana Steiner School in Canberra, Australia is organized in two campuses, the Hill Campus and the Forest Campus. Of these, the Forest Campus, in particular, works as an integrated whole. Each of its two clusters of buildings relates to the outdoor spaces, and the flow between the indoor and outdoor spaces occurs naturally for students and visitors alike. Unlike the Forest Campus, which was purpose-built, the Hill Campus was purchased with the facilities already in place, and work still needs to be done to make it more unified. This work—detailed in a master plan—has been discussed and scheduled with extensive consultations of the kind that extend beyond formality into the realm of real conversation.

Dwelling Companions

I share David Orr's (1992) horror that it is possible to insulate oneself from the natural world entirely, living in suburbs or apartments, driving cars, working in buildings where not a breath of fresh air is to be found, where there are no animals, and where even the plants are synthetic. In many of the more vibrant schools I have visited, there are animals of all kinds, fulfilling what must be, as a friend of mine claims, a basic human need to be in contact with other creatures (L. Scanlan, personal communication, September 12, 2005).

Jamie Campbell teaches at an alternative high school near Ottawa, Ontario— meaning there are no other alternatives left for those students, except the streets and prisons. One winter morning, he found himself contemplating whether he would bring his beloved dog to school. His alternatives were two-fold: leaving his dog alone at home for the long winter days or bringing it to school and risking the chance of some unfortunate incident with one of the troubled teenagers. He decided in favour of the latter. There were no unfortunate incidents: in fact, the students thrived in the presence of such a gentle creature. Students who had been rough and difficult became sweet and generous during the time they spent in his classroom (J. Campbell, personal communication, October 3, 2005). This outcome will come as no surprise to parents whose children have pets: most children form undeniably strong connections with animals. Our own animals presently number two cats, a dog, a guinea pig, and dozens of fish in an outdoor pond. I can no longer imagine a home without animals—animals the children feed, interact with, and build nooks and shelters for, and whose companionship they seek when they feel sad or misunderstood or simply long for unconditional affection.

Creating Dwellings for Living and Learning: From the Inside Out

Most people are not only insulated from nature, but are also insulated almost entirely from the process of building, whether it is the building of their own homes or the schools that their offspring attend. Contractors often refuse jobs when homeowners want to have a hand in the building (perhaps the urge to decorate and renovate—as evidenced by the burgeoning number of television shows dedicated to the topic—is an indication of a deep desire to shape one's home and shelter). Schools where parents and students are involved in construction are the exception rather than the rule. Earlier I suggested that the Newtonian approach to science has had the indirect effect of distancing us from being intimately involved in our natural surroundings. What other knowledge do we no longer possess, as a result of our continual distancing from the natural world and from the very processes required to provide food and shelter and clothing? In this section, I examine three ways that we can be more closely involved with the creation of our dwellings. I begin with places that provide intimate sanctuary and a setting for working and learning, followed by an example of community involvement in raising a school, and ending with a description of the physical labour and creative impulses associated with two public buildings—a national monument and a housing project for low income residents.

Finding Sanctuary

Some places for work and learning are places of sanctuary. When I was writing the first draft of this book, I was not working in my familiar surroundings. Up until then, for many years, I had the privilege of writing in a university office located in what was once the home of a prison gardener, built in the latter part of the 19th century, out of stones carved by hand. In the Stone House, the woodwork was elaborate, the ceilings were high, and rooms were beautifully proportioned. I painted my office walls a salmon colour, and the adjoining seminar room—which was once the great room of the house—was painted in the same shade. There was original art on the walls—a mixture of watercolours and mixed media creations. There were plants thriving in every room. I taught many of my graduate courses in the Stone House, and my students were immediately taken with the beauty of the rooms. At the beginning of the second class of each course I teach, I invite students to talk about one thing they remember from the first class. When I was teaching in the Stone House, invariably there was at least one person who, somewhat sheepishly, said that what he or she remembered best was the room—the woodwork, the high ceilings, and the sound of birds in the nearby trees.

But, as I say, that place was not available to me as I began to write this book while serving as a visiting scholar at the Australian National University in Canberra. Instead, I had a more typical university office—square, small, and grey, although not windowless, for I looked out onto a large seminar room, and if I stretched my neck a little, I could see the city landscape. I was grateful for this space, because university space is at a premium, and private offices for visiting scholars are often hard to come by. I hung art on the walls and tried to keep a plant there, although it suffered from the dearth of natural light and fared poorly. I brought in a large table, so that I could put out books and articles and papers in piles as I pleased, something that was essential given the wide variety of sources I used in assembling this work. The office had the further advantage of being close to the offices of colleagues whom I grew to admire and respect, and who offered encouragement and advice as the book unfolded. But there were days when I simply could not write there. I found it ironic, to say the least, to be writing a book about school architecture and finding myself in a place that did so little to nurture me.

I came to the point where I had to find a different place to write. Fortune smiled. University House—right across the street from where I lived—is the type of building where university conferences are held, accommodation for visiting guests is provided, and where there is often a pub and a garden— throwbacks to the English colleges that were established in the 13th and 14th centuries. This University House was no exception, having all of the requisite amenities, in addition to a lovely old library. The library was not large, but the furniture was comfortable and wooden, the books were old enough to smell right, and the generous windows looked out onto a courtyard lined with a long pond on the library side. I had found a place to write.

I was often alone in the University House library. This made me think about other places that I have undertaken large writing projects over the years. I completed my doctoral dissertation in a small cottage on an island. I often write at the pine table in our cabin in the woods. In a book called *Harvest of a Quiet Eye: The Cabin as Sanctuary*, Lawrence Scanlan (2004) wrote about one of the most humble sanctuaries of all—the cabin—and how the cabin has long provided many people with a certain kind of setting that is conducive to producing books and other forms of creative work. For many people, part of the magic of the setting comes from creating the space in the first place. With mesmerizing prose, Scanlan described the process of giving new life to an old square-timbered log cabin that he moved to his secluded acreage not far from Kingston, Ontario. This process involved the toil and commitment of many workers, friends, and family members, and more often than not, it seemed an unending act of folly. But the cabin became a place of sanctuary, a place to revel in the sweet satisfaction of physical toil, a place to join voices with a long line of others who have found solace in their shelters in the woods.

I know what it means to have a cabin in the woods where one can dwell in the deepest sense of the word. Because of our own cabin, I also know something about the other creatures dwelling there. Before building the cabin, and spending season upon season there, I would have been hard pressed to name even two or three wintering birds. Or to tell you about any of the edible plants that can be found in the forests and meadows, or about the prevailing winds, or about the soil and stone surrounding my humble edifice. The cabin is, indeed, a fine place to write.

It gives me pleasure to read about how others describe how the places where they write are important to the evolution of their work. Thinkers like Capra or Lovelock, for example, are moved by the places in which they write, and this reinforces the role that place has to play in the evolution of work of all kinds, not only in the sense of place-based education as examined earlier. Lovelock (1987) begins the preface to *Gaia: A New Look of Life on Earth* with the words:

> I first started this book when on holiday in Ireland in 1975. Most of it came to mind when walking or sitting on the warm, red sandstone slabs of Hungry Hill. There was one rock that had an unusually pleasing prospect of Bear Island and the end of Bantry Bay as it merged into the broad Atlantic. I would sit there on sunny days and plan the way the book would go. (p. vii).

While I do not claim to keep company with the likes of Capra or Lovelock, the final stages of this book benefited greatly from many stretches, sometimes weeks on end, of cabin dwelling. The writing was punctuated by physical labour—chopping wood, preparing meals, and washing clothes with a washboard in an old tin tub. I played too, swimming in the glacier-formed lake with my family, wandering through the woods gathering sticks and acorns, making music by the evening fire. The days developed an easy rhythm. They stretched out, passing in a languid and serene way. I was happy at the close of every day, tired and full from the day's physical—and mental—activities.

Building Schools

Involvement in planning the school or campus can go beyond discussion to taking part in the actual building process. Sometimes it is parents and teachers who build alongside local tradespeople, as in the examples described earlier, such as the Evangelische Gesamtschule Gelsenkirchen-Bismarck (Evangelical Community School of Gelsenkirchen-Bismarck), the Cologne Waldorf School, Tarramah School near Hobart, Tasmania, and the Seabird Island Community School in British Columbia.

When I spoke with one of the Kindergarten teachers at the Willunga School near Adelaide in South Australia, her love for the building was evident in every word and gesture she used in describing the space, from the larger elements— like the sweeping curved roofs (reminiscent of a German fairy tale)—to the smallest of details, like the wood trim around the window by the classroom door. As she was talking about the curved woodwork, she paused, and said, "The tradespeople loved working here; the workmen were inspired." She spoke at length about a Dutch carpenter who took great joy in bringing the buildings to fruition—such joy, in fact, that he continued to seek out work that would give him opportunities to "work out the puzzles and corners and tricky bits." That the tradespeople loved working at Willunga was confirmed in my conversation with one of the designers of the Kindergarten, Jeremy Keyte, who, along with another parent, Andrew Bragg, designed this and other classrooms at Willunga. Teachers, parents, and designers were justifiably proud that their project was completed within the budget set by the local education authorities.

Sometimes students are also involved with building. At the Orana Steiner School in Canberra, a group of Grade 3 students built a "chook house" for the chickens. (Australians call chickens *chooks*.) One of the parents involved in the project playfully dubbed it the "Gertieanum," harking back to Steiner's Goethe-anum and the legacy of Goethe. While some teachers thought the term irreverent, I cannot help but think that Goethe would have been pleased—or as they say in Australia, chuffed. Chuffed with the chooks. When the children built the Gertie-anum, they first created the mud-baked bricks that they would later use to form the walls of the chook house. After the firestorm of January 2003 only the chook house remained on the Kindergarten site. With a new biodynamic garden in the works for the former Kindergarten site, the chook house is sure to be filled with chickens once again. It is almost impossible to gauge the long-term benefits of building something like the Gertieanum by hand and then filling it with chickens, free to roam the Kindergarten yard.

Figure 15. Willunga Kindergarten Gate (photo by author)

Creating Public Buildings

It is easy to overlook the pride and care that can be involved in the building of structures much larger and more public than wilderness cabins or chook houses or even schools like Seabird Island or Willunga. I offer two examples of how public buildings can also be erected with pride and creativity.

On Easter Sunday, when we were living in Canberra, our family had a picnic on the lawns of Aspen Island where the National Carillon is located. The Carillon was a gift from Britain to Australia to commemorate the first 50 years that Canberra served as Australia's capital city. A large carillon by world standards, the tower originally housed 53 bronze bells. With the addition of two new bells in 2003, the Carillon now boasts a full four-and-a-half octave range. Public concerts are given during weekday lunch hours and on holidays, and visitors and tourists alike bike or walk across the footbridge to the island to admire the building and hear the bells.

The Carillon Tower is a stunning monument and landmark. The tower was designed by the Western Australian architects Cameron, Chisholm, and Nicol, and comprises three triangular columns, the tallest of which rises 50 or so meters into the sky. Each of the three columns is clad with quartz and opal chip and each serves a different function—one is an elevator, one is a steel staircase, and the third a service shaft. The first floor, about halfway up the tower, contains the clavier that operates the bells above; above the carillon there is another chamber, a small viewing and functions room, dwelling-like in proportions and feel.

The grounds surrounding the Carillon Tower are equally attractive, with architectural elements in the natural environment that complement both the tower and the land.

Figure 16. Carillon Tower, Canberra, Australia (photo by author)

The bridge to the island, which everyone must cross, is a simple concrete walkway with pebbled circles of various sizes embedded in the path. The railings appear to be almost ephemeral—wispy spindles open out to a flat railing where birds perch and children run their hands along the smooth steel surface. As we were lunching on the grass, my then seven-year-old son commented that the bridge was "perfect, because you see lake, then the bridge is hardly there, and you see the lake on the other side."

As we were leaving the Carillon Tower, the rest of my family detoured for a drink of water at the fountains. Waiting alone next to the footbridge, I was approached by a man who looked to be in his late sixties. He was unshaven and unkempt, and I dreaded the exchange I expected would follow. As he neared, he asked if I was a visitor or a local. An odd question, I thought to myself, as I answered with "local." He launched into a long and involved tale about the Carillon. As it turned out he was one of the workers who had built the towers and pulled up the bells, bells ranging in weight from seven kilograms to six tonnes. The pride he evinced in telling his tale was palpable. His eyes sparkled as he told story after story about the construction of the Carillon Tower, stories of triumph, and a story of tragedy, too. By the time my husband and children returned, I had learned that this man's cousin was involved in the addition of the two new bells in 2003, and of his pleasure that the Carillon was "still in the family." This was the first time he had visited the Carillon since its completion some 35 years previously—and, no doubt, the last. As soon as our conversation ended, he walked over the footbridge and disappeared into the park. I felt privileged to hear his story. He obviously needed to talk to someone (a local, preferably), and in so doing, to reconnect in yet another way with the building he had helped shape. It was not the architects alone who created the Carillon Tower.

The meeting at the tower reminded me of tales about the construction of the Hundertwasser House in Vienna. The Hundertwasser House, which opened in

Figure 17. Hundertwasser House, Vienna, Austria (photo by author)

1985, was commissioned by the city as a public housing initiative. The result was a series of 50 dwelling units in a village that also contained a meeting-place, café, book-shop, and shopping area. The collection of buildings is Hundert-wasser's art and architecture writ large. When I visited in 2007, I found rooftops covered with greenery, charmingly irregular win-dow and door alignments, buildings created from a giddy mixture of straight and wavy lines, rooftop domes shaped like giant onions, and painted surfaces featuring a wildly eclectic array of bright colours. In almost every way, the Hundertwasser House looks completely unlike the Carillon Tower I have just described. But the two structures are united in a significant way: they were built by tradespeople who took pride in their work.

The bricklayers who built Hundertwasser House were reported to have experienced creative freedom and sheer joy in constructing the edifices. As French art critic and cultural philosopher Pierre Restany (2003) observed, "The workers realized they were not the slaves of the grid system and of prefabrication. The bricklayers and tilers took individual initiatives that were in their reach, and became creative. … On Sundays they brought their families to show them the results of their labours" (p. 47). The bricks and tiles of the Hundertwasser House, the slabs of quartz and opal of the Carillon, the mud bricks of the Gertieanum, the roughly hewn logs of Scanlan's cabin—these materials were fashioned by human hands. In the making, something of the human spirit remains in the buildings, too. And that spirit invites us in—to dwell.

Dwelling Activities and Dwelling Tools

There is a school in Llanycefn, a village in Wales, called the Nant-y-Cwm Steiner Nursery. Of all of the school photographs and plans that I have shared with hundreds of people in the writing of this book, the photographs of this school are received with the most joy and enthusiasm. When people see the pathway leading up to the school door, their shoulders relax and they smile. They describe the school as inviting, safe, embracing, soft, earthy, and cosy. One teacher likened the school to a secret garden. Another teacher said she hoped to live in a place like this when she was older, "pottering about" in the garden. Photographs of the school's interior draw similar comments. Another teacher talked about how the room imbued a sense of gathering around the hearth, a feeling of belonging. She suggested that the room would tell its occupants, "We can easily do what we need to do here. We will look after this space, and it will look after us." Like many other examples I have cited in this book, this building, too, involved a number of self-build projects taken on by teachers and parents.

Contrast the responses to the Nant-y-Cwm Steiner Nursery to those made about a Kindergarten in Stuttgart—a Kindergarten I found, to my surprise, prominently featured in one of Mark Dudek's (2000) fine books. This is a school filled with oblique lines, and if we take the work of Rittelmeyer seriously, then it should come as no surprise that the building leaves most of the people I talked to with a sense of being unbalanced. The more polite and constrained observers called the building "chaotic and confusing," saying it had "too much line and angle" and "didn't look safe." Some commented that it would take them a while to approach the building, partly because it did not seem inviting, partly because they could not identify the entryway. A graduate student commented that it looked like a CIA installation of some sort and said that he would be nervous about going in there. One bold undergraduate student remarked: "Insofar as train wrecks inspire creativity, it is probably a fine learning space."

In talking with people about schools, I was struck, time and again, by how lay people's responses to school buildings primarily revolved around issues of warmth, balance, and beauty. They describe the schools they like as "warm" and the schools they don't like as "prison-like." The same was true for architects. Although architects, not surprisingly, also point to elements of structure and form, many of their initial comments are often also about warmth, balance, and beauty. In the schools described by lay people and teachers as "warm," the next comments invariably focused on what they would do there—such as "potter about in the garden," "read books," or "share meals around a table big enough for the entire class." These are dwelling activities that dwelling places naturally invoke.

In 1995, American educator and cultural critic Neil Postman argued that schools should teach children how to make a life, not how to make a living. In the same year, Clifford Stoll (1995) wrote a book called *Silicon Snake Oil: Second*

Thoughts on the Information Highway. In it he talked of daily life as being about cooking, driving, visiting, negotiating, eating, hiking, dancing, and gossiping, baking bread, playing touch football, piecing a quilt, building a stone wall, reciting a poem or saying a prayer—activities that do not require a computer or a digital network but are the activities that make up a large part of our lives. When I read Stoll's book, I was reminded of the time I lived and worked in a small fishing village in Sierra Leone, just a few years before civil strife ripped the country apart. I had no modern technology to speak of—even electricity was scarce. Every other day, I would walk a couple of miles to the market for fresh food. On the way, I met people from the village and the Milton Margai Teachers College, where I was working, and in what seemed to me, then, only casual conversations, we made plans for opening an arts centre. In the days between, I wrote, often by hand, producing papers and reports. The work was done without computers, without telephones, and without fax machines. It was the social network created in living a life that supported the intellectual work of the community.[34]

Even when I was writing this book—which involved hour upon hour of research with computers and using technological tools of every conceivable description—I still spent most of my waking hours away from the computer screen, in conversation with others, cooking meals, chopping wood at the cabin, and reading stories or making art with my children. These are dwelling activities: these are activities for life and they ought to be activities for school.

Dwelling activities require particular tools, and it is the work of Ivan Illich I find particularly helpful when thinking about tools. Ivan Illich—a 1970s critic of Western institutions—coined the term *convivial tools.* By convivial, he meant tools that could be easily used by many people, "as often or as seldom as desired, for the accomplishment of a purpose chosen by the user" (Illich, 1973, p. 23). Philip Jackson (1968), an American educator and philosopher, claims that chalkboards and textbooks have been good tools for teaching because they are simple, durable, flexible, and responsive. The chalkboard allows the teacher to write, draw, erase, and store materials for weeks on end, and the material can be diagrams, notes, assignments, or records of spontaneous class discussions. By Illich's reckoning, the chalkboard would be a convivial tool. Dutch architect Harman Hertzberger (1969) also thought about the role that tools and objects play in the education of a child. Resonating with the thoughts of Jackson and Illich, Hertzberger observed that things made for one purpose only suppress individuals because they dictate how the thing is to be used.

Illich gave hand tools as one example of convivial tools. A hammer, for example, can be just as convivial for ten-year-olds building birdhouses as it can be for adults building a shed or hanging art on their living room walls. Hammers require little skill at the entry level but become more useful as skill level increases. Hammers—whether purchased at lumber stores or fashioned by choosing the right kind of rock in the forest—are accessible. New uses for hammers are constantly being developed (often by enterprising four-year-olds).

---

[34] See also Todd Oppenheimer's (1999b) article titled *The Computer Delusion.*

Hammers are used to make things: objects of practicality or of beauty or both (Upitis, 1999).

Illich (1973) described two types of non-convivial tools: tools for expediency and tools that are malignant, manipulative and/or addictive. Of the latter type, Illich included multi-lane highways and—most interestingly for the purposes of the present discussion—compulsory school systems. These tools, he claimed, "increase dependence, exploitation, or impotence, and rob not only the rich but also the poor of conviviality" (p. 27).

While Illich called for the abolishment of malignant tools, he recognized the place for tools of expediency and suggested the need for a balance between tools of expediency and tools of conviviality. Tools of conviviality, I hasten to add, can also do harm—take, for example, the hammer, which can both build and destroy. The same can be said for tools for communication. In the best of worlds, e-mail and instant text messaging allow students to communicate freely with a whole host of friends without using the family phone. But for students who are bullied, threatened or harassed by others using interactive technologies of this type, the results can be devastating, leading to dropping out of school or even suicide. Principal Jordan Tinney (2005) of Claremont Secondary School in Saanich, British Columbia, claimed that 80% of the conflicts occurring at his secondary school involve cyberbullying in some way.

What about convivial school buildings? Presumably, convivial schools accommodate a multiplicity of dwellers, from the very young to the elderly, each engaged in purposeful work and involved in the creation of artifacts and ideas. Examples of convivial schools appear throughout this book, and it is this idea that I will now invoke to bring this book to a close.

Raising a School

Many of the images I have described in this book have been rural ones. I have spoken about mountains and hillsides, cabins and forests, chickens and guinea pigs, neighborhoods and villages, waterways and trees. In these contexts, one can imagine how schools can be created in concert with the natural environment, where the values of beauty, truth, and goodness can be honoured. But our future lies in sustainable, socially cohesive, and convivial cities. Architect Dolf Schnebli (1998) says that if we try to see how a city can be a good place for a child to grow up in, "we will start again to build cities for people to *live* in" (p. 14). He wrote about school buildings, in particular. He lamented that schools have been built on an increasingly larger scale for reasons of efficiency, and he made the sobering observation that the industrial language of the school "plant" has replaced the image of what used to be the school "house." He implored school designers to think about ways in which schools might thrive as smaller communities intersecting with larger urban centres, where children and old people might meet in natural ways, such as on the steps of an amphitheater-like plaza where informal meetings, community festivals, or political gatherings might occur. Schnebli—and Jane Jacobs, Nezar AlSayyad, Paul Downton, Kevin Lynch, Karen Malone and others—have called for the same thing: city living rich in social, cultural, and environmental dimensions. That means developing housing complexes that generate more electricity than they consume and use greywater to replenish their community gardens. It means creating roof gardens with native plantings, to attract back the birds and insects that fled our cities long ago. It means designing schools that function as communities within communities, supporting deep learning, learning that is truthful, beautiful and good.

I once heard Canadian First Nations architect Douglas Cardinal speak about how he had solved a structural design problem by spending an afternoon watching a spider weave its web. The building was the Canadian Museum of Civilization, an impressive structure that sits on the Ottawa River in Hull, Québec. Cardinal then spoke about the "magical power" that humans possess, that of creativity. "But," he admonished, "we operate from fear and we are so fearful we do not even take responsibility for our lives. We give responsibility away to others, to all the institutions that we have created, to groups and individuals that have a vested interest in keeping us small" (Cardinal, 2001, p. 41).

It is time for us to take responsibility for the schools we create, to seriously heed the notion that first we shape our schools, and afterwards our schools shape us. It is time to be anything but small. Schools ought to shape the ideas of the people who dwell in them in ever-expanding ways, leading students to unpredictable and creative encounters with ideas, with one another, and with the natural world. For it is only in encounters like these that students will receive the education they require for living both joyfully and responsibly.

Raising a school means creating a convivial school, a school where students can work and play, where they can sit comfortably as they engage in conversation, where they can prepare meals from food they have grown in the school's own gardens, where they can sew and carve, where they can read books and write and have access to resources of all kinds, where they can feel the afternoon sunlight on their shoulders, where they can ask hard questions and find ways to answer them, where they can be provoked by the challenges of nature and be calmed by its beauty, and where they can be warm and sheltered. Then we will have raised—at last—a school.

References

Abramson, P. (2006). The 11th Annual Construction Report. *School planning and management*. Retrieved September 14, 2006, from http://www.peterli.com/spm/resources/rptsspm.shtm

Abramson, P. (2007). The 12th Annual Construction Report. *School planning and management*. Retrieved May 12, 2008, from http://www.peterli.com/spm/resources/rptsspm.shtm

Adams, E. (1991). Back to basics: Aesthetic experience. *Children's Environments Quarterly, 8*(2), 19–29.

Alexander, C., Ishikawa, S., & Silverstein, M. (1977). *A pattern language: Towns, buildings, construction*. NY: Oxford University Press.

Allison, L. (2002). *The Value of Water: Inquiry into Australia's Management of Urban Water*. Report of the Senate Environment, Communications, Information Technology and the Arts References Committee. The Parliament of the Commonwealth Australia.

AlSayyad, N. (2004). *The end of tradition*. London, NY: Routledge.

Andersen, S. (1999). *The relationship between school design variables and scores on the Iowa Test of Basic Skills*. Unpublished doctoral dissertation, University of Georgia, Athens, GA.

Ardalan, N., & Bakhtiar, L. (1973). *The sense of unity: The Sufi tradition in Persian architecture*. Chicago: The University of Chicago Press.

Baker, K. (1998). Education construction projected to grow: School districts have aggressive expansion plans. *AI Architect*, April, 1998. Retrieved October 5, 2005, from http://www.e-architect.com/new/aiarchitect/apr98/education.asp

Bai, H. (2003). Learning from Zen arts: A lesson in intrinsic valuation. *Journal of the Canadian Association for Curriculum studies, 1*(2), 39–52. Retrieved on July 28, 2005, from http://www.csse.ca/CACS/JCACS/V1N2/jcacs-V1N2.html

Bandura, A., & Walters, R. H. (1963). *Social learning and personality development*. New York: Holt, Rinehart, & Winston.

Banham, R. (1996). *A critic writes: Essays by Reyner Banham*. Berkeley: University of California Press.

Bateson, G. (1972). *Steps to an ecology of mind: A revolutionary approach to man's understanding of himself*. NY: Ballantine Books.

Bateson, G. (1980). *Mind and nature: A necessary unity*. Toronto, ON: Bantam

Bateson, M. C. (1990). *Composing a Life*. NY: Plume Books.

Bateson, M. C. (1994). *Peripheral visions: Learning along the way*. NY: HarperCollins.

Barnard, H. (1848). *School Architecture*. Cincinnati, OH: H.W. Derby & Co.

Barnes, H. (1991). Learning that grows with the learner: An introduction to Waldorf education. *Educational Leadership, 49*(2), 52–54.

Bauman, Z. (2000). Social issues of law and order. *British Journal of Criminology, 40*, 205–221.

Beckstead, D. (1998). *Composers in electronic residence: Music, technology, and textual presence*. Unpublished doctoral dissertation, Simon Fraser University, Burnaby, British Columbia.

Belanger, J. August 3, 2005. School Bus Cuts Rile Parents: They Say the Decision Made Behind Closed Doors Will Kill After-Class Activities. *The London Free Press*. Retrieved August 9, 2005, from http://www.canoe.ca/NewsStand/LondonFreePress/News/2005/08/03/1157349-sun.html

Berner, M. M. (1992). Building conditions, parental involvement, and student achievement in the District of Columbia Public School System. *Urban Education, 28*(1), 6–29.

Berry, T. (1988). *The dream of the earth.* San Francisco: Sierra Club Books.

Berry, T. (1996). Ethics and ecology. *Paper presented to the Harvard Seminar on Environmental Values*, Harvard University, April 9, 1996.

Berry, W. (1981). *The gift of good land.* San Francisco: North Point Press.

Berry, W. (1983). *Standing by words.* San Francisco: North Point Press.

Bettelheim, B. (1976). *The uses of enchantment: The meaning and importance of fairy tales.* NY: Knopf.

Bigelow, W. (1996). How my schooling taught me contempt for the earth. *Rethinking schools, 11*(1), 14–17.

Bingler, S. (1995). Place as a form of knowledge. In A. Meek (Ed.). *Designing places for learning* (pp. 23–30). Alexandria, VA: Association for Supervision and Curriculum Development.

Bingler, S. (1998). E pluribus unum: The new American community school. *Mass Magazine: Architecture and Children, Learning Environments and Design Education, 11*(Fall) 9–11.

Bingler, S. (2001). *The School Construction News and Design Share Awards Commentary.* Retrieved October 20, 2004, from http://designshare.com/Awards/2001/Commentary.htm

Bingler, S. (2002). Designing public schools: A blueprint for success. *Connections, 9*(1), 14–16. Retrieved October 14, 2004, from http://www.concordia.com/files/designing_public_schools.doc

Black, R., Morris, S., & Boyce, J. (2003). Where and why are 10 million children dying every year? *The Lancet, 361*, 2226–2234.

Blundell-Jones, P. (1986). Forward. In Lucien Kroll *The Architecture of complexity.* (Peter Blundell-Jones, trans.). London: Batsford.

Blundell-Jones, P. (1999). Social engagement: Peter Hübner's design of the Waldorf school in Cologne Germany. *Architectural Review, February, 1999.*

Blundell-Jones, P. (2004). Human Hübner: Steiner school, Kirchheimunter Teck, Germany. *Architectural Review*, February, 2004, 44–51.

Blundell-Jones, P., Petrescu, D., & Till, J. (Eds.). (2005). *Architecture and participation.* Independence, KY: Spon Architecture Price Book.

Bogle, R. E., & Diamond, B. M. (2004). Schools as centers of community: A new approach to school design serves students and communities alike. *Learning by design.* Retrieved October 22, 2004 from http://www.asbj.com/lbd/2004/essay-schools-as-centers.html

Borgia, E. (1991). *Impressions of Reggio Emilia.* (ERIC Document Reproduction Service No. ED 338386).

Bortoft, H. (1996). The wholeness of nature: Goethe's way of science. Edinburgh: Floris Books.

Boss, S. (2001). Breaking out of the box, *Northwest Education Magazine, 6*(4). Retrieved October 22, 2004, from http://www.nwrel.org/nwedu/summer01/

Bowers, C. A. (1995). Educating for an ecologically sustainable culture: Rethinking moral education, creativity, intelligence, and other modern orthodoxies. Albany, NY: State University of New York Press.

Bowers, C. A. (2001). *Educating for eco-justice and community.* Athens, GA: The University of Georgia Press.

Boyle, C. (2004). *Sustainable buildings in New Zealand.* Unpublished manuscript, International Centre for Sustainability Engineering and Research, Auckland, NZ.

Bradley, J. (n.d.). Does the classroom assist or impede the learning process? *Canadian Language and Literacy Research Network Project*, University of Ottawa. Retrieved August 9, 2005, from http://www.cllrnet.ca/Docs/RESOURCES/Lay_paper_02_international-modified.pdf

Bradley, J. (2005). Does the classroom assist or impede the learning process? *Canadian Association of Principals Journal, 13*(1), 32–34.

Bradley, W. S. (1998). *Expecting the most from school design.* Unpublished manuscript, Thomas Jefferson Center for Educational Design, University of Virginia, Charlottesville. Retrieved on October 22, 2004 from http://curry.edschool.virginia.edu/class/edlp/800/papers/principles/principles.html

Brett, A., Moore, R. C., & Provenzo, E. F. (1993). *The complete playground book.* Syracuse, NY: Syracuse University Press.

Brosterman, N. (1996). *Inventing Kindergarten.* NY: Harry N. Abrams, Inc.

Broudy, H. S. (1972/1994). *Enlightened cherishing: An essay on aesthetic education.* Urbana: University of Illinois Press.

Brown, J. (2000). Goethe's science, History of Science Discussion Group, unpublished manuscript, Seattle, WA: University of Washington. Retrieved February 15, 2010, from http://worldroots.com/gitte/goethe1.htm

Brubaker, C. W. (1998). Lessons in high school planning and design. *MASS Magazine: Architecture and Children, Learning Environments and Design Education, 11* (Fall), 26–33.

Bruun, O., & Kalland, A. (Eds.) (1995). *Asian perceptions of nature: A critical approach.* Richmond, Surrey: Curzon Press.

Bullock, A. A., & Foster-Harrison, E. (1997). Making the best decisions: Designing for excellence. *Schools in the Middle, 7*(2), 37–39.

Burgess, G. (1996). Collaborative balance: Beyond the rhetoric. *Presented at the 1996 Convention of The Royal Australian Institute of Architects,* March, 1996, Adelaide, Australia, 61–64.

Burgess, G. (2004). The multiplicity of the whole. A. S. Hook address delivered at the University of Melbourne, July 16, 2004. *Architecture Australia,* November/December, 2004, 98–100.

Burgess, G. (2005). Unpublished convocation address upon receiving an honorary doctorate from the University of Melbourne, Melbourne, Australia.

Burriss, K. G., & Boyd, B. F. (Eds.) (2005). *Outdoor learning and play.* Olney, MD: Association for Childhood Education International.

Canizares, A., & J. Fajardo (Eds.). (2007). *Kindergarten, schools, and playgrounds.* Barcelona, Spain: Loft Publications.

Cannon, W. B. (1937). *The wisdom of the body.* NY: Norton.

Cantley, D. (1992). Aerodynamic school. *Progressive Architecture, 73,* 142–147.

Capra, F. (1984). *The turning point: Science, society, and the rising culture.* NY: Bantam Books.

Capra, F. (1996). *The web of life: New scientific understanding of living systems.* NY: Anchor Books.

Capra, F. (1998). Ecology and community. *Mass Magazine: Architecture and Children, Learning Environments and Design Education,* 33–40.

Capra, F. (2005). Speaking nature's language: Principles for sustainability. In M. K. Stone & Z. Barlow (Eds.), *Ecological literacy: Educating our children for a sustainable world* (pp. 18–29). San Francisco: Sierra Club Books.

Cardinal, D. (2001). Innovative architect says we must confront our fears as enlighten "spiritual warriors." In Richard I. Doyle (Ed.). *Renaissance II: Canadian Creativity and Innovation in the New Millennium* (pp. 38–47). Ottawa: National Research Council of Canada.

Carey, K. D. (2001). Hearing the public voice: Involving the community in school planning. *Learning by Design.* Retrieved October 22, 2004, from http://www.asbj.com/lbd/2001/inprint/public.html

Carlton, P. (1987). An interview with Eugene Goodrich, The Oral History of Principalship. Retrieved August 9, 2005, from http://scholar.lib.vt.edu/faculty_archives/principalship/g/104goodrich.html

Carson, R. (1962). *Silent spring.* Boston, MA: Houghton Mifflin Company.

Chan, T. C. (1980). *Physical environment and middle grade achievement.* Greenville, SC: Office of School Facilities Planning. (ERIC Document Reproduction Service No. ED 198645)

Chattin-McNichols, J. (1992). *The Montessori controversy.* Albany, NY: Delmar.

Cheesman, R. (1986). *Patterns in Perpetuity: New Towns in Adelaide, South Australia.* Adelaide: Thornton House.

Churchill, W. (1943). 28 October 1943 to the House of Commons (meeting in the House of Lords). Retrieved January 12, 2009, from http://www.winstonchurchill.org/i4a/pages/index.cfm?pageid=388#Shape_our_ Buildings

Clemmer, D. (1940). *The prison community.* NY: Holt, Reinhart, and Winston.

Clifford, A. J., & Takacs, C. (1993). *Maria Montessori schools of Cleveland follow-up study of urban center pupils years 1991 and 1992.* Retrieved July 14, 2004, from http://www.montesorri-namta.org/NAMTA/geninfo/rschsum.html

Cobble, J. E. (2000). The 100-Year School: How to design schools that will last a century. *Learning by Design,* Retrieved November 22, 2004, from http://www.asbj.com/lbd/2000/00inprint/00cobble.html

Cold, B. (1986). *Architecture as a Quality in the Learning and Teaching Process.* (ERIC Document Reproduction Service No. ED 284345)

Coles, R. (1969). Those places they call schools. *Harvard Educational Review, 39*(4), 46–57.

Cook, M. (2002, May 16). "Modest excellence" in architecture: Beautiful architecture needn't be "precious" or "extravagant" says the Governor General's Award panel in announcing 2002 winners, *The Ottawa Citizen,* p. A4.

Cook, M. (2005, April 23). A focused man: One of Canada's most talented architects is a master of designing buildings that are in dialogue with the landscape. *The Ottawa Citizen,* p. J12.

Corrigan, P. (2004). Room temperature: A tribute to Gregory Burgess. *Architecture Australia, 93*(2), 2004, 84.

Cosco, N., & Moore, R. C. (1999). Playing in place: Why the physical environment is important in playwork. *Paper presented at the 14th Play Education Annual Play and Human Development Meeting, Ely,* Cambridgeshire, UK, January 27–29, 1999. Retrieved on February 9, 2006, from http://www.naturallearning.org

Cox, D., McMaster, I., & Obuch, J. (1990). *Grounds for learning.* Surrey Hills, Victoria, Australia: Dellasta Pty Ltd.

Crumpacker, S. S. (1995). Using cultural information to create schools that work. In A. Meek (Ed.). *Designing places for learning* (pp. 31–42). Alexandria, VA: Association for Supervision and Curriculum Development.

Csikszentmihalyi, M. (1990). *Flow: The psychology of optimal experience.* NY: Harper & Row.

Cuito, A. (Ed.). (2001). *Kindergarten architecture.* Barcelona, Spain: Loft Publications.

Curtis, E. (2003). *School builders.* West Sussex, England: Wiley-Academy.

Daniell, K. A., Kingsborough, A. B., Malovka, D. J., Sommerville, H. C., Foley, B. A., & Maier, H. R. (n.d.). *Sustainability assessment of housing developments: A new methodology.* CABM-

HEMA-SMAGET. Retrieved June 18, 2005, from http://smaget.lyon.cemagref.fr/contenu/SMAGET%20proc/PAPERS/Daniell.pdf

d'Aquili, E., Laughlin, C., & McManus, J. (1979). *The spectrum of ritual: A biogenetic structural analysis.* NY: Columbia University Press.

Davis, B. (2004). Inventions of teaching: A genealogy. Mahwah, NJ: Lawrence Erlbaum Associates.

Davis, B., & Sumara, D. (2006). Complexity and education: Inquiries into learning, teaching, and research. Mahwah, NJ: Lawrence Erlbaum Associates.

Davis, B., Sumara, D., & Luce-Kapler, R. (2007). *Engaging minds: Learning and teaching in a complex world* (2nd ed.). Mahwah, NJ: Lawrence Erlbaum Associates.

Davis, B., & Upitis, R. (2004). Pending knowledge: On the complexities of teaching and learning. *Journal of Curriculum Theorizing, 20*(3), 113–128.

Davis, J., Smithrim, K., Anderson, M., Upitis, R., Ogden, H., Brook, J., Troop, M., & Peterson, A. (2009). If I Could Design My School: Students' Perceptions of Their Learning Spaces. *Paper presented at the Canadian Society for the Study of Education Annual Conference,* Ottawa, Ontario, May 23–26, 2009.

Day, C. W. (2000). Trends in School Design. *Learning by Design.* Retrieved October 22, 2004 from http://www.asbj.com/lbd/2000/00inprint/00day.html

Day, C. W. (2001). Rethinking school design. *Learning by Design.* Retrieved October 22, 2004 from http://www.asbj.com/lbd/2001/inprint/reviewers.html

de Botton, A. (2006). *The architecture of happiness.* NY: Pantheon Books.

Deforestation of Amazon is on the rise, *UN Wire,* June 26, 2003. Retrieved on December 12, 2005, from http://www.worldwatch.org/features/timeline/tlitems/14.htm

Dewey, J. (1933/1989). Utopian schools. In J. A. Boyston (Ed.), *Volume IX: The later works 1925–1952,* (pp. 136–140). Carbondale and Edwardsville: Southern Illinois University Press.

Dewey, J. (1900/1956). *The child and the curriculum and the school and society.* London: The University of Chicago Press.

Doelle, L. L. (1972). *Environmental acoustics.* NY: McGraw-Hill.

Dillard, A. (1974). *Pilgrim at Tinker Creek.* NY: Harper's Magazine Press.

Disaster Center (n.d.) United States Crime Rates. Retrieved January 12, 2009, from http://www.disastercenter.com/crime/uscrime.htm

Dissanayake, E. (1988). *What is art for?* Seattle, WA: University of Washington Press.

Dissanayake, E. (1998). *Homo Aestheticus: Where art comes from and why.* Seattle, WA: University of Washington Press.

Dovey, K. (2004). Art, community, environment, spirit: An appreciation of Gregory Burgess on the occasion of the A.S. Hook Address. *Architecture Australia, 93*(6), 101.

Downton, P. (2005). Inner city living. *Green Places, 15,* May, 2005, 26–28.

Driver, R., Asoko, H., Leach, J., Mortimer, E. F., & Scott, P. (1994). Constructing scientific knowledge in the classroom. *Educational Researcher, 23* (7), 5–12.

Driver, R., & Bell, B. (1986). Students' thinking and the learning of science: A constructivist view. *School Science Review* March, 443–456.

Dudek, M. (2000). *Kindergarten architecture: Space for the imagination* (2nd ed.). Independence, KY: Spon Press.

Dudek, M. (2002). *Architecture of schools: The new learning environments.* Oxford: Architecture Press.

Dudek, M. (2007). *Schools and Kindergartens: A design manual.* Basel, Switzerland: Birkhaeuser Verlag.

Duit, R. (1993). The constructivist view: A fashionable and fruitful paradigm for science education research and practice. In L. P. Steffe (Ed.) *Epistemological Foundations of Mathematical Experience* (pp. 124–159). NY: Springer-Verlag.

Economou, A. (1999). The symmetry lessons from Froebel's building Gifts. *Environment and Planning B: Planning and Design, 26,* 75–90.

Edwards, C. P. (2002). Three approaches from Europe: Waldorf, Montessori, and Reggio Emilia. *Early Childhood Research and Practice, 4*(1), 1–21. Retrieved December 22, 2004, from http://ecrp.uiuc.edu/v4n1/edwards.html

Edwards, C. P., Gandini, L., & Forman, G. (1993). *The hundred languages of children: The Reggio Emilia approach to early childhood education.* Norwood, NJ: Ablex.

Edwards, C. P., Gandini, L., & Forman, G. (1998). *The hundred languages of children: The Reggio Emilia approach – advanced reflections* (2nd ed.). Greenwich, CT: Ablex.

Ellen, R., Parkes, P., & Bicker, A. (2000). *Indigenous environmental knowledge and its transformations: Critical anthropological perspectives.* Amsterdam: Harwood Academic Publishers.

Everdell, W. R. (1997). *The first moderns.* Chicago, IL: University of Chicago Press.

Fensham, P. J., Gunstone, R., & White, R. (Eds.). (1994). *The content of science: A constructivist approach to its teaching and learning.* London: Falmer Press.

Fisher, T. (1995). Design as a form of inquiry. *Progressive Architecture, 76,* 52–61.

Fiske, E. B. (1995). Systemic school reform: Implications for architecture. In A. Meek (Ed.). *Designing places for learning* (pp. 1–10). Alexandria, VA: Association for Supervision and Curriculum Development.

Fleener, J. (2002). *Curriculum dynamics: Recreating heart.* NY: Peter Lang.

Fontanesi, G., Gialdini, M., & Soncini, M. (1998). The voice of parents: An interview with Lella Gandini. In C. Edwards, L. Gandini, & G. Forman (Eds.). *The hundred languages of children: The Reggio Emilia approach – Advanced reflections* (2nd ed., pp. 149–160). Greenwich, CT: Ablex.

Ford, A. (2007). *Designing the sustainable school.* Melbourne, Australia Images Publishing Group.

Fox Keller, E. (1983). *A feeling for the organism: The life and work of Barbara McClintock.* NY: W.H. Freeman & Co.

Frangos, A. (2003, November 10). More women design their way to the top. *The Wall Street Journal.*

Franklin, U. (1992). *The real world of technology.* Concord: Anasi.

Friedman, J. B. (2005, January). Thoreau's number and other measures: Value and visibility in humanism. *Paper presented at the 3rd International Conference of the Arts and Humanities,* Honolulu, HI. Retrieved January 31, 2005, from http://www.hichumanites.org

Friedman, T. L. (2008). *Hot, flat, and crowded: Why we need a green revolution and how it can renew America.* NY: Farrar, Straus, & Ciroux.

Frost, J. L. (1992). *Play and playscapes.* Albany, NY: Delmar Publishers.

Fulford, R. (1998, August 19). Canadian science writing undernourished, inferior. *The Globe and Mail.* Retrieved August 10, 2005 from The Globe and Mail via Factiva. http://global.factiva.com/en/arch/display.asp

Gale, F., & Gale, C. (1975). *Experiences with plants for young children.* Palo Alto, CA: Pacific Books Publishers.

Gale, F., & Gale, C. (1982). *Experiences with animals for young children.* Ann Arbor, MI: West Hawk Industries Publishers.

Gale, F., & Gale, C. (1984). *Experiences in the natural environment for young children.* Ann Arbor, MI: West Hawk Industries Publishers.

Gandini, L. (1998). Educational and caring spaces. In Edwards, C. P., Gandini, L., & Forman, G. (Eds.). *The hundred languages of children: The Reggio Emilia approach – advanced reflections* (2nd ed., pp. 161–178), Greenwich, CT: Ablex.

Gardner, H. (1999). *The disciplined mind: What all students should understand.* NY: Simon & Schuster.

Gibson, E. J., & Pick, A. D. (2000). *An ecological approach to perceptual learning and development.* London: Oxford University Press.

Gilliam, F. D., & Bates, S. N. (2001). Strategic frame analysis: Reframing America's youth. *Social Policy Report: Giving Child and Youth Development Knowledge Away, 15*(3), 3–6.

Giradet, H. (2003). Urban design as if people and planet mattered. In B. Fowles, M. Corcoran, H. Laz Erdel-Jan, S. Roaf, & F. Stevenson (Eds.). *Report of the UK Sustainability Special Interest Group (Architectural Education).* Cardiff: Cardiff University Centre for Education in the Built Environment. Cardiff, Cardiff University.

Gislason, N. (2009). *School design: History, case studies, and practice.* Unpublished doctoral dissertation, University of Toronto, Toronto, Ontario, Canada.

Gisolfi, P. (2004). The idea of campus, *Learning by Design: A School Leader's Guide to Architectural Services.* Retrieved on July 20, 2005, from http://www.asbj.com/lbd/2004/essay-the-idea-of-campus.html

Glasson, G. E., Frykholm, J. A., Mhango, N. A., & Phiri, A. D. (2006). Understanding the earth systems of Malawi: Ecological sustainability, culture, and place-based education. *Culture and Comparative Studies, 90*(4), 660–680.

Goad, P. (2004). One hundred years of discourse, *Architecture Australia,* January/February 2004.

Gradel, M. F. (2001). *Creating capacity: A framework for providing professional development opportunities for teaching artists.* Washington, D.C.: The John F. Kennedy Center for the Performing Arts. Retrieved October 22, 2004, from http://www.kennedy-center.org/education/partners/creating_capacity.html

Gradle, S. (2007). Spiritual ecology in art education: A re-vision of meaning. In L. Bresler (Ed.), *The international handbook of research in arts education* (pp. 1501–1516). NY: Springer.

Grover, S. (2004). *At-risk Female High School Students' Perspectives on Factors Affecting Their School Success.* Unpublished master's thesis, Queen's University, Kingston, Ontario, Canada.

Growing Schools. (n.d.). Retrieved on June 18, 2007, from http://www.schoolsgarden.org.uk

Guy, S. (1997). *Alternative developments: The social construction of green buildings.* Centre for Urban Technology, University of New Castle: Royal Institution of Chartered Surveyors.

Haeg, F. (2007). *Edible estates: Attack on the front lawn.* NY: Metropolis Books.

Haines, A. M. (2000). Montessori in early childhood: Positive outcomes among social, moral, cognitive, and emotional dimensions. *NAMTA Journal, 25*(2), 27–59.

Hamilton, L. (2000). *Cypress for farm industry.* State of Victoria, Australia Department of Primary Industries. Retrieved May 7, 2005, from http://www.dse.vic.gov.au/dpi/nreninf.nsf/LinkView/C9F2C1E148B28204CA256BCF000BBDE15F35DFAFEA9EE75E4A256DEA00276C0F

Hamann, C. (2004). Invitation to the dance. *Architecture Australia. 93*(2), 2004, 88–95.

Hart, R. (1987). Children's participation in planning and design: Theory, research and practice. In C. S. Weinstein, & T. G. David. (Eds.). *Spaces for children: The built environment and child development* (pp. 217–237). NY: Plenum.

Hart, R. (1993). Summer in the city. *International Play Journal, 1*(3).

Haslett, A. N. (n.d.). Properties and utilization of exotic specialty timbers grown in New Zealand. Part III: Cypresses. *FRI Research Bulletin 119.*

Hathaway, W. (1995). Effects of school lighting on physical development and school performance. *The Journal of Educational Research, 88*(4), 228.

Hawken, P., Lovins, A., & Lovins, L. H. (1999). *Natural capitalism.* Snowmass, CO: Rocky Mountain Institute.

Hawkins, D. (1965). Messing about in science. *Science and Children, 2*(5), 5–9.

Healy, J. (1990). *Endangered minds: Why children don't learn and what we can do about it.* NY: Simon & Schuster.

Henry, M. (1993). *School cultures.* Norwood: Ablex.

Herrington, S. (2001). Kindergarten: Garden pedagogy form romanticism to reform. *Landscape Journal, 20*(1), 30–47.

Hertzberger, H. (1969). Montessori Primary School in Delft, Holland. *Harvard Educational Review: Architecture and Education, 39*(4), 58–67.

Hill, F. (1997). Harmony in design: It's a people process. *Schools in the Middle, 7*(2), 34–36.

Holmes, W. (1946). Relating style of school architecture to the environment of a rural area. *The School Executive,* April 1946, 68–71.

Honeyman, D. S. (1998). The condition of America's schools. *School Business Affairs, 64*(1), 8–16.

Hosoda, H. (1998). A case history of a community school in Sendai, Japan. *Mass Magazine: Architecture and Children, Learning Environments and Design Education, 11* (Fall), 23–25.

Hübner, P. (2005). *Children make their school: Evangelische Gesamtschule Gelsenkirchen.* Stuttgart, Germany: Edition Axel Menges.

Hyer, T. (2001). Designing places for discovery, *Northwest Education Magazine, 6*(4). Retrieved October 22, 2004, from http://www.nwrel.org/nwedu/summer01/

Illich, I. (1973). *Tools for conviviality.* NY: Harper & Row.

Illich, I. (1984). Dwelling. *Co-Evolution Quarterly 41*(Spring), 22–27.

International Development Research Centre (n.d.) Retrieved July 28, 2005, from bulletin-dl@lyris.idrc.ca (also available at www.idrc.ca/en/ev-1-201-1-DO_TOPIC.html).

International Symposium on Environment, Behaviour, and Society (2006). Program Notes. Faculty of Architecture, University of Sydney, February 9–11, 2006, Sydney, Australia.

Jacobs, J. (1961/1984). *Death and life of great American cities.* Harmondsworth: Penguin.

Jackson, P. (1968). *Life in classrooms.* NY: Holt, Rinehart & Winston.

Jilk, B., Copa, G. H., & Pease, V. H. (1992). *Learning environment: An architectural interpretation of a new designs archetype high school.* National Center for Research in Vocational Education. (ERIC Document Reproduction Service No. ED 352518).

Johnson, S. (2001). *Emergence: The connected lives of ants, brains, cities, and software.* NY: Scribner.

Kaufmann, E. (1981). "Form became feeling": A new view of Froebel and Wright. *Journal of the Society of Architectural Historians, 40*(2), 130–137.

Keaney, B. (1993). *English in the school grounds.* Crediton, UK: Southgate.

Killeen, J. P., Evans, G. W., & Danko, S. (2003). The role of permanent student artwork in students' artwork in students' sense of ownership in an elementary school. *Environment and Behaviour, 35*(2), 250–263.

Kilpatrick, W. H. (1916). *Froebel's Kindergarten principles critically examined.* NY: MacMillan.

King, S. (1989). *Co-Design: A process of design participation.* NY: Van Nostrand Reinhold.

Kohn, A. (1992). *No contest.* NY: Houghton Mifflin.

Kollar, L. P. (1960). The architect and the spirit in man. *Architecture in Australia*, December, 1960, 99–102.

Kollar, L. P. (1985). On postmodern architecture. Research Paper No. 3. School of Architecture, The University of New South Wales, 1–8.

Kolleeny, J. (2003). K–12 Schools: As good as it gets. *Architectural Record, 191*(3), 131.

Korobacz, K. (2005). *Artesian springs: The impact of place on the education of children.* Unpublished manuscript, The University of New England, NSW, Australia.

Kraemer, J. (2003). The School Bus: Abundant Everywhere May Soon Be Gone. Retrieved August 9, 2005, from http://www.geocities.com/Heartland/Flats/3125/ata0302.htm

Kroll, L. (1986). *An architecture of complexity* (P. Blundell-Jones, trans.). London: Batsford Ltd.

Kronlid, D. (2003). *Ecofeminism and environmental ethics: An analysis of ecofeminist ethical theory.* Uppsala, Sweden. Uppsala University Library.

Küller, R., & Lindsten, C. (1992). Health and behavior of children in classrooms with and without windows. *Journal of Environmental Psychology, 12*, 305–317.

Lakoff, G., & Johnson, M. (1999). *Philosophy in the flesh: The embodied mind and its challenge to Western thought.* NY: Basic Books.

Lamm, Z. (1986). The architecture of schools and the philosophy of education. *Paper presented at the Edusystems 2000 International Congress on Educational Facilities, Values, and Contents,* Jerusalem, Israel, November 16–21, 1986. (ERIC Document Reproduction Service No. ED 283287)

Lane, B. (2004). Light but sure touch. *The Australian*, p. 1. Retrieved July 20, 2005, from http://www.theaustralian.news.com.au/common/story_page/0,5744,9159560%255E276 46,00.html

Lave, J., & Wenger, E. (1991). *Situated learning: Legitimate peripheral participation.* Cambridge, UK: Cambridge University Press.

Leacock, S. (1922/1961). *My discovery of England.* Toronto: McClelland & Stewart Ltd.

LeCuyer, A. (1992). Native wit. *Architectural Review, 193*, 47–52.

Lee, R. (n.d.) About the Shakuhachi. Retrieved June 6, 2005, from http://www.rileylee.net/biography.html

Leuthold, S. (1998). *Indigenous aesthetics: Native art, media, and identity.* Austin: University of Texas Press.

Lezotte, L. W., & Passalacqua, J. (1978). *Individual school buildings do account for differences in measured pupil performance.* (ERIC Document Reproduction Service No. ED 164695).

Lightman, A. (2005). *A sense of the mysterious: Science and the human spirit.* NY: Pantheon Books.

Loeffler, M. H. (1992). *Montessori in Contemporary American Culture.* Portsmouth, NH: Heinemann.

Lovelock, J. (1987). *Gaia: A new look at life on earth.* Oxford: Oxford University Press.

Lovins, A. (1991). If it's not efficient, it's not beautiful. *Fine Homebuilding, 66*, 4. Newtown, CT: The Taunton Press.

Lucas, B., & Mountfield, A. (1995). *A guide to fundraising for school grounds.* Winchester, Hampshire, UK: Learning Through Landscapes Trust.

Luckiesh, M., & Moss, F. (1940). Effects of classroom lighting upon educational progress and visual welfare of school children. *Illumination Engineering, 35*, 915–938.

Luke, D. (1964). *Goethe: Selected verse.* NY: Penguin.

Lynch, K. (1977). *Growing up in cities.* Cambridge, MA: MIT Press.

MacCormac, R. (1974). Froebel's Kindergarten Gifts and the early work of Frank Lloyd Wright. *Environment and Planning, 1*, 29–50.

Malone, K. (2001). Children, youth and sustainable cities. *Local Environment, 6(1),* 5–12.

Margulis, L., & Sagan, D. (1997). *Slanted truths: Essays on Gaia, symbiosis, and evolution.* NY: Copernicus.

Matsunobu, K. (2007). Japanese spirituality and music practice: Art as self-cultivation. In L. Bresler (Ed.), *The international handbook of research in arts education* (pp. 1425–1437). NY: Springer.

Maturana, H., & Varela, F. (1987). *The tree of knowledge: The biological roots of human understanding.* Boston: Shambala.

Mazzone, A. B. (1995). *"Islands of culture": Waldorf (Rudolf Steiner) schools in Australia – their origin and development.* A project submitted in partial fulfillment of the requirements of the degree of Master of Educational Studies at the University of Adelaide.

McKay, D. (2001). *Vis à vis: Fieldnotes on poetry and wilderness.* Wolfville, Nova Scotia: Gaspereau Press.

Meek, A. (1995a). Crow Island School: 54 years young. In A. Meek (Ed.). *Designing places for learning* (pp. 51–58). Alexandria, VA: Association for Supervision and Curriculum Development.

Meek, A. (1995b) (Ed). *Designing places for learning.* Alexandria, VA: Association for Supervision and Curriculum Development.

Miller, D. (1995). *Goethe: Scientific studies* (2nd ed.). Princeton: Princeton University.

Miller, J. P. (1996). *The holistic curriculum.* Toronto: OISE Press.

Miller, L. B., & Bizzell, R. P. (1983). Long-term effects of four preschool programs: Sixth, seventh, and eighth grades. *Child Development, 54,* 727–741.

Mitchell, M. (2009). *Complexity: A guided tour.* Oxford, U.K.: Oxford University Press.

Mock, E. (1944). (Ed.). *Built in the USA: 1932–1944.* NY: Museum of Modern Art.

Moore, G. T., & Lackney, J. A. (1993). School design: Crisis, educational performance and design applications. *Children's Environments, 10,* 99–112.

Moore, R. C., & Cosco, N. G. (n.d.) *Developing an Earth-Bound Culture Through Design of Childhood Habitats.* Unpublished manuscript. Retrieved on February 9, 2006, from http://www.naturallearning.org

Moore, R. C., & Wong, H. H. (1997). *Natural learning: Creating environments for rediscovering nature's way of teaching.* Berkeley, CA: MIG Communications.

Mueller, B. (1952). *Goethe's botanical writings.* Honolulu: University of Hawaii Press.

Muir, M. (2001). A model program in a remodeled building, *Northwest Education Magazine, 6(4).* Retrieved October 17, 2004, from http://www.nwrel.org/nwedu/summer01/

Mumford, L. (1939). *The social responsibilities of teachers.* Presented to the Bennington Planning Conference of the American Council of Education, August, 1939.

Mumford, L. (1946). *Values for survival: Essays, addresses, and letters on politics and education.* NY: Harcourt, Brace & Co.

Mumford, L. (1975). Architecture as a home for man. In J. Davern (Ed.). *Architecture as a home for man: Essays for Architectural Record.* NY: Architectural Record.

Mumford, L. (1986). *The Lewis Mumford reader.* NY: Pantheon.

Munby, H., Hutchinson, N., & Chin, P. (2000). "I know how to do it": Research priorities for co-operative and career education in Canada's secondary schools. In Lenoir, Y., Hunter, W., Hodgkinson, D., de Broucker, P. & Dolbec, A. (Eds.). *A pan-Canadian education research agenda* (pp. 37–54). Ottawa, ON: Canadian Society for the Study of Education.

Murphy, J. M. (2003). Findings from the evaluation study of the Edible Schoolyard. Report to The Center for Ecoliteracy, Berkeley, CA.

Nakagawa, Y. (2000). *Education for awakening: An Eastern approach to holistic education.* Brandon, VT: Foundation for Educational Renewal.

Nair, P. (2002). But are they Learning? School Buildings—The Important Unasked Questions. *Paper presented at the International Workshop on Educational Infrastructure,* Guadalajara, Mexico, Feb, 2002. Retrieved October 22, 2004, from http://www.designshare.com/Research/Nair/Are_They_Learning.htm (ERIC Document Reproduction Service No. ED 464479)

Nair, P., & Fielding, R. (2005). *The language of school design: Design patterns for 21st century schools.* Minneapolis: DesignShare.

Nair, P., Fielding, R., & Lackney, J. (2010). *The language of school design: Design patterns for 21st century schools (2nd ed.).* Minneapolis: DesignShare.

Naydler, J. (Ed.). (1996). *Goethe on science.* Edinburgh: Floris Books.

New, R. (2000). *Reggio Emilia: Catalyst for change and conversation.* Champaign, IL: ERIC Clearinghouse on Elementary and Early Childhood Education. ED447971.

Newburg, A., d'Aquili, E., & Rause, V. (2001). *Why God won't go away: Brain science and the biology of belief.* NY: Ballantine.

Noddings, N. (1992). *The challenge to care in schools: An alternative approach to education.* NY: Teachers College Press.

Noddings, N. (2007). War, violence, and peace in the arts. In L. Bresler (Ed.). *The International Handbook on Arts Education.* (pp. 1021–1030). Dordrecht, The Netherlands: Springer.

Oberlin College. (2005). Adam Joseph Lewis Center for Environmental Studies at Oberlin College. Retrieved on February 22, 2005, from http://www.oberlin.edu/

Oberman, I. (1997). Waldorf History: Case Study of Institutional Memory. *Paper presented at the Annual Meeting of the American Educational Research Association,* Chicago, IL, March 24–28, 1997.

Olds, A. R. (2001). *Childcare design guidelines.* NY: McGraw-Hill.

Oppenheimer, T. (1999a). Schooling the imagination. *Atlantic Monthly, 284*(3), 71–83.

Oppenheimer, T. (1999b). The computer delusion. *Atlantic Monthly, 280*(1), 45–62.

O'Reilley, M. R. (1993). *The peaceable classroom.* Portsmouth, NH: Heinemann.

Organization for Economic Co-operation and Development. (2008). *OECD factbook 2008: Economic, environmental and social statistics.* Retrieved May 5, 2008, from http://ocde.p4.siteinternet.com/publications/doifiles/08-01-01-g1.xls

Orr, D. W. (1992). *Ecological literacy: Education and the transition to a postmodern world.* Albany, NY: SUNY.

Orr, D. W. (1999). Reassembling the pieces: architecture as pedagogy. In Steven Glazer (Ed.). *The heart of learning: Spirituality in education* (pp. 139–149). NY: Penguin.

Paley, V. G. (1997). *The girl with the brown crayon.* Cambridge, MA: Harvard University Press.

Papert, S. (1993). *The children's machine: Rethinking school in the age of the computer.* NY: Basic Books.

Parken, D., Jahn, G., Andresen, B., Landorf, C., & Goad, P. (2004). RAIA gold medalist 2004 Greg Burgess. *Architecture Australia, 93*(2), 82–86.

Patkau School Lauded, (2002, May 20). *The Province,* p. A14.

Patteson, A. (2004). *Present moments, present lives: Teacher transformation through art-making.* Unpublished doctoral dissertation, Queen's University, Kingston, Ontario.

Patteson, A., Upitis, R., & Smithrim, K. (2002). *Sustainable Teacher Development In and Through the Arts.* Proceedings of the International Society for Education Through Art 31st World Congress, New York City, August, 2002.

Patteson, A., Upitis, R., & Smithrim, K. (2005). *Learning Through the Arts: Five year longitudinal study, Regina, Saskatchewan*. Toronto: The Royal Conservatory of Music.

Perez, P. & Batten, D. (Eds.) (2006). *Complex science for a complex world: Exploring human ecosystems with agents*. Canberra, Australia: Australian National University Press.

Peters, P. (2003). Here for the children. *Texas Architect, 53*(1), 22–25.

Peterson, A. & Upitis, R. (2009). Picturing Meaning: A Case Study of Icelandic Secondary School Architecture. *Paper presented at the American Educational Research Association Annual Conference,* San Diego, CA, April 13–17, 2009.

Plummer, H. (2003). Rudolf Steiner: Goetheanum. In Henri Purama (Ed.). *Masters of light: Twentieth century pioneers* (pp. 254–257). Tokyo: E ando Yu.

Plympton, P., Conway, S., & Epstein, K. (2000). Daylighting in schools: Improving student performance and health at a price schools can afford. *Paper presented at the American Solar Energy Society Conference,* Madison, Wisconsin, June 16, 2000.

Postman, N. (1995). *The end of education: Redefining the value of school.* NY: Alfred A. Knopf.

Powell, K. (2004). The apprenticeship of embodied knowledge in a Taiko drumming ensemble. In Liora Bresler (Ed.). *Knowing bodies, moving minds: Towards embodied teaching and learning* (pp. 183–195). Dordrecht: Kluwer Academic Publishers.

Putnam, R. (2000). *Bowling alone: The collapse and revival of the American community.* NY: Simon Schuster.

Raab, R. (1980). Rudolf Steiner as architect. *Architectural Association Quarterly, 12*(3), 48–55.

Rainforest Information Centre Educational Supplement. (1991). Lismore: The Australian Rainforests Memorandum. Retrieved on June 27, 2007, from http://www.rainforestinfo.org.au/background/rainfwld.htm

Raintree Nutrition. (2007). The Disappearing Rainforests. Retrieved on June 27, 2007, from http://www.rain-tree.com/facts.htm

Reicher, D. (2000). *Nature's design rules: Leading the way toward energy-efficient schools.* Learning by Design: A lesson in excellence. Retrieved October 22, 2004, from http://www.asbj.com/lbd/2000/00inprint/00reicher.html

Reitzes, L. B. (1998). Review of the book Kindergarten architecture: Space for the imagination. *Journal of Society of Architectural Historians, 57,* 477–480.

Restany, P. (2003). *The power of art: Hundertwasser, the painter with five skins.* Köln, Germany: Taschen.

Rhydderch-Evans, Z. (1993). *Mathematics in the school grounds.* Crediton, UK: Southgate.

Rice, A. H. (1953). What research knows about color in the classroom. *Nation's Schools, 52*(5), 1–8.

Riley-Taylor, E. (2002). *Ecology, spirituality and education: Curriculum for relational knowing.* New York: Peter Lang.

Rittelmeyer, C. (1992). Healthy schools. *Paper presented at the International Seminar organized by the Austrian Federal Ministry of Education and Art, the Austrian Institute for School and Sports Facilities, and the Organisation for Economic Cooperation and Development (OECD) Programme on Educational Building,* Vienna, Austria, October 5–8, 1992. (ERIC Document Reproduction Service No. ED 355646).

Rittner-Heir, R. M. (2002). Color and light in learning. *School Planning and Management, 41*(2), 57–58, 60–6.

Romney, B. (1975). *The Effects of Windowless Classrooms on the Cognitive and Affective Behavior of Elementary School Students.* (ERIC Document Reproduction Service No. ED 126622)

Rothenberg, J. (1989). The open classroom reconsidered. *The Elementary School Journal, 90*(1), 68–86.

Rubin, J. S. (1989). The Froebel-Wright Kindergarten connection: A new perspective. *The Journal of the Society of Architectural Historians, 48*(1), 24–37.

Ryan, J, C. (1992). Worldwatch paper #108: Life support: Conserving biological diversity. Retrieved on July 22, 2005, from http://www.worldwatch.org

Sawin, J. (2005). Climate change indicators on the rise. Retrieved on July 22, 2005, from http://www.worldwatch.org

Scanlan, L. (2004). *Harvest of a quiet eye: The cabin as sanctuary.* Toronto: Viking.

Schafer, R. M. (1977). *The tuning of the world.* Toronto: Random House.

Schnebli, D. (1998). Environments for children. *Mass Magazine: Architecture and Children, Learning Environments and Design Education,* 12–17.

Seamon, D., & Zajonc, A. (Eds.). (1998). *A phenomenology of nature.* Albany, NY: SUNY Press.

Shepherd, R. (1999). Crow Island School. Retrieved July 28, 2005, from http://rogershepherd.com/WIW/solution5/crow1.html

Sherman, L. (2001). Lighting the way to learning, *Northwest Education Magazine, 6*(4).

Shields, C. (2001). Afterword. In Shields, C. & Anderson, M. (Eds.). *Dropped threads* (pp. 343–347). Toronto: Random House.

Sloan, J. L. (2002). Frank Lloyd Wright's "light screens" and the Froebel Kindergarten. *Chicago Architectural Journal, 10,* 68–73.

Smithrim, K., & Upitis, R. (2004). Music for life: Contaminated by peaceful feelings. In L. R. Bartel (Ed.). *Questioning the music education paradigm* (pp. 74–86). CMEA Biennial Series, Research to Practice, Volume II, L. R. Bartel, Series Editor. Toronto: The Canadian Music Educators' Association.

Stairs, A. (1994). Indigenous ways to go to school: Exploring many visions. *Journal of Multilingual and Multicultural Development, 15*(10), 63–76.

Statistics Canada (n.d.) Crime Statistics. Retrieved January 12, 2009, from http://www.statcan.gc.ca/daily-quotidien/040728/dq040728a-eng.htm

Stedman, R. C. (2003). Is it really just a social construction? The contribution of the physical environment to sense of place. *Society and Natural Resources, 16,* 671–685.

Steiner Farm School. (1979). *Rudolf Steiner Farm School, Hawthorne Valley.* Ghent, NY: Steiner Farm School.

Steiner, R. (Ed.). (1921). *Goethe. Naturwissenschaftliche Schriften.* Stuttgart: Union Deutsche Verlagsgesellschaft.

Stine, S. (1997). *Landscapes for learning: Creating outdoor environments for children and youth.* NY: John Wiley & Sons.

Stoll, C. (1995). *Silicon snake oil: Second thoughts on the information highway.* NY: Doubleday Books.

Stone, M. (2007). Educating for Sustainability at Marin Academy. Retrieved on June 24, 2007, from http://www.ecoliteracy.org/

Stormshak, E. A., Kaminski, R. A., & Goodman, M. R. (2002). Enhancing the parenting skills of Head Start families during the transition to Kindergarten, *Prevention Science, 3*(3), 223–234.

Swentzell, R. (1992). *Children of play: A family of Pueblo potters.* Minneapolis, MN: Lerner Publications.

Swentzell, R. (1998). Learning is being alive. *Mass Magazine: Architecture and children, learning environments and design education,* 11(Fall), 7–8.

Tanner, T. (1980). Significant life experiences. *Journal of Environmental Education, 11*(4), 20–24.

Tanner, C. K. (2000). The influence of school architecture on academic achievement. *Journal of Educational Administration, 38*(4), 309–330.

Tanner, C. K., & Andersen, S. (2002). Toward a pattern language theory of middle school design. *Educational Planning, 13*(3), 3–20.

Tanner, C. K., & Lackney, J. (2006). *Educational facilities planning: Leadership, architecture, and management.* NY: Pearson Education, Inc.

Tanner C. K., & Langford, A. (2003). *The importance of interior design elements as they relate to student outcomes.* Dalton, GA: Carpet and Rug Institute. (ERIC Document Reproduction Service No. ED 478177).

Tapscott, D. (1997). *Growing Up Digital: The Rise of the Net-Generation.* NY: McGraw-Hill Ryerson.

Tarr, P. (2001). *Aesthetic code in early childhood classrooms: What art educators can learn from Reggio Emilia.* Minneapolis, MN: Design Share, Inc. Retrieved October 22, 2004 from http://www.designshare.com/Research/Tarr/Aesthetic_Codes_1.htm

Taylor, A. (1995a). Physical environments do affect learning and behavior of students. *Journal of the School of Architecture and Planning, 9*(1), 46–54.

Taylor, A. (1995b). How schools are redesigning their space. In A. Meek (Ed.). *Designing places for learning.* (pp. 67–76). Alexandria, VA: Association for Supervision and Curriculum Development.

Thomas, G. (1993). *Science in the school grounds.* Crediton, UK: Southgate.

Thomson, S. (1999). Advocacy in the arts: A Canada Council perspective. In B. Hanley (Ed.). *Leadership, advocacy, communication: A vision for arts education in Canada* (pp. 137–144). Summary of Proceedings of the National Symposium on Arts Education. Victoria: The Canadian Music Educators Association.

Thoreau, H. D. (1886). *Walden.* London: W. Scott Ltd.

Tinney, J. (2005). e-Bullying: Implications for schools. Adminfo: Journal of the British Columbia Principals' and Vice-Principals' Association. Retrieved October 4, 2005, from http://www.bcpvpa.bc.ca/adminsfo/Articles00405/jtinney0405.pdf

Totterdell, P. (n.d.). *Plan for the Promotion and Implementation of Waterharvesting.* Clearwater Environmental Design Business Plan. Downer, Australia.

Totterdell, P. (2004). *Blue Lake.* Unpublished manuscript, Canberra, Australia.

Tomasello, M. (2000). *The cultural origins of human cognition.* Cambridge, MA: Harvard University Press.

Trancik, A., Evans, G. (1995). Spaces fit for children: Competency in the design of day care center environments. *Children's Environments, 12,* 311–319.

Trends in International Math and Science Studies (n.d.). Retrieved January 23, 2009, from http://nces.ed.gov/timss/

Uline, C. L. (1997). School architecture as a subject of inquiry. *Journal of School Leadership, 7*(2), 194–209.

UNICEF (1996). Children's rights and habitat. Retrieved on March 14, 2006, from http://www.childfriendlycities.org/pdf/habitat_cfc.pdf

United Nations Economic Commission for Europe (n.d.). Retrieved March 14, 2005, from http://www.unece.org/

United Nations Food and Agriculture Organization (FAO), Deforestation continues at a high rate in tropical areas: FAO calls upon countries to fight forest crime and corruption. Press release, Rome: 3 October 2001.

Unique Saanich school wins architecture award, May 20, 2002, *Victoria Times Colonist,* p. B3.

Upitis, R. (1990). *This too is music.* Portsmouth, NH: Heinemann.

Upitis, R. (1999). The impact of information technology on education: Possibilities for the coming millennium as seen through an artist's eye. In R. Boyce (Ed.). *Policy Implications for Information Technology* (pp. 153–172). Montreal: McGill-Queen's Press.

Upitis, R. (2001). Spheres of influence: The interplay between music research, technology, heritage, and music education. *International Journal of Music Education, 37*(1), 44–58.

Upitis, R. (2003). In praise of romance. *Journal of the Canadian Association of Curriculum Studies* 1(1), 53–66.

Upitis, R. (2009). Complexity and design: How school architecture influences learning. *DESIGN Principles & Practices: An International Journal, 3*(2), 123–134.

Upitis, R., Davis, J., Smithrim, K., Anderson, M., Upitis, R., Ogden, H., Brook, J., Troop, M., & Peterson, A. (in press). If I Could Design My School: Students' Perceptions of Their Learning Spaces. *UNESCO Observatory on Multi-Disciplinary Research in the Arts.*

Uyechi, L. (1995). University *Taiko*: Roots and Evolution. *Paper presented at the Symposium on North American Taiko,* Stanford University.

Valentine, J., Wilson, O., Halstead, M., Dodd, G., McGunningle, K., Hellioer, A., & Wood, J. (n.d.). *Classroom acoustics – A New Zealand perspective.* Unpublished paper available from Marshall Day Acoustics and the National Audiology Centre. Retrieved on April 20, 2005, from http://www.marshallday.com/downloads/8_ Classroom_Acoustics_A_New_Zealand_Perspective.pdf

van Matre, S. (1990). *Earth education: A new beginning.* Cedar Cove, WV: The Institute for Earth Education.

Varela, F. J., Thompson, E. & Rosch, E. (1993). *The embodied mind: Cognitive science and human experience.* Cambridge, MA: MIT Press.

Vygotsky, L. (1934/1978). *Mind in society: The development of higher psychological progress.* Cambridge: Harvard University Press.

Walsh, D. (2004). Frog boy and the American monkey: The body in Japanese early schooling. In L. Bresler (Ed.). *Knowing bodies, moving minds: Towards embodied teaching and learning* (pp. 97–111). Dordrecht: Kluwer Academic Publishers, p. 97.

Walsh, E. May 10, 2003. Area Schools' Budgets Bad, Could Get Worse. *North County Times.* Retrieved August 9, 2005, from http://www.nctimes.com/articles/2003/05/11export10233.txt

Ward, R. (1998). School designs suffer with B.C. budget cuts: Education Minister Paul Ramsey says the design of schools doesn't matter any more—their cost does, April 8, 1998, *The Vancouver Sun*, p. C4.

Ward, B., & Dubos, R. (1972). *Only one earth.* NY: W. W. Norton.

Waters, A. (2003). Slow food, slow schools: Transforming education through a school lunch curriculum. Retrieved on March 13, 2005, from http://www.edibleschoolyard.org/alice_message.html

Wells, M. (1982). *Gentle architecture.* NY: McGraw-Hill.

Wells, M. (1992). Upside-down architecture. *Fine Homebuilding, 73,* 4. Newtown, CT: The Taunton Press.

Wente, M. (2004). *An accidental Canadian: Reflections on my home and (not) native land.* Toronto: HarperCollins.

Westerkamp, H. (1980). *The new Museum of Anthropology in Vancouver: An acoustic dump.* Retrieved on April 20, 2005, from http://www.sfu.ca/~westa/writings/acousticdump.html

Whitehead, A. N. (1929). *The aims of education.* NY: Free Press.

Wilson, S. (1967). The "Gifts" of Friedrich Froebel. *American Society of Architectural Historians, 26*(4), 238–241.

Wilson, S. (1969). Early educational reformers and contemporary architectural education. *Architectural Science Review, December, 1969,* 99–104.

Wilson, W. R. (n.d.) *Central Algoma Secondary. School crises in the making.* Sault Ste. Marie, Ontario: Central Algoma Board of Education.

Wisniewski, R. (1998). Beginning professors and college reform. In A. L. Cole, E. Rosebud, & J. G. Knowles (Eds.). *The heart of the matter: Teacher educators and teacher education reform* (pp. 387–396). San Francisco: Caddo Gap Press.

Wood, C. (2005). The value of play as a developmental mechanism in pre- and early adolescence. In K. G. Burriss & B. F. Boyd (Eds.). *Outdoor learning and play* (pp. 71–76). Olney, MD: Association for Childhood Education International.

Wright, F. L. (1943). *Frank Lloyd Wright – An autobiography.* NY: Duel, Sloan and Pearce.

Yarbrough, K. A. (2001). *The relationship of school design to academic achievement of elementary school children.* Unpublished doctoral dissertation, University of Georgia. (ERIC Document Reproduction Service No. ED 475272)

Acknowledgments

A book with a single author named on the cover belies the fact that there is no book—or building, for that matter—created by an individual. A number of people have helped raise this book. I owe much to them all.

It is my good fortune to work with many sensitive and wise colleagues both at my home institution, Queen's University, and at sister institutions in Canada, the United States, and Australia. My closest colleague and friend, Katharine Smithrim, is owed special thanks. I also collaborate with exceptionally hard-working and insightful graduate students, several of whom made important contributions to this work. I extend sincere thanks to Marie Anderson, Julia Brook, Christine Chapman, Jennifer Davis, Jordana Garbati, Scott Hughes, Roseann Kerr, Holly Ogden, Anna Peterson, and Meagan Troop, among others.

This book was enriched by conversations I have enjoyed (and occasionally have been troubled by) with teachers, administrators, architects, students, parents, builders, tradespeople, gardeners, artists, and other people intimately associated with educational communities. Many of these people I number as lifelong friends. In particular, I thank Rachel Alves, Annie Ball, Paul Barnett, Mark Baxter, Bronwyn Bellemore, Yvette Breytenbach, Gregory Burgess, Jamie Campbell, Rob Cheesman, Ian Cleworth, Deborah Crisp, CJ Dalton, Paul Downton, Angela Elster, David Jacobson, Alex Keats, Gracie Kelly, Gary Kembel, Margaret King, Stanley King, Konrad Korobasz, Harald Lehmann, Rebecca Luce-Kapler, Serena Manson, Callista Markotich, Robin Moore, James Morrison, John Patkau, Ann Patteson, Eileen Phillips, Lynn Rainboth, Jane Rodgers, Larry Scanlan, Barbara Schreiner, June Simonson, Paul Stapleton, Paul Totterdell, Kim Turnbull, Libbi Turner, Helen Tyas Tunggal, Lyn Walker, Samara Warren, Wendy Warren, John Webber, Jennifer West, John Whisson, and Lynda Wilde. I am sure there are names I have missed.

Other friends and colleagues supported me personally and helped develop this book in concrete ways. I am indebted to those who provided translations, read the manuscript in its many stages, and gave encouragement when I needed it most. I owe the deepest thanks to Philip Abrami, David Murphy Haglund, and Helen Turnbull.

I want to give special recognition to my husband, Gary Rasberry, and our children, Zinta Upitis and Hayden Rasberry, for their unfailing faith in "the book." Their insightful observations about how schools influence our lives are contained throughout the volume you now hold in your hands. I also thank my parents, Zigfrids Reinholds Upitis and Valda Daila Upitis, for teaching me that being engaged in learning is one of life's great pleasures.

Index

Aboriginal teachings, 14, 68, 132, 134–136, 180

Aesthetic value, x, 14, 52, 84, 92, 119

African schools, 178

Air quality, 160, 166, 169

Alexander, Christopher (architect), 79–80, 86, 99, 146

American schools, ix, x, 1–5, 10–11, 13, 16, 29, 47, 49, 77, 81, 83–84, 97, 115–116, 121–122, 129, 146, 148–149, 152–153, 156–157, 164, 167, 169

Animals in schools, 40, 82, 85, 129, 150–151, 167–168, 170–171, 174

Apprenticeships, 91, 98, 100, 105

Architectural drawings, 27, 30, 38, 39

Architecture as teacher, 3, 8–10, 12, 16, 20, 123, 138

Artistic expression, 21–22, 38, 46, 48, 53, 57, 92

Arts teaching, 23–24, 51–52, 82–83, 85, 93, 97, 105, 112, 169. *See also music teaching, dance*

Assessment methods
   Documentation and observation, 24, 112–113
   Reflective practice, 113
   Standardized, 112

Australian schools, x, 1, 9–10, 13, 18, 25–26, 29, 31, 34, 58–60, 73, 82–88, 99–100, 114, 118–119, 122, 125, 131–134, 141, 145–146, 156, 158, 164, 170, 173–174, 191

Ball, Annie (playground designer), 56–59, 63, 144

Barnett, Paul (architect), 14–16, 80, 88, 119–122

Bateson, Gregory (anthropologist), 6–7

Bellemore, Bronwyn (architect and teacher), 11, 31–32

British schools, 10–11, 48–49, 152

Building costs, 1, 17, 109, 117–118

Burgess, Gregory (architect), 15, 21, 34–37, 42, 68, 88–89, 120–121, 156

Campus, 29, 95, 99–100, 118, 127, 156, 163, 169–170, 173

Canadian schools, x, 7, 10, 18, 34, 43, 74, 81, 85–87, 98–99, 129, 134–139, 153–154, 173

Capra, Fritjof (scientist), 67–70, 74, 139, 150, 173

Caring for objects, 54–55

Carpentry, x, 22, 28, 155, 174. *See also skilled trades*

Cheesman, Rob (architect), 30, 73, 80, 99–100, 117, 145

Cologne Waldorf School, 37–38, 173

Colour, 2, 14, 20, 38, 46, 57, 68, 71–73, 88, 159, 161, 164–165, 168, 171

Communication, 13, 21–22, 24, 26, 30–31, 76, 100. *See also conversation*

Community, x, 7–8, 17, 22, 31–34, 37–42, 61, 74, 79, 83–86, 88, 93–94, 97, 100, 110–113, 118, 120–121, 124–125, 128, 133–136, 139–141, 144, 147, 153, 156, 158, 164, 167–171, 178–179

Complexity theory, 4, 36, 50, 65, 67–68, 74–85, 87, 89, 101, 106, 121–122, 126, 136, 144, 147, 150, 167

Construction trends and practices, ix–x, 5, 9, 16, 33, 38, 61–62, 99, 109, 116, 122–124, 139, 143, 152, 156, 163, 175–176

Conversation, x, 18, 21–22, 24, 27, 30, 33–34, 38, 56, 68, 92, 99, 106, 119, 125, 138, 144, 162, 164, 167, 170, 174, 178, 180. *See also Dewey, occupations of childhood*

Crime, 1, 5–7, 11, 13, 19, 159

Dance, 3, 24, 35–36, 47–48, 51, 75, 105. *See also music teaching, arts teaching*

Davis, Brent (educator), 74–77, 106–107, 166

Deplacement, 134, 144–145, 147. *See also Orr*

Dewey, John (educational philosopher), 21–22, 24, 33, 38, 40,

45, 49, 52–53, 55, 63, 74–75, 81–84, 92, 139, 141, 144, 153, 155–156, 158, 164, 167
   Occupations of childhood, 21–22, 38, 55, 92, 125

Dominance over nature, 10, 20, 39, 69, 87, 89, 130, 139, 141, 145, 152–154

Dudek, Mark (architect), 9–12, 32–33, 40, 45–47, 49–52, 54, 56, 60, 63, 71–73, 82, 136–138, 159, 168, 177

Ecosystems, 63, 67, 74, 130, 140, 145, 173. *See also Capra*

Edible Schoolyard, 129, 147, 149–153, 167. *See also school gardens*

Embodied knowledge, x, 15, 24, 43, 47, 50–51, 54, 91–95, 98, 101–105, 107, 115, 142, 161–162, 168

Energy-efficient building, 117–118, 124

Engagement in learning, x, 98, 100, 105, 109, 121. *See also lifelong learning*

Entryways, ix, 14–15, 27, 55, 136, 167, 177

Environmental impact of construction, 109, 122, 149
   Paints and finishes, 122

Evangelical Community School of Gelsenkirchen-Bismarck, 37–42, 60, 97, 116, 169, 173, 188

External accounting, 112, 115, 118, 122

Factory metaphor, ix, 10, 13, 16

Fielding, Randall (architect), 82, 169

Froebel, Friedrich (Kindergarten), 12, 34, 45, 47–51, 54, 59, 63, 68, 140

Froebel's Gifts, 48–51

Furniture, ix, 10, 14, 26, 33, 37, 40–41, 46, 51–52, 82–83, 155, 159, 164–167, 169, 172. *See also home-like atmosphere*

Gaia hypothesis, 70–71, 85, 127, 140, 173

Gardner, Howard (educator), 25, 52–53, 63, 75, 109, 110, 112–113, 142

Gathering places, 52, 58, 66, 79–83, 86–87, 93, 116, 120, 136, 138, 169

German schools, x, 11, 37–42, 48–50, 60, 62, 67, 71, 97, 116, 166, 169, 173

Graffiti, 7, 41–42, 73

Green spaces, ix–x, 4, 80, 84, 99, 137, 152, 166–169, 176

Hard architecture, 13, 165, 168

Hennigan School, 1–5, 77, 156

Home-like atmosphere, 19, 33, 40, 42, 52, 81, 106, 134, 156–158, 165, 166–168

Hübner, Peter (architect), 21, 37–40, 42, 116, 169

Human relationships, ix, 25, 52, 57, 87, 140, 147, 159, 170

Humble architecture, 34, 41, 47, 95–96, 149, 156–157, 168, 172–173

Improvisation, 28, 101

Indoor-outdoor connections, 19, 39–40, 51, 56, 66, 80, 84–87, 121, 129, 133, 136–138, 154, 172. *See also outdoor classrooms*

Internal accounting, 112, 114, 122, 127, 138. *See also external accounting*

Japanese schools, 49, 55, 85, 102, 106

Kindergarten, x, 9, 11–12, 26–27, 34, 36–37, 45–49, 51, 53–54, 56–58, 68, 74, 82, 84–85, 103, 118, 121, 123, 132, 135, 144, 157, 161, 173, 177

Kitchens, 85, 150. *See also school gardens*

Learning through social interactions, 18, 22–23, 60, 75, 78, 87, 93, 104, 137, 143, 151

Lifelong learning, x, 34, 66, 91–92, 152–153. *See also engagement in learning*

Lifetime value, 118. *See also internal accounting, external accounting*

Lloyd Wright, Frank (architect), 33, 45–46, 49–51

Lovelock, James (scientist), 70, 139–140, 173, 189

Making things by hand, 21–22, 48, 50, 53, 99–101, 130, 141–142, 153, 155, 173, 177. *See also Dewey, occupations of childhood*

McClintock, Barbara (geneticist), 65, 69–70, 186

Modern architecture, 50, 60

Modernism, 12

Montessori schools, 1, 11–12, 34, 50–51, 54–55, 63, 112, 114, 141, 153, 159

Moral development, 46–47, 54–55, 149, 151, 154

Mumford, Lewis (historian and architectural critic), 70, 111, 114–115, 119, 140–142, 144, 147, 149, 153–154, 159, 165. *See also regional survey*

Music teaching, x, 78, 95, 102, 107, 111
Composition, 92
Private studio teaching, x, 2, 5, 67, 92
School music, x, 3, 78, 85, 96, 97
School musicals, 3–4. *See also arts teaching, dance*

Nair, Prakash (architect), 82–83, 169

Natural light, ix, 6, 19, 35, 46, 51–52, 68–69, 72, 80, 86, 89, 104, 116–118, 121, 124, 137–138, 155, 157, 159–160, 165–167, 169, 172

Natural materials, 15, 17, 35, 37, 52, 56, 82, 85, 88, 95, 123, 136, 141, 157, 172

Natural surveillance, 9, 87

Newtonian science, 68–69, 111, 171

Noddings, Nel (educator), 18, 25, 54–55, 139–140

Open concept schools, 81, 87

Orana Steiner School, 17, 25, 36–37, 84, 88, 125, 127, 170, 174

Organic architecture, 12, 31, 35, 37, 51, 60, 72, 82

Orr, David (environmentalist), 10, 13–14, 29, 109, 131, 134, 139, 141, 144, 147–149, 154, 170

Outdoor classrooms, 10, 45, 49, 54, 56–60, 79–80, 84, 103, 129, 143–144, 152, 168–169. *See also school gardens, indoor-outdoor connections*

Parental involvement, 38

Parkour, 7

Participatory design and building, x, 21–22, 32–35, 37, 38–40, 59, 87, 116, 121, 135–136, 148, 167, 170–172, 174

Pathways, 12, 40, 58–59, 66, 80, 85, 87, 116

Patterns, 50, 65, 67–72, 74, 76, 78–80, 84, 86–87, 102, 111, 115, 146–147, 150, 167

Place-based education, ix, 40, 52, 57, 85, 131–132, 135–137, 140, 143–145, 151, 173

Plants in classrooms, 17, 40, 49, 52, 59, 70, 85, 129, 133, 144, 147, 151, 153, 166–168, 170–171

Play, x, 3, 6–7, 9, 22, 28, 33, 45–49, 52–59, 63, 66, 75, 80, 86, 92, 96, 100, 110, 113, 122, 125, 136, 143, 151–152, 155, 166, 169, 173, 178. *See also Dewey, occupations of childhood*

Preparing meals, 9, 134, 136, 142, 150–151, 168, 177, 180. *See also kitchens, school gardens*

Prisons and schools, 1, 5, 12–13, 19, 157

Progressivism, 12, 33, 60, 75, 111

Recycled materials, 37, 115, 124, 130

Reggio Emilia approach, 1, 11, 12, 21, 24–25, 34, 40, 45, 50, 52, 55, 81, 83, 93, 112–113, 186

Regional survey, 140–141, 144, 147, 149, 153. *See also Mumford*

Romanticism, 49, 59, 65–67, 74, 87–88, 92

Roof gardens, 61–62

School gardens, 36, 48–49, 57, 59, 85, 99–100, 129, 137, 147, 149–154, 167, 174, 180. *See also outdoor classrooms*

School renovations, ix, 14, 16, 96, 116, 119

School violence, 2, 8–9, 17–18, 42, 122

Scottish schools, 47

Seabird Island School, 129, 134–138, 145, 173–174

Shearwater Mullumbimby Steiner School, 85, 114, 131–132, 141, 164

Skilled trades, 28, 29, 43, 119–120, 122, 133, 136, 173–176. *See also carpentry*

Small acts of beauty, 1, 14, 16–17, 38, 157, 173

Smell, ix, 4, 17–18, 57, 168, 172

Socialization, 5, 9–10, 13

Solar power, 61, 116, 118

Sound, 17, 31, 39, 46, 81, 95–96, 98, 101–102, 106–107, 128, 133, 159, 162–166, 168, 172

Spaces between buildings, 60–62, 80, 84, 170

Specialized languages and symbols, 23, 25–27, 43, 120
Architectural drawings, 27–28, 33

Spiritual knowledge, 7, 31, 48–49, 52–53, 55, 63, 84, 88, 92–93, 95, 102, 106–107, 131–132

Steiner (Waldorf) schools, 1, 9, 11–12, 17–18, 25–26, 31, 32, 35, 37, 45, 48, 51–52, 65, 71–73, 75–76, 81–85, 88, 98, 99, 113–114, 131–132, 141, 153, 156–157, 159, 164–165, 170, 173–174, 177

Steiner, Rudolf (philosopher, architect, educator), 11, 48–51, 63, 71

Stewardship, 131, 152–153

Strawberry Vale Elementary School, 137–139.

Student academic achievement, ix, 16, 41, 46, 72, 80, 81, 84, 109–110, 122, 150–160, 168
  and colour, 161
  and lighting, 160
  and sound, 163

Student artwork, 25–26, 59, 164

Students' views, 19, 84, 161, 165–166

Sustainable or green building, 123–124, 148, 153

Swiss schools, 48

Taiko drumming, 91, 93–98, 100–106

Tanner, Kenneth (architect), 9, 32–33, 80–81, 84, 87, 116, 151, 159, 162, 193–194

Teachers' views, 75, 138

Technology, 3, 14, 16, 22–24, 28, 30, 82, 85, 93, 97, 99–101, 144, 149, 177–178

Toilets, 9, 17–20, 27, 41–42, 87, 120, 159

Transmission teaching, 33, 60, 75, 80

Universal design, 57, 116, 127, 137

University teaching, x, 6, 8–9, 13–14, 16, 18, 29–31, 78, 104, 171

Upitis, Rena (educator), 3, 23, 66, 75, 77, 101, 105, 166, 178

Urban environments, ix, 3, 7, 15, 19, 25, 54, 59, 61–63, 79, 99, 113, 115, 124–126, 145–146, 150–151, 154, 156, 158–159, 169–170, 179, 184

Ventilation, 95, 138

von Goethe, Johann Wolfgang (poet and scientist), 65, 67–72, 74, 76, 92, 120, 159, 161, 174

Warm colours, 14–15, 17, 38, 51, 159, 164

Water recycling, 17–18, 39–40, 51, 55, 61–62, 69, 124–126, 132, 137, 139–140, 145, 153, 166

Waterharvesting, 112, 125–127

Whitehead, Alfred North (educational philosopher), 66–67, 75, 79, 141, 153

Willunga Waldorf School, 9, 73, 99–100, 173–174

Windows, 13–14, 21, 26, 28, 33, 51, 78–80, 88, 115, 117–118, 129, 137, 157, 159–161, 163, 165, 168, 172

Made in the USA
Charleston, SC
19 July 2010